CROSSCURRENTS *Modern Critiques*

CROSSCURRENTS *Modern Critiques*
Harry T. Moore, *General Editor*

William Van O'Connor

The Grotesque:

AN AMERICAN GENRE
AND OTHER ESSAYS

WITH A PREFACE BY

Harry T. Moore

Carbondale

SOUTHERN ILLINOIS UNIVERSITY PRESS

MIDDLEBURY COLLEGE
LIBRARY

TRANSFER 155470

PS
121
02

Quotations from Complete Poems of Robert Frost. *Copyright 1916, 1921, 1923, 1928, 1930, 1934, 1939 by Holt, Rinehart and Winston, Inc. Copyright 1934, 1936 by Robert Frost. Copyright renewed 1944, 1951, © 1956, 1962 by Robert Frost. Reprinted by permission of Holt, Rinehart and Winston, Inc.*

Copyright © 1962 by Southern Illinois University Press.
All rights reserved.
Library of Congress Catalog Card Number 62–15004
Printed in the United States of America
Designed by Andor Braun

To Professor Irène Simon

AND MY FORMER COLLEAGUES AT THE

UNIVERSITY OF LIÈGE

PREFACE

THESE ESSAYS on American literature by one of the outstanding critics in that area of studies were written separately but represent a single point of view. In one way or another, they are variations on the theme of the opening chapter, "The Grotesque: An American Genre," which quite properly gives the present volume its title.

William Van O'Connor has been publishing books on literature for some twenty years. Before he became involved with specifically American writing, he brought out The New Woman of the Renaissance (1942), Climates of Tragedy (1943), and Sense and Sensibility in Modern Poetry (1948). The second of these was written in collaboration with his wife; the third was a revision of his doctoral thesis. In 1950 Mr. O'Connor wrote The Shaping Spirit: A Study of Wallace Stevens, followed by An Age of Criticism (1952), The Tangled Fire of William Faulkner (1954), and a collection of short stories, Campus on the River (1959). Mr. O'Connor, after fifteen years of teaching at the University of Minnesota, in 1961 became Professor of English at the University of California at Davis. He has been an extremely influential editor, notably in association with Allen Tate and Robert Penn Warren in the University of Minnesota Pamphlets on American Writers series. A volume Mr. O'Connor edited in 1948, Forms of Modern Fiction, has remained in print as a significant contribution to the understanding of the novel of our time.

Mr. O'Connor brings to literary studies his natural endowments, which were almost certainly augmented by the excellence of his training at an exciting time in the development of modern criticism. Just before World War II, he was one of the younger men deeply involved in the new-critical movement which was just then invading American universities. The virtue of its method, to students of his generation, was that it emphasized an author's work as the focal aim of criticism rather than the secondary matters which had too long attracted primary attention in college literature courses.

So far, so good—the application of the newer criticism generally improved such courses when the teachers attempted to maintain some kind of balance or at least didn't entirely disregard the secondary phases which do have some relevance in criticism. In the years immediately after World War II there was danger that the newer methods would be carried too far, for some extremists in the movement behaved as if the works of an author existed in a vacuum, and as if environmental, biographical, linguistic, and other influences were of no significance in understanding or judging literature—indeed, the very mention of these elements became in some quarters a critical sin. As Mr. O'Connor's writings show, he is not one of these extremists. He has made good use of the more reasonable declarations of the newer critics—leading to what he calls analytical criticism—and he doesn't emphasize background considerations at the expense of what properly belongs in the foreground; on the other hand he doesn't go to the extreme of ignoring the plain fact that the authors he examines lived in certain climates of thought, in certain historical periods of the language in which they wrote, or in certain tropisms of human experience that conditioned their work. Mr. O'Connor's level-headed essay on modern criticism is an important part of the present book, which continually displays his good sense as well as his trained sensibility.

To speak further of the newer criticism, the observation may be safely made that recent biographical and environmental approaches to authors have received friendlier treatment than they would have in the days when so many of the younger literary purists were pitching most exercises in scholarship into classroom bonfires. In the last few years, huge literary biographies such as Richard Ellmann's of James Joyce, Mark Schorer's of Sinclair Lewis, and Arthur and Barbara Gelb's of Eugene O'Neill have stirred many critics to enthusiasm. One of the reasons for this is that although these books deal mostly with the lives of the authors in question, the biographers have an expert critical understanding of the works of the men they are writing about and can relate these works to the men's lives. Indeed, literary studies of all kinds are more organic now than they promised to be a few years ago—once again, William Van O'Connor learned from the newer criticism without indulging in its excesses.

In his own academic training, Mr. O'Connor no doubt benefited from having studied with Lionel Trilling, Marjorie Hope Nicolson, and William York Tindall, who were the advisers for his Columbia University doctoral dissertation—which, as mentioned earlier, was published as Sense and Sensibility in Modern Poetry. Professors Trilling, Nicolson, and Tindall in their various ways dealt primarily with the writings of the authors they taught, but were also aware that those writings have distinct connections with the milieu in which they were produced. In the last section of the present book, "The Hawthorne Museum," Mr. O'Connor gives us an interesting flash of reminiscence of Columbia when he was a graduate student there.

During his years of pre-war study at Columbia, William Van O'Connor served as an instructor at Louisiana State University, a crucible of the newer criticism. He married one of his colleagues, Mary Theresa Allen; they taught in the same department as Cleanth Brooks and Robert Penn Warren, whose new-critical anthology, Understanding Poetry, was just then beginning to exert its important influence on the explication of verse in colleges and universities across the United States. Mr. O'Connor also gives us some glimpses of his Louisiana associates in "The Hawthorne Museum."

Printed here for the first time, this fantasy makes use of a form too long neglected: the dialogue. Mr. O'Connor shows us anew the possibilities of this medium, for his dialogue contains not only the previously mentioned elements of autobiography and fantasy, but also some penetrating criticism. The critical comments often arise informally out of the reminiscences, as when Mr. O'Connor is telling the momentarily resurrected Hawthorne about some more recent writers: Karl Shapiro in New Guinea in wartime, Sinclair Lewis baring the raw wound of his egotism at a party in Minneapolis, David Garnett speaking gentle memoirs in the Reform Club in London. Mr. O'Connor's Hawthorne Museum, with its literary props which include Crusoe's parrot and Shelley's skylark, evaporates as its twentieth-century visitor steps away from its door, but fortunately the dialogue itself remains to be reread, a piece of grotesquerie at once instructive and entertaining.

Grotesquerie: the opening essay in this volume, also published here (in full) for the first time, establishes the central thesis of the book, as pointed out earlier. In this essay, Mr. O'Connor refers back to the ancestry of the grotesque, such as the works of Poe, but he spends most of his time with the present-day exponents of this genre, with special emphasis on the Southern writers.

His other chapters deal mostly with the American novel, but some of them concentrate on poets—Dickinson, Stevens, Frost. Mr. O'Connor's treatment of topics such as "The Writer and the University" is of special interest, adding variety to the book and increasing its scope. He is a skillful practitioner of the comparative method which so often serves to bring out salient critical points through the exploration of similarities and differences: witness the "common ground" between Hawthorne and Faulkner which Mr. O'Connor so valuably surveys for us. Some of his comparisons are founded on scholarship of the most fruitful kind: he is able to show us much about Eliot's poem "Gerontion" by holding it up beside Cardinal Newman's "The Dream of Gerontius," and he is able to cast fresh light on Hemingway's story "The Snows of

Kilimanjaro" by putting it alongside Bayard Taylor's poem about that literarily attractive mountain.

Altogether, eighteen essays make up the present book; perceptive and stimulating, they provide a significant addition to modern American criticism.

HARRY T. MOORE

May 30, 1962

CONTENTS

PREFACE   *vii*

INTRODUCTION   *xv*

1   The Grotesque: AN AMERICAN GENRE   3

2   Traditions in American Literature   20

3   A Note on the American Novel   32

4   The Novel-of-Experience   37

5   The Novel and the *Truth*
    About America   47

6   Hawthorne and Faulkner:
    SOME COMMON GROUND   59

7   The Narrator as Distorting Mirror   78

8   Plotinus Plinlimmon and the
    Principle of Name Giving   92

9   Emily Dickinson:
    THE DOMESTICATION OF TERROR   98

10 *Huckleberry Finn* and the
    Great American Novel   *109*

11 Two Views of Kilimanjaro   *119*

12 "Gerontion" and "The Dream
    of Gerontius"   *125*

13   Wallace Stevens: IMAGINED REALITY   128

14   Robert Frost: PROFANE OPTIMIST   137

15   Some Notes on Modern Literary Criti-
       cism   155

16   Art and Miss Gordon   168

17   The Writer and the University   177

18   The Hawthorne Museum:
       A DIALOGUE   193

INTRODUCTION

INTRODUCTIONS ARE frequently occasions for an author to move from self-explanation to self-justification. Therefore I shall try to be brief, in the hope that denying myself words will minimize my temptations.

The essay on the grotesque is new, although a few sentences in it are from a short article in College English. "The Hawthorne Museum: A Dialogue" is wholly new, as is the essay on Frost. There are changes and additions in most of the others. Although the various pieces have been written at different times, I believe the collection has a certain homogeneity, and that is one way to justify it. But there are other reasons too. One does not want to have certain articles lost in the files of magazines, or, in this case, to let two continue in the limbo of anonymity imposed by the Times Literary Supplement.

Critical tags sometimes claim too much. I hope I have not claimed too much for the term grotesque—nor on the other hand too little. Further investigations of the concepts suggested could of course lead to insights and formulations that have eluded me. I could justify "The Hawthorne Museum: A Dialogue" at some length, but I'll content myself by saying the dialogue, although rarely employed today, should not be abandoned.

A number of these pieces were done in 1953–54, when I was a Fulbright lecturer at the University of Liège. It was this occasion, followed by a summer in England, that started me thinking about the American-ness of American literature. And that I suppose is the chief subject of this book.

"Traditions in American Literature" first appeared in an April 1959 issue of the Times Literary Supplement. "Emily Dickinson: The Domestication of Terror" was also in the Times Literary Supplement, September 1955. "A Note on the American Novel" was a preface written for The Idea of the American Novel, edited by L. Rubin and J. R. Moore and published by T. Y. Crowell in 1961. "The Novel-of-Experience" was published in Critique in 1956. "Hawthorne and Faulkner: Some Common Ground" was published in Virginia Quarterly in 1957. "The Novel and the Truth About America" first appeared in English Studies in 1954. "The Narrator as Distorting Mirror" appeared under a different title in Revue des langues vivantes, 2, 1954. "Huckleberry Finn and the Great American Novel" first appeared in College English in 1955. "Two Views of Kilimanjaro" was published in History of Ideas News Letter in 1948. "Some Notes on Contemporary Literary Criticism" appeared in Contemporary Literary Scholarship, edited by Lewis Leary, and published by Appleton-Century-Crofts. "Wallace Stevens Imagined Reality" appeared in Western Review in 1948. "Art and Miss Gordon" appeared in South, a Doubleday anthology edited by L. Rubin, 1961. "The Writer and the University" was published in The Texas Quarterly, 1960. To the various editors and publishers I am grateful for permission to use my articles.

Ralph Ross gave me a few helpful suggestions about the grotesque as a genre. Philip Young gave me a couple of hints about the incest theme in Hawthorne. Harry T. Moore suggested several novels employing an untrustworthy narrator. Celeste Wright and Robert Wiggins, my colleagues, helped me on the Melville chapter. Leonard Unger, Joseph Kwiat, Allen Tate, Jack Ervin, and Lewis Leary have often been helpful in discussing literary, as well as other, matters with me. My wife, as all authors say, has been of inestimable help. In my case, it happens to be true.

WILLIAM VAN O'CONNOR

University of California, Davis

The Grotesque:
AN AMERICAN GENRE
AND OTHER ESSAYS

1 THE GROTESQUE:
AN AMERICAN GENRE

AMERICANS IDENTIFY themselves as children of the Enlightenment, with sentiments from the Romantic movement. To the rationality of the eighteenth century we
added humanitarian sympathy, thus satisfying both head
and heart. One might therefore expect Americans to have
produced a literature of neoclassical clarity, warmed by
a sense of human brotherhood, like the work of certain
late eighteenth-century English writers.

But we have not produced such a literature. Critics and
literary historians have observed that our novel is not, unlike the English novel, domesticated. We write the "romance," what Richard Chase calls "a profound poetry of
disorder" and F. Frohock calls "the novel of violence."
Whereas we might expect neatly ordered novels ours tend
to churn and dream and writhe. Our poets try to contain
disorder, even Whitman, and in the twentieth century
poets have reached back to touch the hands of Poe and
Baudelaire, each of whom was profoundly aware of irrationality. As citizens we seem satisfied to be children of
the Enlightenment and of the Romantic movement. Yet
our literature is filled with the grotesque, more so probably than any other Western literature. It is a new genre,
merging tragedy and comedy, and seeking, seemingly in
perverse ways, the sublime.

Tragedy depends on a moral universe, one not wholly
inscrutable. Twentieth-century man no longer feels any
intimate moral kinship with the universe. The farther

science goes in describing the motions of the universe, its laws, the less sure the human being seems to feel about himself. We are not certain how we ought to feel, but we do suspect that Oedipus and Hamlet are a little over-powering, a little too magnificent. Our own writers have insisted that the universe is neutral, unaware of man's moral searchings, and this of course has led to trying to discover moral sanctions within himself.

Comedy as a genre does not insist on a moral order, but it does insist on rationality, especially a rational social order. Again, our writers are less certain than their prede-cessors have been about the nature of rationality, codes, and a fixed social order.

Tragedy implies a moral universe, and comedy is ulti-mately dependent upon human rationality and social codes. Our writers are terribly preoccupied with the irra-tional, the unpredictable, the bizzare, with the grotesque.

Several critics in the nineteenth century discussed the grotesque in literature. Victor Hugo in his Preface to *Cromwell* (1827) held that the grotesque is relatively un-important in classical art but very important in Christian and romantic art. John Ruskin, in *The Stones of Venice*, says the true grotesque merely plays with the fearful and the awesome; it recognizes the moral nature of the uni-verse. The false grotesque concentrates and mocks all things "with the laughter of the idiot and the cretin," and is usually obscene. In 1864 Walter Bagehot published "Pure, Ornate, and Grotesque Art in English Poetry." His "grotesque" is Browning. (The twentieth-century reader is likely to feel that monsters of Browning's are rather nice monsters.) Bagehot believes literature should treat the normal, and that the abnormal, a deplorable variation, is the grotesque. Nature, Bagehot says, is striving to elimi-nate the grotesque. John Addington Symonds' "Carica-ture, The Fantastic, The Grotesque" (1890) comes closest to viewing the grotesque as modern writers do. "Nowhere," he says, "is there an abrupt chasm in man's sentient being. Touch, taste, smell, sex" all run together in the great concert.

The nineteenth-century critics tend to separate the phys-

ical and the spiritual, normal and abnormal, just and unjust, moral and immoral into readily describable categories.
Symonds is not so sure. Neither are the creators of the
modern grotesque. In one of his essays in *Past Masters*
Thomas Mann has this to say about the prevalence of the
grotesque in modern literature:

> For I feel that, broadly and essentially, the striking feature
> of modern art is that it has ceased to recognize the cate-
> gories of tragic and comic, or the dramatic classifications,
> tragedy and comedy. It sees life as tragi-comedy, with the
> result that the grotesque is its most genuine style—to the
> extent, indeed, that today that is the only guise in which
> the sublime may appear. For, if I may say so, the grotesque
> is the genuine anti-bourgeois style; and however bourgeois
> Anglo-Saxondom may otherwise be or appear, it is a fact
> that in art the comic-grotesque has always been its strong
> point.

Mann did not develop this statement or point to works
that he considered examples of the grotesque. Even so, he
has said several things that seem to be true of the grotesque: that the sharp division between tragedy and comedy has broken down; that the sublime sometimes lurks
behind weirdly distorted images; and that the literature
of the grotesque is in reaction against the sometimes
bland surfaces of bourgeois customs and habits.

Since the seventeenth century many sensitive men have
been suspicious of a system of thought, the scientific revolution, that gave them a sense of being estranged, that
gave them a sense of finiteness, asked them to be impersonal agents in an all-embracing mechanical order, and
stressed material things. This intellectual revolution gave
rise to the industrial order, and with it the bourgeois
world and the bourgeois mentality. Almost all of modern
literature, as one knows, is a protest in one form or another against a too easy faith in progress, against the
literal-mindedness and smugness that this mentality invited. As soon as one uses the phrase "the alienated artist"
a whole range of writers asks to be listed.

It is also an old story in literary history and criticism
that literary conventions shift and change as the beliefs

and myths of an age change and take new form. Thus the stage emulated the shape and function of the glass slide during the period when science was explaining or seemed to be explaining the nature of man. Today when we are trying rather to explain both the nature of science and its relationship to ourselves, the shape of the stage again is changing. In other words, the literary conventions shift with shifts in our view of ourselves. Conventions in the novel or in fiction undergo similar changes.

The grotesque has developed in response to our age, to atom bombs and great social changes. The century just before ours learned that man had evolved from a lower biological species, and certain of its philosophers stressed both the irrationality of human nature and the ways in which our actions are determined by forces beyond our control.

The grotesque is not the sole form expressing the nature of modern man, but it is a widely prevalent form. In America it has clear antecedents in Edgar Allan Poe; it has antecedents in the Literary Naturalists, Crane, Norris, London, and in those other protestants against the genteel mind, Edgar Saltus and Ambrose Bierce.

Perhaps the South has produced more than its share of the grotesque. The writers are easily listed: Erskine Caldwell, William Faulkner, Robert Penn Warren, Eudora Welty, Carson McCullers, Flannery O'Connor, Truman Capote, and Tennessee Williams. Some of the reasons are clear enough; the old agricultural system depleted the land and poverty breeds abnormality; in many cases people were living with a code that was no longer applicable, and this meant a detachment from reality and loss of vitality. But there are reasons beyond these. The grotesque has been seen everywhere in American life and fiction, and beyond them. Sherwood Anderson found it in the small town in Ohio. Nathaniel West saw it in New York City, Vermont, and in Hollywood. Nelson Algren finds it in Chicago and in New Orleans. Paul Bowles finds it in Africa.

Sherwood Anderson called his preface to *Winesburg, Ohio* "The Book of the Grotesque." In this preface he speaks of a writer, an old man, who held a theory about grotesques: "The old man had listed hundreds of truths in his book. . . . There was the truth of virginity and the truth of passion, the truth of wealth and of poverty, of thrift and profligacy, of carelessness and abandon. Hundreds of truths and they were all beautiful." He adds that people snatched up one or more of these truths. "It was his notion that the moment one of the people took one of the truths to himself, called it his truth, and tried to live by it, he became a grotesque and the truth he embraced a falsehood." The theory is not really worked out, but clearly Anderson was preoccupied with the frustrations that turn trusting, aspiring, decent people into grotesques.

In most of the stories the protagonists suffer from an inability to communicate, to express their affections and to be loved in return, or to fulfill themselves creatively. Wing Biddlebaum, in "Hands," instinctively expresses his affections with his hands, he speaks with his hands, and he can use them with a marvelous dexterity. But as a young teacher, accustomed to touching students, indeed anyone, he had been misunderstood, brutally beaten, and driven out of town. He is shown prematurely aged, living alone, and fearful that his hands will get him into more trouble. Alice Hindman, in "Adventure," is a twenty-seven-year-old spinster. At sixteen, she had been in love with a Ned Currie. He had left Winesburg for Cleveland and later Chicago, promising to send for her, but as the months, then years, went by, she knew he would not keep his promise. Her life is an empty one. As she undresses one evening, she hears the rain spattering on the window pane, and she follows an impulse to run naked out onto the lawn. "She thought the rain would have some creative and wonderful effect on her body." Walking along the sidewalk is an old man, and she calls out to him, wanting to go with him. The old man is deaf, and does not understand her. Suddenly frightened, she falls to the ground and crawls across the grass and up the stairs into the house.

Sometimes it is said that Anderson was writing about the "village virus," or that he felt there had been some general failure or breakdown of brotherhood in American life, or that an original innocence had been lost. Although their presence is sometimes hinted at, none of these theories is present in any significant way in *Winesburg, Ohio*. There would be no remedy in any society for certain of his grotesques; their minds are twisted or they simply lack intelligence. Others suffer from frustrated affections, inability to communicate their feelings, or to express their creative impulses. On the other hand the possibility of normality seems almost always present, and George Willard, who appears in many of the stories, is its representative.

Nathaniel West once wrote that he had based the technique of *Miss Lonelyhearts* on the comic strip. "Each chapter," he wrote, "instead of going forward in time, also goes backwards, forwards, up and down in space like a picture." West's mention of the comic strip is an important clue to the peculiar nature of his stylization. The characters are one dimensional. Each represents one thing only, tends to be obsessed, and moves through the action with the sort of inertia common to comic strips.

Miss Lonelyhearts presents various promises of escape from the destruction wrought by time and suffering. Shrike, the cynical editor, enumerates them: the soil, the South Seas, hedonism, art, suicide, drugs, and Christ. Each is seen as a form of self-deception. The modern world, the book says, offers only disbelief, sterility, frustration. The fact that these characters are looked at or presented as cartoon characters adds to the frightening sense of emptiness that pervades *Miss Lonelyhearts*.

A Cool Million is so wildly exaggerated a caricature of the Horatio Alger myth that it hardly can be considered seriously. *The Day of the Locust*, a more objective, distanced conception than the two earlier novels, is centered on Hollywood hangers-on, those who have only dreamed the celluloid dreams of Hollywood success, and on the great mass or crowd who know no sense of direction or purpose in their lives. Faye Greener, a sexually attractive but moronic girl, has ambitions to be an actress. She has a pathetic ex-comic father, and a drugstore cowboy for a lover. A gratuitous touch is a mean-spirited dwarf. One of the scenes is a fight between the cowboy and the dwarf: "The dwarf let go his hold and Earle sank to the floor. Lifting the little man free, Miguel shifted his grip to his ankles and dashed him into the wall, like a man killing a rabbit against a tree. . . . He was unconscious. They carried him into the kitchen and held him under the cold water." Hollywood crowds are described as people who have discovered that "sunshine isn't enough. . . . Their boredom becomes more and more terrible. They realize they've been tricked and burn with resentment. Every day of their lives they read the newspapers and went to the movies. Both fed them on lynchings, murder, sex, crimes, explosions, wrecks, love nests, fires, revolutions, wars." These are the people who compose the strange half-human mob which riots. *The Day of the Locust* is about the California dream world, and beyond that about the search for meaning and about the modern confusions of illusion with reality.

"The Face on the Barroom Floor, or Too Much Salt on the Pretzels" is a fairly characteristic Algren story. In it there is a legless strongman, named Shorty, his girl friend Venus, and others. The chief setting of the action is a bar run by Brother B. The habitués drink "to fill the emptiness in their lives," and regularly two of them fight (Brother B. lowers the shutters, locks the door) for their self-respect. After violent, bloody fights in which the participants can be maimed "everyone would feel that something had at least been achieved that day."

The Man with the Golden Arm is filled with people of the same sort: petty thieves, morphine addicts, and drunks, all of them inexorably pulled toward their own destructions and deaths. The central character, Frankie Machine (Majcinek), ex-soldier, card dealer, addict, moves toward his own destruction with such intensity that, perversely, his suicide takes on a strange dignity; in dying by his own hands he avoids the even greater degradation of death in a jail hospital. Some unseen current carries him toward destruction. He and all the others live in a shadowed world of bars, cheap honky-tonks, jail, illicit love making, occasional gestures or even periods of loyalty, frequent betrayals, and irrational violence. They make no effort to escape, as though in some dark recess of their minds was a determination to enjoy their own destruction.

Somebody in Boots and *Never Come Morning,* early Algren novels, are social protest novels, and occasionally in *The Man with the Golden Arm* and *A Walk on the Wild Side* there is a gesture in the direction of social protest. But, at bottom, Algren is not a social-protest writer. He seems to be fascinated by the grim comedy of lives lived violently, soddenly, desperately.

In *A Walk on the Wild Side,* the most recent novel, Algren's setting is New Orleans—and this provides Algren with even more bizarre possibilities. Its humor is essentially zany and unrealistic. Dove Linkhorn, the central character, is a would-be Horatio Alger hero. Although illiterate and ingenuous, he shows a remarkable capacity —he is a kind of male Moll Flanders—for making the best of his opportunities. With his various talents, he might have been a "success," but Algren chooses to have him blinded and injured in a fight similar to that in "The Face on the Barroom Floor." The episodes, some of them extremely funny, are merely strung together. When he remembers that he is supposed to be motivating the action, Algren refers to the "Hoover depression" but usually he forgets about this. About the need for violence of derelicts, cripples, panders, and prostitutes he says, as he had in *Neon Wilderness,* "each fresh blow redeemed that blow his life had been to him."

Algren is an inconsistent theorizer. In *Neon Wilderness* he uses a viewpoint foreign to the motives of the character he is describing. In *Man With the Golden Arm* there is no outside world, except that suggested occasionally by Algren's comic asides or ironic comments on a character's motives or actions. In *A Walk on the Wild Side,* the injuries characters inflict on one another are retaliatory for injuries inflicted on them, but many of the episodes are so bizarre that the world inside the book is strangely distant from the ordinary world, even the ordinary world of pimps, junkies, and pick pockets, and not very relevant to it. One can believe in Frankie Machine but Dove Link-

horn is credible only as a theatrical creature. Algren's grotesques are the maimed, the crippled, the defrauded, but
Algren is not always certain about how they should be
viewed.

What Bowles seems to be saying in *The Sheltering Sky*
is that Kit (it could as easily have been her husband) is
a kind of Kurtz. The desert finds her out, echoes inside
her hollowness, as the jungle had found him out. Both
give themselves to a primeval animalism. Kurtz had died
saying, "the horror, the horror!" and Kit loses her mind.
(Unfortunately Bowles' novel evokes memories of many
melodramatic stories about desert sheiks and fair maid-
ens.) Kurtz is a far more memorable character than Kit,
and one of the reasons for this is that Kurtz had at least
thought of himself as deeply committed to morality before going to the Congo; it was there that he had learned
the depth of his hypocrisy. Kit has no moral center, and
her experiences merely confirm what was already known
about her.

Dyar, the amoral American who is the central figure in
Let It Come Down, is a lesser Decoud. Conrad's Decoud
has the dignity of a scepticism born of worldly knowledge.
Terror stricken at his own emptiness in the face of the
sand, the sky, the ocean, Decoud kills himself, and one
has witnessed a moral struggle. Dyar is devoid of moral
sensitivity. He has no gratitude or respect for those who
are kind to him. And he has no skill. When he becomes
a spy, the authorities are immediately aware of it, and
when he becomes a thief he is an ineffectual thief. Tan-
giers, with its maze of streets, opportunistic business deal-
ings, and its mysterious mores is a proper background for
seeing Dyar. And the mountainous Spanish coast, to which
he escapes, is a proper background for his horrendously
unnatural act, the murder, during a hashish dream, of the
Arab Thami.

> The mountain wind rushed through his head, his head
> that was a single seashell full of grottoes; its infinitely
> smooth pink walls, delicate, paper-thin, caught the light
> of the members as he moved along the galleries. "Melly
> diddle din," he said, quite aloud, putting the point of

the nail as far into Thami's ear as he could. He raised his
right arm and hit the head of the nail with all his might.
The object relaxed imperceptibly, as if someone had said
to it: "It's all right."

Kit Moresby's sexual orgies are an attempt to close her
ears to the ticking of time, and to escape her own emptiness. Dyar does not know what he wants, much less what
he is. Still lost in his dream, he considers Thami's body
and says: "I've come back. . . . Thami has stayed behind.
I'm the only survivor. That's the way I wanted it." When
Daisy, his mistress, finds him, she also finds Thami. In
horror, she retreats, telling Dyar she will not tell anyone
where he is. He is left, as he said he wanted to be, as the
only survivor. "Out in the murk there was no valley, there
were no mountains. The rain fell heavily and the wind
had begun to blow again. He sat down in the doorway
and began to wait. It was not yet completely dark."

It is Daisy who tells us what Dyar signifies. Dyar, she
says, does not really exist; he is dead. " 'Oh, not dead!'
she said impatiently. 'Just not alive. Not really. But we're
all like that, these days, I suppose. Not quite so blatantly
as you, perhaps, but still . . .' " She adds that today all of
us are capable of monstrous acts which, even one hundred years ago, were almost beyond human contempla-
tion. Whether this is so or not, it is true that however
ambiguous the moral order was for Conrad, it was a much
more fixed and stable order than it is for Bowles.

Thomas Mann's point that the grotesque is an anti-
bourgeois style as already suggested, could be assented
to for the wrong reasons or rather for oversimplified reasons. Among American literary historians there is, or has
been, a group that has been content to account for literary forms largely or solely in social and political terms.
They could say, for example, that grotesques occur because of unjust treatment of the Negro, of the tenant
farmer, or of the immigrant forced to live in a slum. In
other words, they would study the grotesque as a social
phenomenon and as a problem to be solved. They might
select for their thesis such writers as Stephen Crane, Anderson, West, Caldwell, and Algren.

But behind Crane's rage at human injustice and stupidity, there is a backdrop of cosmic pointlessness. Behind Anderson's theory that somewhere along the line America had failed her citizens is the dark suspicion that his grotesques, and perhaps all of us, stand facing a thick wall. Behind West's bitter satire on the American preoccupation with material things, or the simple minded Horatio Alger myth, is a deep suspicion that all beliefs are demonstrably illusory and false. Mixed with Caldwell's condemnation of certain of his villains is a detached delight in the complications of the villainy itself. Nelson Algren occasionally protests in social and economic terms, but the violence in his stories is a protest against a sense of emptiness and meaninglessness. Undoubtedly the more significant sources of the grotesque in most of their stories are well below the level of social and political injustice.

Many of the writers who have emerged, or whose reputations have grown, since World War II seem far removed from nineteenth-century morality. In Eudora Welty's stories morality and righteousness are not principles, but sentiment and sympathy are principles. Her characters seem to live in a land of dreams where everything is eerie and often incongruous. She creates comic grotesques. In Carson McCullers' stories the controlling factor is psychological motivation. Almost invariably the motivations are abnormal or perverse, but Miss McCullers seems to ask that they be taken as "normal." Some of the characters are almost mannequins, and their actions seem only a parody of human actions. The Truman Capote world is quite similar to McCullers' world in that what most of us would take to be normal is presented as monstrous. The nice people are sexually abnormal, demented or eccentric. The young frequently have the wizened appearance of midgets, civilization is decayed, and everything moves at a lethargic pace.

As with any other literary convention, the grotesque can be imitated. One can feel that Faulkner's grotesques, or the Southern grotesque in general, is easily turned into pastiche. Serious insights become almost stereotypes and sincere emotions give way to calculated effects.

As I Lay Dying is a good example of the morally serious grotesque. Addie, seemingly bent on shocking her
neighbors, those pious advocates of human dignity, is
getting ready to be dead a long time. She refuses to be
put into the ground without having seen the blood flow
along the earth in a meaningful torrent. The weird funeral
journey, the rough box falling into the stream, Cash's riding on the box with his broken leg, the putrescent corpse,
the belated struggle of Jewel and Darl for Addie's love—
all of this represents a journey of involvement, the painful
search for dignity and meaning.

The Hamlet is also a good example of the morally serious grotesque. Ike Snopes, idiot, is in love with a cow.
Seen in one way, his "affair" with the cow would seem
only a grotesque case of rural sodomy. But Ike, bemused
though he is, truly loves the cow. The "normal" people
in the novel do not love each other. Their "love affairs"
arise out of self-aggrandizement and perversity. Ike
Snopes' relationship with the cow has in it more affection
and is more sacred than any other relationship in *The
Hamlet*. The idiot Benjy functions similarly.

Warren, another serious creator of the grotesque, sees
man's reason and man's desire for realms of the spirit
involved in inextricable ways with nature and his own
biological organism. Warren is fascinated by the perfidies
committed by men most dedicated to rationality and to
idealism. For example, there is Jeremiah Beaumont, in
World Enough and Time.

Jeremiah is the very spirit of quixotic virtue. When he
learns that Colonel Cassius Fort, his friend and benefac-
tor, had seduced Rachel Jordan and that she had borne a
dead child, he is desolate. "Could a man not come to
some moment when, all dross and meanness of life is con-
sumed, one could live in the pure idea? If only for a moment?" Out of this desire he makes himself the defender
of Rachel Jordan; out of his need to pursue the pure idea,
he courts her, wins her love, and unwittingly forces her
to request that he kill Fort. Compromising voices warn or
try to warn him from his course. Even the landscape of
frontier Kentucky seems to warn him.

Eastward, cutting off the past, rose the wall of the mountains, and westward the wilderness stretched away forever
with its terror and its promise. . . . Here a man might
plunge into nature as into a black delirious stream and
gulp it and be engulfed. Or he might shudder with horror
at the very flesh he wore, at the sound of his guts or the
pulse in his blood, because whatever of himself he could
touch or feel was natural too.

Jeremiah's first attempt on Fort's life had been the offer
of a duel, a gesture of fealty to Virtue, but the second and
successful attempt is outright murder, committed in darkness and in stealth. The ensuing trial presents a tangle of
lies, half-truths and truths. Though enraged by the lies
told for heinous ends, Jeremiah contributes his own, main-
taining silence about the murder even with his lawyers,
concocting a body of false testimony intended to catch a
lying witness. Unfortunately the latter plan, which he
put into the form of a document and sent to his wife, is
stolen and presented to the court. In the end Jeremiah is
found guilty. Rachel joins him in the dungeon-like cell.
Attempts at appeal fail, but Wilkie Barron, who poses as
his friend, helps them escape to a distant swamp hide-
away near the Mississippi, the domain of a decayed old
river pirate, the humped-back La Grand' Bosse.

There in almost primeval slime Jeremiah experiences
what it is to live *in* nature. He becomes thoroughly de-
bauched, indifferent to the idealism that had driven him
there. Rachel, who has become an old woman as the result
of her experiences, loses her mind and takes her own life.

On the way back to Frankfort with One-Eye Jenkins,
Jeremiah comes to a resolution, in keeping with and as
romantic perhaps as his earlier actions; he will not seek a
pardon from the governor but will acknowledge his own
guilt. He writes a final passage in the journal he has kept,
reviewing his life and his terrible preoccupation with the
idea of justice: "I no longer seek to justify. I seek only to
suffer. I will shake the hangman's hand, and will call him
brother, at last."

Jeremiah never reaches home. He is overtaken and
killed by One-Eye, who carries Jeremiah's hacked off head

back to Frankfort. Wilkie Barron, true to form, arranges burial for Rachel, whose body is also brought back, and for Jeremiah, or rather for Rachel's body and for Jeremiah's head. The symbolism is gruesome but apt; for Jeremiah is the protagonist of the pure idea.

A more recent literary arrival, James Purdy, is an acute observer and creator of the grotesque. For example, his "63: Dream Place" suggests *As I Lay Dying,* not because Faulkner influenced Purdy, but because both understand the way in which the sublime lurks within the grotesque. Two boys from West Virginia arrive in New York City and try to catch on. Fenton, a handsome boy, and his sick little brother Claire are introduced to a bizarre world of poverty, lechery, perversity, and fear. Fenton, who is attractive both to homosexuals and some wealthy elderly women, loves and hates his brother because Claire refuses, out of sickness, tiredness and disgust, to allow Fenton to sell himself. Fenton "wanted desperately to be rid of Claire and even as he had this feeling he felt more love and pity for him than ever before. As he sat there gazing at Claire he knew he loved him more than any other being. He was almost sure that he would never feel such tenderness for any other person. And then this tenderness would be followed by fury and hatred and loathing, so that he was afraid he would do something violent, would strike the sick boy down and harm him." In a paroxysm of mixed hatred and protectiveness, Fenton chokes Claire. For days, the memory is blocked out, and he wanders the street. Finally, in another violent scene, he rejects the diseased and bizarre world that Claire had rejected, and returns to the abandoned house where Claire's body remains. He is trying to surface the recognition that Claire is dead.

Finally he does realize that Claire can't drink the coffee he has brought him because he is dead, and that he has killed him. There comes to Fenton the solacing idea that Claire must be buried. In the attic he finds an old chest. Inside is an old wedding veil. The box was not a fit resting place, he says to himself, but it would have to do. Finally there is this paragraph: "It took him all night to get himself ready to carry Claire up, as though once he had put him in the chest, he was really at last dead forever. For part of the night he found that he had fallen asleep over Claire's body, and at the very end before he carried him upstairs and deposited him, he forced himself to kiss the dead stained lips he had stopped, and said, 'Up we go then, motherfucker.'" Human dignity has rarely been expressed in such an unlikely scene or human love in such unlikely language.

There is of course a deeply existentialist drift in modern fiction, European and American. Medieval or Renaissance man could dream of the harmonies implicit in the doctrine of the microcosm-macrocosm relationship. Citizens in Pope's world could dream of the harmonies of a mechanistically ordered universe. Shelley and Byron could reassert that man was a Prometheus. Herbert Spencer and others testified to having observed that evolution is biological, social, and moral. Common to all of these doctrines is the belief that man may rely on spiritual and rational forces in the universe. There was an order of things upon which he could depend for succor, a sense of purpose, and the assurance that he was rational. The modern writer seems certain only of uncertainty.

Our writers believe that man carries in his unconscious mind not merely wilfulness or the need to indulge himself, but a deep bestiality and dark irrationality. In civilization a convention or a mode may be sloughed off, forgotten, or become a detritus. But whatever was once in man's mind remains there. Impersonal civilization, free from biology, helps man, and conscious man strives to follow its "laws." In the nineteenth century civilization had the appearance of natural law. Looking back at the novels of the eighteenth and nineteenth centuries one might recall these lines from *Owl's Clover:*

> *The solid was an age, a period*
> *With appropriate, largely English furniture*
> *Barbers with charts of the only possible modes,*
> *Cities that would not wash away in the mist.*

A generation or two later, with Conrad, Joyce, and Mrs. Woolf, civilization has quite a different look. In their fiction we sometimes seem to be seeing cities (the symbols of civilization) as though they were under water. In a good deal of American fiction the city appears as a destructive force (this is true as far back as *McTeague* and *Maggie: A Girl of the Streets*), a mechanical wilderness or a jungle (*The Man With the Golden Arm*), a maze ("The Artificial Nigger" in *A Good Man Is Hard to Find*), a place of frightening purlieus and back alleys (*Sanctuary* or *A Walk on the Wild Side*), or a stage set (*The Day of the Locust*). More often than not there are small town or rural settings. These phenomena may be fortuitous. More likely there is a reason for them, namely, that the city is no longer a symbol of civilization, and civilization is no longer an expression of natural law. For the modern creator of the grotesque, man is an inextricable tangle of rationality, irrationality, love and hatred, self-improvement and self-destruction. He appears caught in his own biological nature.

The search for identity of course runs through Joyce and Virginia Woolf, as well as through the writers we have been discussing. But a distinction needs to be made. Whim, will, emotional pulls, and levels of consciousness complicate the nature of identity in their fiction, yet there seems to be a promise of "Where Id was, there shall Ego be." Not so with certain creators of the modern grotesque. They present the human mind as bemused. Others, however, as we have seen, do search for new formulations, new beliefs.

A frequent, and probably an essential, factor in this newer literature, especially in its more serious manifestations, is that one category tends to erupt inside another category. In Addie Bundren, as we have already seen, a woman is trying desperately to find a sense of significant being through conduct that on the surface seems perverse. Addie is a prototype of the modern grotesque. The most deliberately idealistic figures in Warren's novels find themselves performing base acts, usually with a half-accepted sense of their own righteousness. In his fiction Warren strives to resolve ambiguities and contradictions in moral issues, and in the process grotesque actions and characters evolve. In Flannery O'Connor's fiction, to take a final example, one finds Catholic orthodoxy erupting inside an amoral commercialism and an ill-defined and sometimes not very vigorous Southern Protestantism. The consequences are such strange villain-heroes as the Misfit, the Bible salesman, and that grotesque saint, Hazel Motes.

Categories, as we all know, have a way of not being absolute. Our rational selves want the category, want it fixed and stable. But we also want to recognize the ironic, the paradoxical, the ambiguous, the conflict of equal or almost equal claims. It is not wholly fortuitous that the terms irony, paradox, ambiguity, synthesis, tension, and so many others are the staple terms of modern criticism. They are ways of saying that categories merge, break down, and that elements from one category have an odd way of turning up in neighboring categories.

Modern literature has sought to incorporate the antipoetic into the traditionally poetic, the cowardly into the heroic, the ignoble into the noble, the realistic into the romantic, the ugly into the beautiful. Modern literature has heightened and stylized the antipoetic and the ugly. The grotesque, as a genre or a form of modern literature, simultaneously confronts the antipoetic and the ugly and presents them, when viewed out of the side of the eye, as the closest we can come to the sublime. The grotesque affronts our sense of established order and satisfies, or partly satisfies, our need for at least a tentative, a more flexible ordering.

2 TRADITIONS IN AMERICAN LITERATURE

THE AMERICAN WRITER IS a human being before he is an American, and he writes out of his own congenital temperament. The too simple formulation of what is or is not an American expression or attitude has first to explain away the variety in human temperament. Yet he does write inside the American milieu and that milieu influences what he feels and believes. The now standard history of American literature, the *Literary History of the United States* (1948), says in effect that a happy and forward-looking literature has been produced by a happy and forward-looking people:

> It has been a literature profoundly influenced by ideals and by practices developed in democratic living. It has been intensely conscious of the aspirations of the individual in such a democracy as we have known here. It has been humanitarian. It has been, on the whole, an optimistic literature, made virile by criticism of the actual in comparison with the ideal.

It is true that America has envisioned herself as the land of new opportunities and great expectations. As a nation America has been optimistic. It does not follow that the bulk of American literature has been optimistic. Whether intentionally or not the editors of the *Literary History* have imposed a tendentiousness on American literature that it does not, except in small part, actually have. And the reason why they have done so is clear: They desire a literature in the service of democracy.

Most literature, however, is written out of the author's vision of the nature of things, a vision that is much larger and more inclusive than a political system. He may, like Melville, Hawthorne, or Faulkner, create a vision of horror and yet be a democrat. Perhaps most good writers would feel a little uneasy with the label "optimistic," and with some justice they might say that a better word for this state of mind is innocence, the state to which optimism aspires. It is the better word too because it suggests ironic overtones. They could say that many American writers have discovered the tension inherent in the doctrine of innocence, and, furthermore, that many of our best writers have been anything but optimistic.

Probably all American writers are influenced by their country's dream of innocence. The horrors of Poe or Bierce or those in the novel of violence may be darker than they might have been if the authors were not American. Hawthorne and Melville write with the ironic awareness that the received doctrine was that man is innocent. Grotesqueries as they appear in Stephen Crane, Sherwood Anderson, Nathaniel West, Carson McCullers, Truman Capote, Tennessee Williams have lent to them a quality of pathos and shock by their American *mise en scène*. America was not supposed to be like this, to let such things happen! Their grotesqueries are like the corrupted young or the wicked act of the dedicated idealist, doubly a betrayal, doubly evil. Presumably each of these and other writers would not be what they are were it not that innocence is a part of the landscape, a part of the topographical reaches of the American mind. The desire for innocence, aside from the question of the ways it influences American conduct, is a part of the national character.

In Henry Adams' novel *Democracy* (1880) one Baron Jacobi complains bitterly about the American's vision of himself as a citizen of a nation of purity and innocence:

You Americans believe yourself to be excepted from the operation of general laws. You care not for experience I have lived seventy-five years, and all that time in the midst of corruption. I am corrupt myself, only I do have the courage to proclaim it, and you others have not. Rome, Paris, Vienna, Petersburg, London, all are corrupt, only Washington is pure!

He goes on to say that many businessmen and local legislators are corrupt—and why shouldn't Americans acknowledge that evil flourishes among them as much as it does anywhere else. A half century and more later one finds Leslie Fiedler, in the symposium *America and the Intellectuals* (1953), writing a dramatically exclamatory paragraph on the American's horrified reaction when he discovers that all is not innocent:

> Among us, nothing is winked at or shrugged away; we are being eternally horrified at dope addiction or bribery or war, at things accepted in older civilizations as the facts of life, scarcely worth a tired joke. Even tax evasion dismays us! We are forever feeling our own pulses, collecting statistics to demonstrate the plight of the Negro, the prevalence of divorce, . . . the decline of family Bible reading, because we feel, we *know* that a little while ago it was in our power, new men in a new world (and even now there is hope), to make all perfect.

The student of the American temperament could collect innumerable quotations apposite in some way to America's desire for innocence. There is no doubt that the Jeffersonian heritage, among others, has helped to convince many Americans that they are not merely freer from prejudice than Europeans but infinitely freer from political tyranny. Any number of writers, regardless of nationality, have questioned these assumptions. The assumptions remain. The shocked surprise, to take a single example, provoked by exposé volumes—almost an industry in itself —suggests how deeply Americans, in intention, assent to their Jeffersonian doctrines.

The West, the frontiersman, and the cowboy have, of course, played a considerable part in the American's image of himself. The "horse-opera" and books about the cowboy, most of them third or fourth rate or worse, are to the twentieth century what pastoral poetry was to Renaissance Europe. Perhaps no small number of Americans are a little uneasy with Stephen Crane's "The Blue Hotel" or Steinbeck's *Of Mice and Men* because they seem, by the sheer fact of being set in the West, to question the reassurance and hope for which the West as symbol stands.

James Fenimore Cooper's Leatherstocking, especially in *The Prairie*, affords an interesting introduction to the plainsman and to the West as symbols of American innocence. When Leatherstocking inhabits the settled land of New York State, Cooper feels obliged to give him a relatively low place in the social order—his love affairs, if they may be called that, are kept from development by the impropriety of the woodsman courting a genteel, that is upper-class, heroine. But in *The Prairie* the social structure of the East is not greatly in evidence, and Leatherstocking is seen against the backdrop of nature. Susan Cooper said her father wished he had not introduced Captain Middleton and Inez de Certavallos, genteel aristocrats, and his reason is clear: The social hierarchies of civilization interfere with Leatherstocking, freedom and his being apotheosized as a symbol of natural wisdom. Ironically a weakness in stories of this sort is that the tensions of civilization are left behind, and the resulting peacefulness, though momentarily enchanting, seems unengaging because it is undramatic.

William Faulkner's "The Bear" may well be the greatest paean to innocence in all American literature. It belongs, of course, to the latter part of the Faulkner canon, beginning with *Go Down Moses*, of which it is a section, when he turns toward a vision of innocence and hope. Ike McCaslin is a kind of Leatherstocking. He contemplates Nature as bountiful, peaceful, and moral. Civilization, with its lusts and axes and dirt, has destroyed it. Ike dreams a kind of Midsummer Night's Dream of innocence, and of America as it might have been.

The dream of innocence has also contributed to certain reputations, most notable those of Mark Twain and Walt Whitman. Their subject matter is the West and innocence, and it follows (by association though not by logic) that they are the most American writers. Twain wrote a number of declarations of independence from the Old World. He wrote about the common man. He took the tall tale, an indigenous form, and gave it literary eminence. Twain himself came from Missouri, the very heart of America, and he lived near and worked on America's mythic river, the Mississippi. He was a home product, at once comic, shrewd, and innocent. The pathetic irony of his role is that (it is the conflict of visions again) he ended his life terribly disillusioned and pessimistic.

Whitman also was a celebrant of the West as natural innocence, and it is instructive that most propaganda poetry and most "war poetry" has been written in the Whitman idiom. Karl Shapiro in *Essay on Rime* says of epics or would-be epics written by his contemporaries:

> *The bulk of these fall from the sanguine pens*
> *Of Emersonian and Whitmanian bards.*

Thoreau had his own version of the recovery of innocence: One sloughed off old conventions, allowing in their place new organic conventions to reveal themselves. Innocence, too, was Emerson's message: Sorrow is "superficial," and varieties of evil are "the soul's mumps and measles." The Sage of Concord does not speak in tones that sound very compelling to twentieth-century ears, but most certainly he was the dominant figure in his own era, and if he did not begin the Genteel Tradition he was, in part, its prophet and lawgiver.

Almost the whole history of American fiction in the late nineteenth century and the early decades of the twentieth century can be brought to focus by demonstrating ways in which it was in reaction against the Genteel Tradition. Henry James demanded that novelists be free to tell the truth as they knew it. William Dean Howells bridged the world of Emerson and the "new realism," first by insisting that God's goodness and truth are in "reality," then by showing, as in *A Hazard of New Fortunes*, that the business ethics of the new industrialism seemed to have destroyed America's moral idealism. Stephen Crane wrote *Maggie* "to show people to people as they appear to me," and Richard Watson Gilder declined to publish it because, so it is said, he found it "*too* honest." Crane ridiculed sentimental fiction, demonstrated that a bad neighborhood environment and overly righteous people are equally destructive agents, and presented Nature as "alien." Theodore Dreiser's *Sister Carrie* bluntly gainsaid the belief that "virtuous conduct" is rewarded and "immoral conduct" is punished, and so on. Jack London and Frank Norris played with themes borrowed from Zola and produced a fiction of romantic naturalism. The names in the history of "realism" are many: Edward Eggleston, Hamlin Garland, Harold Frederic, Ed Howe. . . . When Sinclair Lewis made his acceptance speech in receiving the Nobel Award in 1930 he announced the final defeat of the Genteel Tradition —of one part of the cult of innocence.

But the tradition of innocence did not die with the rise of realism. One finds it in a variety of fiction, in Sherwood Anderson's search for the American soul and a return to some blessedness that has disappeared, in Thomas Wolfe's romantic search and his anguished cry that he cannot go home again, and in William Saroyan's discovery that people are zany and yet somehow wonderful. Perhaps the weakness in these writers is that each felt he could find or rest in a state of innocence. America's vision of innocence has not invariably passed into literature in forms that seem mature or able to resist skeptical gaze. On the other hand, some of the best of her writers have been preoccupied with it and have found therein a play of forces, moral and intellectual, that has engaged them significantly and seriously.

Charles Brockden Brown, the first American novelist, wrote tales of Gothic horror. Edgar Allan Poe envisioned a universe haunted, malevolent, and in decay. Hawthorne believed in the doctrine of original sin, and he discovered his primary subject in the iron righteousness of the New England conscience. Herman Melville, his contemporary, possessed a profound sense of the human mind as the carrier of long forgotten terrors and violences, and he inclined to be contemptuous of writers who had little or no sense of man's still living in the presence of roaring Niagaras. Twentieth-century literature in America looks backward to Poe, to Hawthorne, to Melville, as much as to Emerson and to Whitman. There is a Hawthorne aspect, as well as a Henry James aspect, to T. S. Eliot's poetry (if he may still be regarded as American). There is a Hawthorne aspect to William Faulkner's *Light in August* and, in part, to *Absalom, Absalom!* There is a Melville aspect to the "Hemingway world" and to the fiction of Robert Penn Warren. In other words, there is a continuity to American literature that envisions worlds of terror or horror.

Poe had sufficient reason for imagining a world shrouded in darkness and threatening disaster. But his decaying castles, slimy tarns, and "clammy virgins" are not merely the projection of a sick mind; they are a version of the world. And it is this—that they are a version of the world—that has caused Allen Tate to speak of "Our Cousin, Mr. Poe." Ambrose Bierce and perhaps Fitzjames O'Brien are the only significant nineteenth-century American writers who seem very close to Poe, probably because it is unnatural constantly to envision the world as mad. But awareness in Poe's fiction of the world as mad or haunted or malevolent finds its echoes in twentieth-century literature, American as well as European. In "Morella" the nature of human identity is discussed very explicitly, and it is clear that Poe was not satisfied with Plato's doctrine of the soul as "one everlastingly, and single." W. B. Yeats in the introduction to the *Oxford Book of Modern Verse* said modern poets are haunted by the idea of the human mind as flux. Instances might be quoted from Pound's *Cantos* or from any number of poems by Conrad Aiken. Again, Poe's generation did not have such terms as sadism, masochism, or the death wish, but Poe understood these phenomena. Gertrude Stein's Melanctha, Faulkner's Miss Emily, and Warren's Lilburne Lewis are all cousins to Mr. Poe.

Nathaniel Hawthorne continued the Gothic tradition in something like direct descent from Mrs. Radcliffe and Charles Brockden Brown. Wizards and witches hold their horrible séances in dark forests, portraits have mysterious powers, a curse hangs heavily in a family line, the wind and even flowers can be malevolent. But Hawthorne was not preeminently a teller of eerie tales. His plots were frequently an embarrassment to him. His interest was the psychology of evil, especially as he knew it, historically and contemporaneously, in New England. He believed profoundly in man's capacity for evil, and he was amused by, or contemptuous of, the doctrines of innocence proposed by his Transcendental friends. He admired moral fibre, but he was fascinated by the iron-like morality of the Puritans and the righteous persecution to which it gave rise.

William Faulkner is also preoccupied with rigidity of spirit, which he suggests by the phrase "iron New England dark" and which he develops at great length in his anti-Calvinist novel, *Light in August*. None of Hawthorne's iron men is more intent on righteous persecution than Simon McEachern, foster father of Joe Christmas, and probably no other modern novel so clearly demonstrates the evil lurking in the righteous mind. *Absalom, Absalom!* also deals with rigidity of spirit, but this time Faulkner, a master of violence, uses a Gothic form: father and brother talking on dim battlefields, brother shooting brother, the decapitation of Sutpen, the "demon," with a scythe, a once great house roaring in flames, a slack-jawed idiot seeming to hover half disembodied in the night. Yet another form of horror is in his *Sanctuary*, with amoral creatures on a cooling ball in space pursuing their meaningless lusts of flesh and spirit, and coming to violent deaths or vacuous ennui. Novel after novel, until rather late in Faulkner's career, say, and in a variety of ways, that life is a condition of violence and of horror.

In Faulkner's work a vision of innocence or the desire for innocence has gradually replaced a vision of horror. In Ernest Hemingway the two visions co-exist, contributing to the dramatic tension and ironic tone of his fiction. The world of childhood is used to evoke a sense of innocence, but set against it are the images of evil, of Africa, Kilimanjaro, the hyenas, the sea, the bullfight, war. There is also something that might be called the Huck Finn aspect; that is, the Hemingway hero will have nothing to do with ordinary civilization, and, like Huck, he takes off for the territory. But, and this is Hemingway's double vision, the evil is there too. If finally the truth is *Nada* it is a truth heard by innocent ears, and the hearer is horror-struck.

One reason behind the renewed interest in Melville and the acceptance of Robert Penn Warren as an important novelist is that both writers have created visions of horror that in some inevitable sense seem true. The thematic similarity between *Pierre or, the Ambiguities* and *World Enough and Time* might suggest that Robert Penn Warren's fiction in some sense derives from Herman Melville's fiction. Warren did write a sympathetic essay on the poetry of Melville, but that appeared long after Warren had established himself as a poet and novelist. The influence of Conrad or Faulkner is more easily demonstrable. More interesting than direct influences are the accidental similarities, in points of view, attitudes, and vision. Both are intensely moralistic writers who have struggled to work out a naturalistic ethic. Both attempt to reconcile profound skepticism with an equally profound idealism. Neither writer belongs to what Warren had called the Captain McWhirrs of literature, the writers who for all their good will or courage never suffer from a vision of horror, who are so lacking in imagination that terror is beyond them. Melville of course created his own Captain McWhirr in the Captain Delano of *Benito Cereno*, and in his essay on Hawthorne he noted his preference for those men who dive deep. And both writers have believed profoundly that nature seems or is alien to man's spirit, that his idealistic side pulls away from nature, and, conversely, that nature exerts a pull to draw man deeply into herself. Nature is neither to be denied nor unresisted, for man is *in* nature, but not *of* it.

In Melville's "The Encatadas" there is one Oberlus who lived with the turtles on a lava island. "So warped and crooked was his strange nature, that the very handle of his hoe seemed gradually to have shrunk and twisted in his grasp, being a wretched bent stick, elbowed more like a savage's war-sickle than a civilized hoe-handle." In Warren's *All the King's Men* Jack Burden observes a row of statutes that line a road leading into a nerve sanatorium:

> Between the regularly spaced oaks stood pedestals on which classical marble—draped and undraped, male and female, stained by weathers and leaf acid and encroaching lichen, looking as though they had, in fact, sprouted dully out of the clinging black-green humus below them— stared out at the passer-by with the faintly pained, heavy, incurious unamazement of cattle. The gaze of those marble eyes must have been the first stage in the treatment the neurotic got when he came out to the sanatorium. It must have been like smearing a cool unguent of time on the hot pustule and dry itch of the soul.

The "dry itch of the soul" and the conjunction of "hot pustule" and "soul" say what Warren's fiction as a whole says, that man is capable of great good and tremendous evil. He is at once in nature and above it—and his conduct, human, natural, ethical, is determined by this fact.

To say that literature is experience may, if it does not seem merely fatuous, seem merely another way of saying that literature is "knowledge" or "power" or "a criticism of life." But the term is useful: Sometimes experience uses a vision of innocence to encourage hope, and sometimes to criticize excesses of hope; it says with Lambert Strether, "Live all you can, it's a mistake not to," discovering refinements of mind, imagination, and sense; it helps define the nature of life as quotidian.

American poets, from Anne Bradstreet to Marianne Moore, present a view of the unusual in the commonplace. In Emily Dickinson, who employed a most homely diction, New England had a poet who domesticated the Old Calvinist vision. In Robert Frost and John Crowe Ransom romantic innocence and romantic horrors are disciplined and restrained. Frost has written, "The fact is the sweetest dream that labor knows," and Ransom, "I am shaken, but not as a leaf." In E. E. Cummings, Kenneth Fearing, and Karl Shapiro contemporary poetry has critics of the Babbitt type of innocence.

Henry James had a whole gallery of American inno-
cents, Christopher Newman, Isabel Archer, Milly Theale,
Daisy Miller, Lambert Strether. Perhaps Newman of
The American is the prototype of them all. He is the
voyager into new experiences, he has great capacities for
hope, and he is trusting. The story may be summarized as
the conflict between Newman's artistic, social and moral
innocence and the Bellegarde's knowingness, strict forms,
restraint, and guile. Newman learns the importance of
self-discipline, of forms, properties, and the implication is
that Europe could learn from him. As with so many of
James's characters, Newman makes terms with necessity
without falling into despondency or hopelessness.

A surprising number of modern fiction writers in
America have found one of their major themes in causing
characters to pursue romantic dreams and absolutes, and
coming to terms with or being destroyed by the consequences. The beginnings seem to be with Henry James,
but those who follow are legion: Edith Wharton, Willa
Cather, Scott Fitzgerald, Glenway Wescott, Caroline
Gordon, Katherine Anne Porter, James Gould Cozzens,
and Lionel Trilling. Each is concerned with the phenomenon Allen Tate called "positive Platonism," that is, a
"cheerful confidence in the limitless powers of man."

Edith Wharton, commonly seen as the most distinguished of the immediate followers of James, may be said
to have found her major theme in explaining the need
for compromise. That certainly is the theme of her *Age
of Innocence*. Mrs. Wharton ordinarily is not especially
witty or humorous, but in "The Other Two" she had written a finely humorous story about compromise. It concerns
the slow and ironic recognition on the part of husband
number three that his wife owes her undoubted charms
to having lived with her two earlier husbands; from the
first, who was lower middle class in taste, she learned
to appreciate delicacy, and from the other, who had had
"advantages" but was a little on the libertine side, she
learned to respect fidelity and loyalty. Husband number
three comes finally to his discovery one afternoon when
circumstances have caused all of them to be present in his

drawing room. The men are embarrassed, but she, who has faced and surmounted difficulties before, is her charming self. He finds his discovery painful, but accept he does, wryly appreciative.

Willa Cather, who also learned a good deal from James, is, though less ironic, like Edith Wharton in understanding muted joys. She understands the strangeness, pain and pleasure of "obscure destinies," and the deep satisfaction in simple, unostentatious, and even hard conditions of life. Miss Cather's knowledge of frontier, village and farm life may have given her an even fuller understanding of the pretentious and the meretricious. Professor St. Peter, in her fine novel *The Professor's House*, tries to understand what had brought him to the edge of suicide, and he says to himself: "Perhaps the mistake was merely an attitude of mind. He had never learned how to live without delight."

Scott Fitzgerald provides a classic instance of romantic innocence defeated. Jay Gatsby is presented as a prototype of American innocence and hopefulness: Defeat is impossible to him and even time can be brought to a standstill, or life can be relived and mistakes refined into nonexistence. Each of his protagonists, like the one in "Babylon Revisited," is asked to recognize that the snow is "real snow." He is subjected to a series of tests which, at long last, force him to face the consequences of living with sentiments that were ill-understood, of having confused illusion and reality. Similar statements, modified to suit their special preoccupations and subject matters, might be made about the fiction of Glenway Wescott, Caroline Gordon, Katherine Anne Porter, James Gould Cozzens—and about still other writers who, consciously or not, write in the tradition of Henry James. However individualized their subject matter and tone, qualities they have in common are the surprise that attends failure and the pathos that attends making friends with death, time and necessity.

AT FIRST young America talked about a national epic. Rome had her *Aeneid*, England her Arthurian legends, and France her *Song of Roland*. Before long, however, Americans were saying that the spirit of the new country would not be caught in the epic—it would be caught in the novel. And in looking back we can see that it is in the novel, rather than in poetry, that America has sought her own image.

America differs from other countries in having been founded on an idea. As some historian has said, it had no pre-history, no dim and mythy past. Seventeenth- and eighteenth-century man, born into the new age when rationality was supposed to have freed him from superstition, now had his chance. During the Renaissance, More, Campanella, Bacon, and others imagined and described utopian societies. Here in North America was the opportunity.

Men, even the men of the Enlightenment, however, are not merely social and political creatures. They study themselves in mirrors, in the memorials they erect honoring their own achievements, and in the dreams constructed inside the covers of their books. Young America was carrying a terrible burden—the need to be a perfect society, or as near perfect as possible. Crèvecoeur, who wrote *Letters from an American Farmer*, a utopian vision of the new society, also wrote *Sketches of Eighteenth Century America*, a disillusioned and bitter account of "patriots" he had known. Significantly, the former was published and widely acclaimed. The latter was put in a trunk and rediscovered, with no great fanfare, only in the twentieth century. There may be a clue here to the American imagination.

With his characteristic perceptiveness, D. H. Lawrence put his finger on a preoccupation of James Fenimore Cooper:

> In his Leatherstocking books, Fenimore is off on another track. He is no longer concerned with social white Americans that buzz with pins through them, buzz loudly against every mortal thing except the pin itself. The pin of the Great Ideal. One gets irritated with Cooper because he never for once snarls at the Great Ideal Pin which transfixes him. No, indeed. Rather he tries to push it through the very heart of the Continent.

To some extent almost every American novelist is haunted by the Great Ideal and by the Continent; they are related. In essence the Great Ideal is a search for innocence, and the virgin continent was the innocent wilderness. Or was it? Man carried himself into the wilderness, and however fast he moved westward he was dogged by a sense that society, reality, and his own instincts were close behind. For the American novelist the dream of innocence is always there in one form or another. If he is a Cooper or a William Saroyan there is no irony in contemplating it. If he is a Hawthorne, a Melville, a James or a Robert Penn Warren the irony may be gentle or harsh.

We are sometimes told the novel begins with *Don Quixote* (1647). Certainly Cervantes understood the kinds of aspiration that were to dominate the American novel. On the one side, in *Don Quixote*, there is the practical world, the sort of world in which a young man will be seen marrying for money, in which innocent servants are seduced, and the master of the household calmly cheats a business associate. On the other side, there is gallantry, love, self-sacrifice, and dedication to noble causes. Which side wins in the lists? Does the practical-realistic man easily unseat the dedicated idealist, or does the conduct of the latter so enliven the former's imagination that they join forces? Presumably the novel is at its best when the understanding of the "illusion" and the understanding of the "reality" are profound or at least sufficiently sophisticated to satisfy our awareness that neither "illusion" nor "reality" is wholly separable and definable—we cannot always tell the dancer from the dance. Put in another way, we want to feel sure that the dedicated idealist is tilting at something more than a windmill.

In *Don Quixote*, Cervantes began on the side of reality; he ridiculed and poked fun at the romantic. Then, in midstream, as we say, he changed horses. He began to see that fantasy can influence the human heart and idealize human conduct. The American novel appears to have reversed Cervantes' procedure. It began with a preference for the ideal, for the dream. But reality has a way of following, nipping at the heels of the romantic-minded hero.

As early as 1828, in "American Literature," Cooper was making the distinction between the novel (by which he meant a treatment of manners, the social novel) and the romance (apart from, or indifferent to, society). The former was European, the latter American. There were, according to Cooper, three reasons for this difference: America offered a "poverty of materials," "no costume for the peasant, . . . no wig for the judge, no baton for the general, no diadem for the magistrate"; there was a heaviness and lack of individuality to the American character; and, anyway, an American publisher would rather pirate British novels than pay any American for his book. Cooper, of course, is not wholly consistent.

One can wonder why Boston, Philadelphia, or Charleston—which cannot have been so greatly different from provincial cities in Europe—produced no social novelists. What if Ben Franklin had been inclined toward fiction? Presumably he'd have written social novels, stories about housemaids and the young master, indentured servants, apprentices, gala dances, the slave quarters out back, the pursuit of learning in an attic room, the pull of Europe, the ways of politicians, and getting on in the world. But

Franklin didn't write novels, nor did anyone of his temperament. As Cooper says, this type had more assured ways of making successful careers. And we can at least speculate that the pull of the collective American imagination was away from the social community because society has a way of dimming and tarnishing the brilliant shine on the dream.

In an interesting essay, "Manners, Morals and the Novel," Lionel Trilling says that snobbery about one's function as well as about one's status, and money, having or not having it, are or should be at the very center of the novel; in others words, the novel ought to be about society. The English and the French novel are centered in society, and even D. H. Lawrence, in comparison with most American writers, is a social novelist. Mr. Trilling says that only Theodore Dreiser and Sinclair Lewis wrote social novels, but he adds that neither handled social difference with sufficient cogency. John Dos Passos, he says, was preoccupied with social forces, but he employed them only as background. Following Mr. Trilling's thesis, we can assume that James has been gathered into "Balzac's bosom." And perhaps we should assign Fitzgerald, especially for *Tender Is the Night*, and Edith Wharton, for *The Age of Innocence*, to the Balzac section in heaven. And more recently, of course, John O'Hara and James Gould Cozzens have written the social novel. As life in the United States becomes "more complex and pressing," to borrow Mr. Trilling's phrase, the American social novel will be more commonly written.

Recently an English critic has said that most American novelists tend to imitate their "own engineers," and to think of the novel in terms of the Empire State Building or the George Washington Bridge—he writes "on a scale other than that of everyday life." Our short novels, incidentally, tend not to sprawl; they have the neatness of a convex mirror. This English critic might have had Thomas Wolfe, William Faulkner, Robert Penn Warren or even Saul Bellow in mind. If he had a nineteenth-century novelist in the back of his head, probably it was Melville.

However important the architecture or the sprawl of

the American novel in accounting for differences, there is another characteristic that may be even more significant. As backdrop, and subject too, the American novelist tends to employ something vast, the sky, the prairie, the wilderness, the ocean, war, humanity, and even eternity. Man-as-American stands in the foreground. As illustrations we may take *Wieland*, *The Prairie*, *The Scarlet Letter*, *The Adventures of Huckleberry Finn*, *Moby Dick*, *McTeague*, *The Red Badge of Courage*, *The Country of Pointed Firs*, *A Farewell to Arms*, *The Professor's House*, *U. S. A.*, *World Enough and Time*, and *A Fable*.

A series of arguments and manifestoes that run through *Idea of the American Novel* have to do with the terms *regionalism*, *nationalism*, and *universality*. By and large, the regionalists have the best of the argument. If a novelist produces a significant work, it inevitably has a wide, a universal appeal. Inevitably too, and unplanned, it has a national character.

In the past few years there has been an effort to locate the American vernacular. Twain, Crane, Anderson, and Hemingway are sometimes said to represent it in its purest or at least its earliest forms. Faulkner, when not employing his high rhetoric, is said to employ it, and even Warren. And, of course, Salinger's *Catcher in the Rye* is the vernacular in its New York City guise. There has also been a search for the American hero—Huck Finn, Nick Adams, Leatherstocking, Ishmael, Pierre, Christopher, Tom Outland, Jay Gatsby, and Holden Cauldfield. Obviously there is a certain family resemblance among all of these characters. Others could be added.

Recently too we have been told by R. P. Blackmur that the American novelist—he is referring mostly to the short novel—tends to express himself in allegories. And we seem to have come full circle back to Cooper with Richard Chase's thesis that the American novel, unlike the English, is romance.

In reading and studying American novels we are involved in the never ending discussion of what it is like to be an American. In the process too we learn something about the adaptability of the novel as an art form.

4 THE NOVEL-OF-EXPERIENCE

AS WE ALL KNOW, many of the modern novelist's preoccupations with form derive from Henry James. We even
speak of the Jamesian novel, which Joseph Warren Beach
describes as the turning of "pictorial matter into drama by
straining it through the consciousness of the leading character." James's formal considerations, as the collected
prefaces show, are many and significant. By the Jamesian
novel we also mean such complicated intellectual and
moral conflicts as may be involved in a particular and
rarefied social world. It doesn't follow, of course, that
everyone in the Jamesian tradition writes about a "rarefied
social world." James's protagonists come to understand
deceit, the seamy side of motives, the urgency of time,
the importance of vivid experience—they reconcile their
innocent vision with the world as it is, and they compromise with the high expectations they had had for themselves. James wrote what might be called the novel-of-
experience, quite distinct, say, from the Conradian novel,
the struggle to understand the very substructure of a
civilization, or the Joycean novel, the presentation of the
mind in all its layers of light and darkness. The phrase
"novel-of-experience" may suggest too much, be too loose
as a category. Even so, it helps to define a line in
twentieth-century American fiction that is quite as distinct,
and perhaps equally as important, as the novel-of-violence.
   Certain of James's shorter works, "The Lesson of the
Master" and "The Beast in the Jungle" are clearly stories

of experience. In the former, St. George, a gifted novelist, sacrifices his talent to "success" and domestic comforts. He advises an equally gifted younger man, Paul Overt, not to involve himself domestically, but to dedicate himself to his art. The young man follows this advice; but when he returns to London, two years later, with a completed manuscript he finds events have taken a most curious turn. He learns that St. George has been widowed and then married to Miss Fancourt, the beautiful young lady he himself had, with great difficulty, given up! At first Overt is outraged and feels that St. George has taken him in, but he has a conversation with St. George and the latter convinces him that he had given him sincere advice. Overt has achieved what he had hoped to achieve as a writer. St. George has not. Despite the literary achievements, however, Paul Overt will live with half a suspicion that the older man, who says he has ceased to write, is mocking him. The story, in the narrator's summary, ends thus:

> When the new book came out in the autumn Mr. and Mrs. St. George found it really magnificent. The former still has published nothing, but Paul doesn't even yet feel safe. I may say for him, however, that if this event were to occur he would perhaps be the very first to appreciate it: which is perhaps a proof that the Master was essentially right and that Nature had dedicated him to intellectual, not to personal passion.

The story would seem to say that moral dedication can never be entirely pure. Clinging to motives are ironic perplexities, ambiguities of intention. In "The Beast in the Jungle" romantic expectations are subjected to the most unromantic of ironies: The protagonist has so exaggerated an idea of what destiny holds in store for him that he cannot even imagine what it might be; ultimately he learns that exactly nothing is in store for him. He is left with the painful realization that he has been a fool. He has missed ordinary happiness, experience, while waiting for something spectacularly above the ordinary.

Perhaps the essential quality in Edith Wharton, James's immediate follower, is the ironic pleasure to be found in defeat and in compromise. In *The Fruit of the Tree* (1907) she wrote: "Life is not a matter of abstract principles, but a succession of pitiful compromises with fate, of concessions to old traditions, old beliefs, old tragedies, old failures." She was especially concerned with the compromises called for in marriage, and with the fact that duty allowed one a superior, though sometimes grimmer, joy than that to be found in romance itself. *Ethan Frome*, it should be said, has in it almost no joy at all; duty is served, as the situation demands that it be, through long and painful years. In *The Age of Innocence* (1920), on the other hand, the joy is muted rather than grim. Although sorely tempted, Newland Archer refuses to leave his wife May for the exotic Ellen Olenska, whom he loves very deeply. Twenty-odd years later, when he is a widower, Archer thinks back over his life:

> His days were full, and they were filled decently. He supposed it was all a man ought to ask.
>
> Something he knew he had missed: the flower of life. But he thought of it now as a thing so unattainable and improbable that to have repined would have been like despairing because one had not drawn the first prize in a lottery . . . He had been what is called a faithful husband; and when May had suddenly died—carried off by the infectious disease through which she had nursed their youngest child—he had honestly mourned her. Their long years together had shown him that it did not so much matter if marriage was a dull duty: lapsing from that, it became a mere battle of ugly appetites. Looking about him, he honoured his own past, and mourned for it. After all, there was good in the old ways.

The last chapter is not, as certain of Edith Wharton's critics have said, an ironic presentation of a man who had sacrificed happiness to conservative conventions. Mrs. Wharton agrees that his conduct was the only moral action possible to him. There is story after story in which she finds her conflict in the indulgence of one's own desires at the expense of someone else. In "The Reckoning," from *The Descent of Man* (1904), a woman says: "If we don't recognize an inner law . . . the obligation that love creates . . . being loved as well as loving . . . there is nothing to prevent our spreading ruin unhindered."

Scott Fitzgerald, who was probably indebted to Mrs. Wharton in various ways, wrote in *The Great Gatsby* a novel that is likely to remain a classic study of American innocence and hopefulness. Gatsby's dream of success belongs in Plato's realm of absolute perfections. Over and over again in the novel there are references to this Platonism. In one of the opening paragraphs there is this:

> If personality is an unbroken series of successful gestures, then there was something gorgeous about him, some heightened sensitivity to the promises of life, as if he were related to one of those intricate machines that register earthquakes ten thousand miles away. . . .—it was an extraordinary gift for hope, a romantic readiness such as I have never found in any other person and which it is not likely I shall ever find again.

Again:

> The truth was that Jay Gatsby of West Egg, Long Island, sprang from a Platonic conception of himself. He was a son of God—a phrase which, if it means anything means just that—and he must be about his Father's business, the service of a vast, vulgar, and meretricious beauty. So he invented the sort of Jay Gatsby that a seventeen-year-old boy would be likely to invent, and to this conception he was faithful to the end.

Gatsby's vision is in a sense sacrilegious, but he does not know that it is. Nor does he realize that his notions of the beautiful or appropriate are vulgar. In his ignorance, Gatsby thinks that huge amounts of money can buy freedom from time, pain or defeat, that having it one should be able to rise above the hot struggles of ordinary humanity. At one point, Carraway warns Gatsby that Daisy having been married to Tom Buchanan for several years is bound to have made compromises and to be a different person from the one Gatsby had known—he tells him, in effect, that time has its way with us whether we will or not:

"I wouldn't ask too much of her," I ventured.

"You can't repeat the past."

"Can't repeat the past?" he cried incredulously. "Why, of course you can!"

When Gatsby had come to love Daisy, he had identified that love with his Platonic vision:

> Out of the corner of his eye Gatsby saw that the blocks of the sidewalk really formed a ladder and mounted to a secret place above the trees. . . . He knew that when he kissed this girl, and forever wed his unutterable visions to her perishable breath, his mind would never romp again like the mind of God. . . . At his lips touch she blossomed for him like a flower and the incarnation was complete.

The rhetoric Carraway uses—"the mind of God," "incarnation," "Platonic ladder"—are obviously intended to suggest the preposterous hope, or even the sacrilege of Gatsby's vision of his destiny. It is in terms of this vision that Daisy lives for him. Thus when he is forced to admit that she had loved Buchanan, he says: "In any case it was just personal." Gatsby's expectations are of course defeated. Whatever Daisy *might* have been married to Gatsby, she *was* something quite different: She is fully as corrupt as Tom Buchanan, and with him, either by design or terrible negligence she helps cause Gatsby's murder. Carraway was right in telling Gatsby that time is compromise and eventually defeat. The closing passage of the novel is this:

> He had come along way to this blue lawn, and his dream must have seemed so close that he could hardly fail to grasp it. He did not know that it was already behind him, somewhere back in that vast obscurity beyond the city, where the dark fields of the republic rolled on under the night.
>
> Gatsby believed in the green light, the orgiastic future that year by year recedes before us. It eluded us then, but that's no matter—tomorrow we will run faster, stretch our arms farther. . . . And one fine morning—
>
> So we beat on, boats against the current, borne back ceaselessly into the past.

Jay Gatsby is an American Don Quixote, more self-interested than his prototype perhaps but like him committed to an absolute romanticism: He is *a* symbolic American: he believes somehow that mortality applies to other people, he believes in the future not in the past, and all achievements are possible to him.

Willa Cather, like Mrs. Wharton and Fitzgerald, was concerned with life as commonplace experience, compromise, and reconciliation with hard circumstance. *The Professor's House*, for example, is an antiromantic novel. It is sometimes read as a story of a family made mean-spirited and selfish by money, and there is some justification for such a reading. Professor St. Peter's receiving a large award for his series of historical studies enables him to build a new house, much more sumptuous than the one he had rented for twenty-odd years. St. Peter dislikes ostentation but his wife is rather given to it, and the house occasions grave disagreements which finally estrange them. In Tom Outland, killed in World War I, St. Peter had had a brilliant student, a close friend, and almost a son-in-law. Outland, who had made an important scientific discovery, left a will in favor of Rosamund St. Peter, the professor's daughter; and her husband, Louis Marsellus, exploits the discovery. The consequences of the wealth of the young couple are many: quarrels between St. Peter and his wife, jealousy and strained relations between Rosamund and her sister Kathleen, difficulties between St. Peter and his daughters, a colleague's ugly recriminations and lawsuit, the near-suicide of St. Peter, and so on.

The various episodes of the novel do suggest the theme that money corrupts. Yet insofar as it is St. Peter's story—"his" story—the theme is deeper than this. After his near-suicide St. Peter examines his life. There had been two great excitements in it: an intensely romantic love for his wife, and the delight in writing a highly original history of the Spanish explorations. Estranged from his wife and having finished his work, he was suddenly empty. And this emptiness had allowed him to welcome the half-accident that nearly ended his life.

The lives of two other people, Tom Outland and Augusta, the seamstress, teach St. Peter he can face the future "without joy, without passionate griefs," and even find it pleasant. Early in *The Professor's House* we learn that Mrs. St. Peter had been jealous of her husband's friendship with Outland and had used Outland's reticence about certain events in his life to justify her dislike of him. When we learn the reason for the reticence, however, we find it not to Outland's discredit. His story, briefly, is this: An orphan, he had been befriended by a man named Roddy, ten years his senior; and together as cowpunchers in New Mexico they had stumbled on an ancient, prehistoric Indian village. There are many beautiful descriptions of the village, interesting speculations on the sort of civilization it must have held, and, in sum, a fine evocation of mankind's part in the eternal march. Outland had gone to Washington for assistance in bringing the village to people's attention, and his discouraging reception there had caused Roddy to sell many of the moveable objects to a German museum. Outland, upon his return, berates Roddy, who had not understood his friend's sense of piety about the village, and Roddy, greatly hurt, leaves. Outland, in relating the story, says: "Anyone who requites faith and friendship as I did, will have to pay for it. I'm not very sanguine about good fortune for myself. I'll be called to account when I least expect it." To Professor St. Peter the story signifies two things: the importance as Outland put it of "faith and friendship," as well as the humble place of the individual in the great expanse of time, and one's need therefore to restrict one's hopes and anticipations.

The life of Augusta is a far cry from the romance of Outland's life. This physical description of her suggests something about the quality of her life: "She herself was tall, large-boned, flat and stiff, with a plain, solid face and brown eyes not destitute of fun." Psychologically, Augusta is a strong character. She is disappointed that her life has not had more romance in it, but she does not sentimentalize her misfortunes. Her strength is suggested by her attitude toward death: "While she ate a generous breakfast, she would reply to his polite questions about the illness or funeral with befitting solemnity, and then go readily to another topic, not holding to the dolorous note. He used to say that he didn't mind hearing Augusta announce these deaths which seemed to happen so frequently along her way, because her manner of speaking about it made death seem less uncomfortable." It is to Augusta that St. Peter turns, or, rather, to his understanding of her: "If he had thought of Augusta sooner, he would have got up from the couch sooner," that is, he wouldn't have encouraged the "accident" that almost caused his death. Although his relations with his family had been seriously injured, "There was still Augusta. . . . a world full of Augustas, with whom one was outward bound."

Katherine Anne Porter, not unlike Miss Cather, has frequently found her theme in the contrast between the dream and the fact. In the novelette, "Old Mortality," Miranda is disillusioned by the falseness she discovers in the "history" of her family. She sees the distortions or transformations as pitiful attempts to hide the truth, and decides that she, at least, will face the truth. The story concludes: " 'I will know the truth,' she said, in her youth, in her ignorance." In "Pale Horse, Pale Rider," Death is the antagonist. A love story, it has as its setting the later days of World War I. Miranda, the heroine, recovers from influenza to discover that Adam, her lover, has also caught it—and died. The war ends and there is much celebrating, but the victory is celebrated thus by Miranda: "No more war, no more plague, only the dazed silence that follows the ceasing of the heavy guns; noiseless houses with the shades drawn, empty streets, the dead cold light of tomorrow. Now there would be time for everything."

Caroline Gordon, Miss Porter's fellow Southerner, is also able to cast a cold eye on excesses, to compare expectation with event, theory with experience, and especially to show us Time as antagonist. Her fine novel *Alec Maury, Sportsman* may be considered as almost the prototype of the novel-of-experience. Alec Maury, professor of Latin, is the humane, disciplined man. He admires the dignity

of classical poetry, and he admires the descipline necessary to the first rate fisherman. He is preoccupied with
Time and refuses to waste a moment of it; but he has no
moralistic notions about activity being the devil's ad-
versary or work being somehow virtuous in and for its own
sake. He brings his talent for fishing to perfection because that activity best enables him to live fully and
humanely. Public notions of success and magnificence he
rejects. He will enjoy the blue sky, the contour of hills,
patches of woods, and the flowing water. He lives for
delight, but a delight he has earned:

> When I had finished eating I went out on the porch and
> lit my pipe. It was still light when I went out. I sat there
> until nearly midnight and during those four or five hours
> I engaged, I imagine, in more introspection than in all the
> rest of my life put together. I knew suddenly what it was
> I had lived by, from the time when, a mere child, I used
> to go out into the woods at night hunting with a negro
> man. I remembered—it must have been when I was about
> eight—looking up in black woods into the deep, glowing
> eyes of the quarry and experiencing a peculiar, an almost
> transfiguring excitement. I had experienced it for the first
> time that night long ago in the woods at Oakleigh and I
> had been seeking and finding it, with mounting excite-
> ment, ever since. I had known from the first that it was
> all luck; I had gone about seeking it, with, as it were, the
> averted eyes of a savage praying to his god. But I had
> brought all my resources to bear on the chase. I had used
> skill and caution—nobody but myself knew what patience
> I had always expended on my careful preparations for my
> sport—and I had succeeded as few men, I told myself now
> with some arrogance, had ever succeeded.

There is a scene near the end of the novel that might
seem merely pleasant description, but it is much more
than that; it is a seventy-year-old man looking back on a
highly successful life:

> The river coming into view between banks covered with
> cane described a sharp bend, then widened out into a
> broad still pool. I went over to the rail and looked down.
> Farther up the water had a perceptible current but here

under the bridge it flowed so gently that the eye could hardly detect the movement. And it was of the most lovely pellucid green I have ever looked upon.

The novelists cited in this brief survey have been mostly women, and one might infer that the novel-of-experience is most frequently written by women. This may be so, but there are a number of men who also fit the category, notably Glenway Wescott and James Gould Cozzens. Wescott's *The Pilgrim Hawk,* for example, develops the theme that even excesses of involvement are preferable to noninvolvement, and Cozzens' quiet but deeply intelligent novel *The Just and the Unjust* shows us a young lawyer in a small town learning to accept human (jury) justice as opposed to the letter of the law.

There are, of course, other novels and other novelists who might be listed. Wright Morris, who writes a similar sort of fiction, once said in an interview that too much modern fiction depends on shock and violence. "In the name of so-called realism writers like James Jones are victimized by the notion that absolute photographic realism is an art form. What they're employing is exposure. The very techniques of exposure require use of shock which invariably cancels out the depth and wider meaning of the subject or the experience. The author suffers most from this; he is cut off from the depth and fullness of his own material." Presumably Morris is not saying that the novel-of-violence is invariably without depth, for that would deny thoughtfulness to such violent novels as *Light In August* and *As I Lay Dying,* or *All the King's Men* and *World Enough and Time,* but merely that the photographically realistic novel denying itself depth feels the need of shock. And all literature, of course, contains some degree of thought, but Morris' point, by extension, would suggest that the novel-of-experience stands or falls by the very quality of its thoughtfulness.

SHERWOOD ANDERSON, sometimes listed among American "realistic novelists," once wrote some interesting comments on fiction that is said to be true to life ("On Realism," *Notebooks*):

> The life of reality is confused, disorderly, almost always without purpose, whereas in the artist's imaginative life there is purpose. There is determination to give the tale, the song, the painting Form—to make it true and real to the theme, not to life . . .
>
> I myself remember with what a shock I heard people say that one of my own books, *Winesburg, Ohio*, was an exact picture of Ohio village life. The book was written in a crowded tenement district of Chicago. The hint for almost every character was taken from my fellow-lodgers in a large rooming house, many of whom had never lived in a village.

Anderson believed there had been some spiritual and emotional failure in modern America, and his sympathies were strongly drawn toward those men and women who were the victims of this failure. He turned them into pathetic grotesques. Presumably a village setting, which ordinarily suggests peaceful simplicity, gave these figures more dramatic contrast than Chicago would have provided. In any case, it is worth observing that there is no little irony in the fact that a specific town in Ohio is frequently mentioned as the "real" Winesburg, and that visitors sometimes go there, as they go to Oxford, Mississippi, to see with their own eyes what Anderson or William Faulkner had shown them in their respective stories about these towns.

Many of the citizens of Mississippi have felt that they and their state have been misrepresented by Faulkner's novels. And Faulkner himself has acknowledged that his fiction has contributed to misunderstanding. Lynchings, rape, fantastic funeral journeys, idiots in love with cows, Snopesism, and the rest, including the pastoral innocence side, are hardly "typical" of Mississippi.

Early in his career as a writer, Faulkner noted an essential difference between life and literature (*New Republic*, May 20, 1931, pp. 23–24). The fiction writer, he said, rather frequently meets people who have a fine story to give him—which they present with the invitation to put it down on paper intact. Unfortunately, Faulkner observed, it is not possible to transfer the story directly to paper: "Somewhere between the experience and the blank page and the pencil, it dies." The reasons why this is so are probably multiple. Only problems of a certain kind tease a writer's imagination. Again, the "world" (not merely the *mise en scène*) of the novel grows or swarms into being out of the novel's germ, and this is, in considerable part, quite a different, or more specialized, world from the one the novelist himself as citizen inhabits. Two novelists in writing about what would seem to be the same subject can project two quite different "worlds." Or, indeed, the same novelist, on different occasions, can project quite different "worlds." This latter observation can be illustrated by reference to Faulkner's *Light in August* and *Intruder in the Dust*.

In *Light in August* Faulkner treats the "Negro problem" in relation to the Protestant tradition in the South, and in *Intruder in the Dust* he treats it as a sectional issue. In both novels the setting is the town of Jefferson in Yoknapatawpha county, but the "worlds" are not the same. It is true that twenty-odd years separate their respective settings, but this does not account in any major way for the difference. In *Light in August* a Calvinistic gloom pervades the action. Episode after episode touches the central irony that a lynching can grow out of Christian righteousness. There are descriptions of church architecture and services, of life in a seminary, expositions of Southern history in relation to the church, speculations about religious and moral conduct, and so on. Collectively such matters make the "world" of the novel. Presumably Faulkner, at the time he wrote *Light in August*, did not believe that the church alone was responsible for cruel and monstrous irony. The monstrous irony makes a fine novel; it is not, sociologically, a full account of the Negro problem in the actual town of Oxford, Mississippi.

Intruder in the Dust is also concerned with a lynching, or rather the threat of a lynching, but its "world" is not Calvinistic: This time Faulkner presents a beleaguered South defending itself ideologically against liberal Yankee opinion. The town is peopled, for the most part, by rather easy-going but thoughtless citizens; not intentionally vicious, they are potentially a mob. Either the wilfully vicious, like the Gowries from Beat Four, or the intelligent and decent, like Gavin Stevens and Miss Habersham, will win them over, will help them decide how the Negro accused of shooting a white man will be treated. Helping to frame and interpret the action are Gavin Stevens and his young nephew Chick. Gavin Stevens explains that North and South are different countries. And one of the images left in the reader's mind is of the United States as a topographical map, with the North being composed of great cities and the South of small towns. Jefferson itself is seen as poor but not genteel. Chick struggles to accept the Negro as human being. In *Light in August*, the action glowers; in *Intruder in the Dust*, it is essentially bright. Whatever their similarities, they are two distinct worlds. Neither Jefferson is Oxford, Mississippi.

In the article referred to above, Faulkner also said that a novelist is free to put into the mouth of a character better speech than an actual person ordinarily is capable of speaking. He might have added that the milieu which exists inside the covers of a book of fiction is a stylized milieu: Each physical presence, each action, and each description serves to dramatize a conception. Faulkner's *Soldier's Pay*, a world-weary and sophisticated novel, belongs in part to the cut-glass artistry of Oscar Wilde and Aubrey Beardsley, and in part to the languorous gesture common to the "lost generation." *Pylon* symbolizes a waste-land world, and its principal characters suggest the near possibility of creatures "incapable of suffering, wombed and born complete and instantaneous, cunning and intricate and deadly, from out some iron bat cave of the earth's prime foundation." *Sanctuary* presents characters either bemused or hypnotized by evil, so that nature herself seems in ripe decay and all modern objects seem metallic, brassy, cheap and vulgar. And so on. Each novel aspires to live in relation to its own premises, its germ, its initial conception. And, as implied earlier, the degree to which it succeeds is an important clue to its value as a work of art. Conversely, the degree in which it fails to create a self-defining image or symbolic world is an indication of its weakness as a novel.

Consequently, it is in "marginal literature," not highly imaginative literature, that one should look for manifestations of a way of life, or sociologically valid descriptions, for "documentation" in studying an historical period, people or place. Certainly it is safer, or, as we say, a more scientific procedure, to examine church, court, and jail records, personal letters, text books, and so on to learn about the life of Shakespeare's England than it is to reconstruct it after reading *A Shoemaker's Holiday* or *As You Like It*. It would seem no less reasonable to be extremely careful in forming ideas about American life from American novels.*

---

* Each of the following makes comments about the general issue raised in this brief paper: Kenneth Burke, "Psychology and Form," *Counter-Statement* (New York, 1931); Joyce Cary, "Including Mr. Micawber," N. Y. *Times Book Review*, April 11, 1951; Harry Levin, "Literature as an Institution," *Accent*, vi (Spring 1946); "Notes on Convention," *Perspectives in Criticism*, ed. Harry Levin (Cambridge, Mass., 1950); Gorham Munson, "The Real Thing," *U. of Kansas City Review*, xvi (Summer 1950); Lionel Trilling, *E. M. Forster* (New York, 1943); Carl Van Doren, "Literature and Document," *Contemporary American Criticism* (New York, 1926); Harry B. Parkes, "Poe, Hawthorne, Melville: An Essay in Sociological

The nineteenth century saw fiction incline toward "realism" and there were apologists for absolute realism, but certain major writers delivered themselves of critical comments which make clear their understanding of fiction as nature, or reality, idealized or transformed. Nathaniel Hawthorne in the introduction to *The House of the Seven Gables* made his famous but probably unnecessary distinction between the Romance and the Novel:

> When a writer calls his work a Romance, it need hardly be observed that he wishes to claim a certain latitude, both as to its fashion and material, which he would not have felt himself entitled to assume had he professed to be writing a Novel. The latter form of composition is presumed to aim at a very minute fidelity, not merely to the possible, but to the probable and ordinary course of man's experience. The former—while as a work of art, it must rigidly subject itself to laws, and while it sins unpardonably so far as it may swerve aside from the truth of the human heart—has fairly a right to present that truth under circumstances, to a great extent, of the writer's own choosing or creation. If he thinks fit, also, he may so manage his atmospherical medium as to bring out or mellow the lights and deepen and enrich the shadows of the picture. He will be wise, no doubt, to make a very moderate use of the privileges here stated, and especially, to mingle the Marvellous rather as a slight, delicate, and evanescent flavor, than as any portion of the actual substance of the dish offered to the public. He can hardly be said, however, to commit a literary crime even if he disregard this caution.

Hawthorne was saying that if he were not free to call what he wrote novels, then he would call them romances; but "Marvellous" does find its way into most interesting fiction—a setting is meaningful, coincidence and irony move in remarkable ways, language is strangely luminous, and character is singular, living only in relationship to the major impulse of the novel.

Melville had reasons enough to disapprove of his audi-

Criticism," *Partisan Review*, February 1949, Katherine Woods, "Remarques sur la littérature américaine," *L'Âge Nouveau*, Summer 1952; and W. V. O'Connor, "The Novel as Social Document," *American Quarterly*, II (1952).

ence, among them the tendency to hold the novelist to the literal truth. At several points in *The Confidence Man* he writes little asides on the problems of fiction, but none is more interesting than Chapter 33:

> But ere be given the rather grave story of Charlemont, a reply must in civility be made to a certain voice which methinks I heard, that, in view of past chapters, and more particularly the last, where certain antics appear, he exclaims: How unreal all this is! Who did ever dress or act like your cosmopolitan? And who, it might be returned, did ever dress or act like Harlequin?
>
> Strange, that in a work of amusement, this severe fidelity to real life should be exacted by anyone, who, by taking up such a work, sufficiently shows that he is not unwilling to drop real life, and turn, for a time, to something different. Yes, it is, indeed, strange that anyone should clamor for the thing he is weary of; that anyone, who, for any cause, finds real life dull, should yet demand of him who is to divert his attention from it, that he should be true to that dullness.
>
> There is another class, and with this class we side, who sit down to a work of amusement tolerantly as they sit down at a play, and with much the same expectations and feelings. They look that fancy shall evoke scenes different from those of the same old crowd round the custom-house counter, and the same old dishes on the boarding-house table with characters unlike those of the same old acquaintances they meet in the same old way every day in the same old street. And as, in real life, the properties will not allow people to act out themselves with that unreserve permitted to the stage; so, in books of fiction, they look not only for more entertainment, but, at bottom, even for more reality, than real life itself can show. Thus, though they want novelty, they want nature, too; but nature unfettered, exhilarated, in effect transformed. In this way of thinking, the people in a fiction, like the people in a play, must dress as nobody exactly dresses, talk as nobody exactly talks, act as nobody exactly acts. It is with fiction as with religion: it should present another world, and yet one to which we feel the tie.

Finally, of course, there is the body of criticism written by Henry James, which, along with his fiction, has been so influential in our own time. The prefaces frequently touch on the question of reality, and in "The Real Thing," a fine short story, he has written a parable of the artist in relation to a fixed reality. Here we may quote a few sentences from "The Art of Fiction," his answer to Mr. Walter Besant, one of those who feel they know what is real and what is not and how the former is to be put into a work of fiction. Henry James said:

> The reality of Don Quixote or of Mr. Micawber is a very delicate shade; it is a reality so coloured by the author's vision that, vivid as it may be, one would hesitate to propose it as a model: one would expose one's self to some very embarrassing questions on the part of a pupil. It goes without saying that you will not write a good novel unless you possess the sense of reality; but it will be difficult to give you a recipe for calling that sense into being. Humanity is immense, and reality has a myriad forms, the most one can affirm is that some of the flowers of fiction have the odour of it, and others have not; as for telling you in advance how your nosegay should be composed, that is another affair.

Should one, for example, read Herman Melville's *Israel Potter* as a trustworthy account of a soldier-hero in the American Revolution? The novel *is* based on a chapbook autobiography, but anyone reading a few chapters into the novel recognizes that this is a picaresque tale. Israel Potter is a tough-muscled New England Yankee, not very literate but adaptable, witty, and inclined to take the world as he finds it. As the years go by it is clear that he has been defeated; poverty and deaths in his family attend his forty-odd years in London, and upon his return to New England not a single member of his family is remembered by name, and the roads, paths, and house Israel knew have disappeared. Technicalities prevent his obtaining a soldier's pension, and soon he is dead. Who is Israel Potter? He is the wanderer (Israel) and he is the common man (potter's field)—and, Melville says in his fierce irony, his reward is what the hero can expect. Certainly this is not history; it is Melville's bitter view of things at a stage in his career when the current was running strongly against him, carrying him, like Israel Potter, toward inevitable defeat.

In an early chapter we see Israel Potter as an escaped prisoner meeting George III, finding the king a pleasant man who refuses to have him arrested. We see him meet John Paul Jones, who is presented as a pursuer of pretty wenches, and, albeit a fine commander, the most unconscionable of braggarts. Israel himself is responsible for much of the damage to the *Serapis*—he blows up the ship's magazine. He also is presented as having introduced Jones to Ben Franklin's *Poor Richard's Almanac*, and it is he who names Jones's ship *Bon Homme Richard*. Franklin, who has an important place in the narrative, talks like an American version of Polonius. How much of all this is trustworthy history? Not much of it certainly, which fact, of course, has nothing to do with whether or not we like the story or, privately, agree that Melville has caught the spirit of Jones or Franklin. Anyone reading *Israel Potter* as a good document of the American Revolution and the reward of heroes would, of course, have an apparitional sense of historical fact.

One might say in reply to this that since *Israel Potter* is a picaresque novel no one would think of reading it for the factual content. What of a novel written about the problems and facts of our contemporary world?

We have lived, or at least Americans in the last generation or two, have lived in a "scientific" milieu which has invited one to put a premium on facts of a certain kind, the kind that can be measured, weighed, and catalogued. This milieu has encouraged the notion that life-as-it-is-experienced or that life-as-it-actually-is can be got inside the covers of a book of fiction. And this milieu has encouraged the notion that certain preoccupations imply coming to terms with, or facing, the actual world and that certain other preoccupations imply a turning away from facts. For example, a novel that tells how to improve race relations is more "real" than a novel showing a young man struggling to decide between a marriage of convenience and a life as a poet. Personal moral struggles are somehow less real than public social questions. This mentality has also helped foster the notion that fiction, at its truest, bears a one-to-one relationship with the society it is treating.

George Santayana says somewhere that exaggeration is an inevitable and necessary part of artistic expression. Stylization involves exaggeration and distortion. The artist who has little or no feeling for stylization usually is not much of an artist. It does not follow, of course, that he does not believe he is telling the truth, at least the truth as it is caught in the distorting mirrors of fiction. As James said, some fiction has the odor of reality and of truth and some does not. It is up to the reader or the critic to see what conventions, what larger-than-life characters, what bejewelled or suggestive patterns of imagery, what qualities of legend, myth or fable it does or does not possess.

Rather frequently the fiction writer who has created a vision appropriate to his theme is asked why he did not give a more "realistic" view. Thus we find Nathaniel West explaining why, in *The Day of the Locust*, he had not included any sincere or honest Hollywood citizens: "If I put into *The Day of the Locust* any of the sincere, honest people who work here . . . those chapters couldn't be written satirically and the whole fabric of the peculiar half-world which I attempted to create would be badly torn by them." As a matter of fact he was not writing only about Hollywood, he was writing about empty lives, about people who learn too late, if they learn at all, that some forms of easy living and materialistic pursuits are the reverse of what they had seemed. All of the characters in *The Day of the Locust* live with a pretense to being something that they are not. Their frustrations increase in intensity until released in cruelty and violence. The characters are grotesques, either pitiful or bizarre dramatizations of artificiality, dishonesty, self-deception, and frustration. The scene being laid in Hollywood makes it relatively easy to introduce other forms of pretense: the movie-sets, the eccentric and assorted architecture, the strange religious sects, and the local worship of glamour. West's image of Hollywood, from one point of view, is unfair. From another, it is eminently just.

This is not the occasion for attempting to classify conventions in the American novel, but a few sentences may suggest the sort of thing that might result from such an attempt. In Nathaniel West, Carson McCullers, Truman Capote, Ernest Caldwell, and Eudora Welty, for example, one finds grotesques, the comedy and pathos of the misfit. In William Faulkner, Robert Penn Warren, Katherine Anne Porter, and Caroline Gordon, one finds the ex-member of the regional world suffering from deracination. Consequently there are in their fiction more regional types (hill-billies, evangelical ministers, "rednecks," sectional patriots, and so on) than a visitor might be aware of in the South, and the nineteenth-century character of the South is caught and stressed more vividly (exaggerated, if one will) than it would be, say, by the average Southern citizen. A sense of the past informing the present is one of the characteristics of their fiction. These writers are dramatizing man suffering from cosmopolitanism and abstraction—and they choose to stress that which serves their theme.

Another group is suggested by the phrase, "the Hemingway world," or, perhaps better, by Edmund Wilson's title, *The Boys in the Back Room.* The stories of Ernest Hemingway, John Steinbeck, John O'Hara, James M. Cain and others suggest common characteristics: the tough, two-fisted hero who believes in little beyond the need to maintain his self-respect, who meets a demanding world on its own terms. Philosophy, rhetoric, or even social graces are pointless in such a world. A group related to these latter writers have made a legend of the harshness of the American city: Theodore Dreiser, James Farrell, Nelson Algren, Willard Motley, or Saul Bellow.

Writers discover symbolic situations and settings, a tone and stance appropriate to what they want to say. Certain things go unsaid. And some things, if it may be so put, are more than said.

In the December 1952 issue of *Commentary* there was an article on the types of short stories appearing in American magazines. The author, after reading a dozen or so collections of short stories published in the last few years, decided that there are two current types: the sophisticated or "Connecticut" story and the Southern or "Yoknapatawpha" story. Connecticut, as a sort of suburb for the upper middle class from New York City (advertising people, successful artists, brokers, etc.) is meant to suggest the urbanite who earns a good salary and is interested in the cultural life: books, theatre, music. He also pays a price for his way of life; he pays for it in anxieties, in worry about his job and about his mode of life. In the "Connecticut" story, everyone is middle-aged, either temperamentally or chronologically; and each day has its crisis, usually a muted or silent crisis—but a crisis none the less. In the Southern story, the setting is rural; if a city is mentioned it is off in the distance, not in the immediate area. The people tend to vegetate, not to think; they seem akin to the sun and the earth. Money does not complicate their lives; the good earth is there to provide them with potatoes and turnips.

Perhaps the sociologist studying regions in America might find fewer anxieties in the people south of Washington, D. C. He might find more. Certainly he would find as much industrialization as in New England, and he would find in the village and town life a greater preoccupation with manners and modes of personal relationship. The two regions, that is, would not fit the image one might anticipate merely from reading current American short stories. An astute reader might find out certain things about the American "psyche" from the stories. The foreign reader would not find out very much about American economic and social geography—and what he might think was fact could turn out to be fiction.

There is nothing essentially new in the above argument, except that we are talking about American fiction. Throughout the history of Western literature, indeed beginning with Plato, one finds philosophers and moralists setting certain terms in opposition to each other—real *vs.* imagined, fact *vs.* fancy, true *vs.* beautiful, and other terms as well. The strictest of these categorizers, or perhaps we should say the most literal minded among them, have not merely favored the first term in each pair but have used "real," "fact," and "true" to berate the poet and the fiction writer because they see them as being preoccupied with the fanciful, the imagined, and the beautiful.

In literary criticism we have had Aristotle, Boccaccio, Sidney, Shelley, or Kenneth Burke attempting to explain to the moralists and the philosophers why the poet or fiction writer finds himself unable and unwilling to accept the dichotomy. Theirs is a statement that apparently has to be made in every generation. Simply, it is that in fiction the "real," the "factual," and the "true" are inevitably caught up in the author's private vision.

It is undoubtedly a tribute to a novelist when a reader believes in the "reality" of his fictional creation, but the reader should not forget what Henry James said, that reality has myriad forms and that the reality of a given piece of fiction is merely one of its guises. Therefore one ought to be wary of finding sociologically valid descriptions of a society in highly imaginative fiction. It would be naïve to reconstruct Elizabethan England after reading *The Shoemaker's Holiday* or *As You Like It*. It would be equally naïve to reconstruct the Spanish-American War, a small town in Ohio, or middle-class life in Connecticut after having read a novel on each of these subjects. Before attempting any such reconstructions one would have to investigate such aesthetic questions as the literary conventions and the nature of the stylization to be found in the given novel, as well as the author's peculiar or individual way of looking at a subject.

STUDENTS OF the American novel and especially the apologists for the fiction of Henry James have frequently pointed to this passage in his biographical and critical study of Hawthorne:

> There is a phrase in the preface to his novel of *Transformation* [*The Marble Faun*], which must have lingered in the minds of many Americans who have tried to write novels and to lay the scene of them in the western world. "No author, without a trial, can conceive of the difficulty of writing a romance about a country where there is no shadow, no antiquity, no mystery, no picturesque and gloomy wrong, nor anything but a commonplace prosperity, in broad and simple daylight, as is happily the case with my dear native land."

But Hawthorne managed to find "gloomy wrongs" in the history of his own Salem, and he knew these "gloomy wrongs" had a way of living on into the "simple daylight" of the present. There is another passage, less frequently quoted, in James's study that puts Hawthorne's assets in the way of time and place very well:

> History, as yet, has left in the United States but so thin and impalpable a deposit that we very soon touch the hard substratum of nature; and nature itself, in the western world, has the peculiarity of seeming rather crude and immature. The very air looks new and young; the light of the sun seems fresh and innocent, as if it knew as yet but weariness of shining . . . I doubt whether English ob-

servers would discover any very striking trace of it in the ancient town of Salem. Still, with all respect to a York and a Shrewsbury, to a Toledo and a Verona, Salem has a physiognomy in which the past plays a more important part than the present. It is of course a very recent past; but one must remember that the dead of yesterday are not more alive than those of a century ago.

Nathaniel Hawthorne's family relationship with Salem was of even longer standing than a century. Major William Hathorne (Nathaniel inserted the *w*) came out to the Puritan settlement about 1630, belonging to the band of John Winthrop. Major William was apparently made of the right stuff for the occasion, doing his duty in disposing both of Indians and Quakers. William became a magistrate of the town of Salem, and he figures in the history of New England as having ordered "Anne Coleman and four of her friends" to be publicly whipped through Salem, Boston, and Dedham. Nathaniel refers to this ancestor in his Introduction to *The Scarlet Letter:*

> The figure of that first ancestor, invested by family tradition with a dim and dusky grandeur, was present to my boyish imagination as far back as I can remember. It still haunts me, and induces a sort of home-feeling with the past, which I scarcely claim in reference to the present phase of the town. I seem to have a stronger claim to a residence here on account of this grave, bearded and sable-cloaked, and steeple-crowned progenitor—who came so early, with his Bible and his sword, and trod the unworn street with such a stately port, and made so large a figure as a man of war and peace—a stronger claim than for myself, whose name is seldom heard and my face hardly known. He was a soldier, legislator, judge; he was a ruler in the church; he had all the Puritanic traits, both good and evil. He was likewise a bitter persecutor, as witness the Quakers, who have remembered him in their histories, and relate an incident of his hard severity towards a woman of their sect which will last longer, it is to be feared, than any of his better deeds, though these were many.

William's son John, a colonel, is even more conspicuous in Salem history because of his part in the burning of witches. To the comments quoted above, Nathaniel adds that the condemning of the witches probably left such a stain "that his old dry bones in the Charter Street burial ground must still retain it, if they have not crumbled merely to dust." In the third generation the family fortunes fell off. Several generations of Hathornes lived on in Salem without contributing in any luminous way to its history. But gradually the family took to the sea, thereby retrieving something of the place in the world that had been lost. Throughout the eighteenth century the Hathornes were professional seamen. Nathaniel said of them: "From father to son, for above a hundred years, they followed the sea; a gray-headed shipmaster, in each generation, retiring from the quarter-deck to the homestead, while a boy of fourteen took the hereditary place before the mast, confronting the salt spray and the gale which had blustered against his sire and grandsire." The last of the shipmasters, Nathaniel Hathorne, died in Surinam in 1808, leaving behind him in Salem a widow, two daughters, and a son, also named Nathaniel.

In this same Introduction, Nathaniel Hawthorne wrote this about his two early ancestors:

> Either of these stern and black-browed Puritans would have thought it quite a sufficient retribution for his sins that after so long a lapse of years the old trunk of the family tree, with so much venerable moss upon it, should have borne, at its topmost bough, an idler like myself. No aim that I have ever cherished would they recognize as laudable; no success of mine, if my life, beyond its domestic scope, had ever been brightened by success, would they deem otherwise than worthless, if not positively disgraceful. "What is he?" murmurs one gray shadow of my forefathers to the other. "A writer of story-books! What kind of a business in life, what manner of glorifying God, or being serviceable to mankind in its day and generation, may that be? . . . And yet, let them scorn me as they will, strong traits of their nature have intertwined themselves with mine.

Of Salem itself, he says he has felt involved in its life as though he were touched by a spell. "It is no matter that the place is joyless for him; that he is weary of the old wooden houses, the mud and the dust, the dead level of site and sentiment, the chill east wind, and the chillest of social atmospheres,—all these and whatever faults besides he may see or imagine, are nothing to the purpose. The spell survives, and just as powerfully as if the natal spot were an earthly paradise."

William Faulkner also lived under the spell of his own family's history and the history of his own town, Oxford. In the family and the local histories were lives lived as high romance, and there were "gloomy wrongs" aplenty. Faulkner's great grandfather, William C. Falkner (William Faulkner, like Nathaniel Hawthorne, was responsible for adding a letter to his name) was probably the most fascinating figure living in North Mississippi during the pre– and post–Civil War periods. A picaresque novel could be written about his life: the journey as a young half-orphaned boy from Tennessee to Mississippi in search of an uncle, finding the uncle in jail on a murder charge, the boy studying law in his uncle's office, fighting as a first lieutenant in the Mexican War, organizing a Mississippi regiment during the Civil War and fighting as its colonel at Harper's Ferry and the first battle of Manassas, being demoted by the will of his men because of his excessive discipline, returning to Mississippi and organizing a group of rangers, serving under General Bedford Forrest, becoming the founder of the first railroad company in North Mississippi, writing successful romantic novels, marrying the girl he had first met as a little boy in search of his uncle, being involved in duels, and dying at the hands of a man who had once been his partner and whom he had recently defeated for a seat in the state legislature. There is a life-sized monument erected to him facing his railroad. . . . It is all there as a string of events for an episodic romantic novel. Faulkner has never written it out in this form, but he has used parts of it in various ways, especially in *Sartoris* and *The Unvanquished*. In *Sartoris*, William C's murder takes this form:

> It showed on John Sartoris' brow, the dark shadow of fatality and doom, that night when he sat beneath the candles in the dining room and turned the wineglass in

his fingers while he talked to his son. The railroad was finished, and that day he had been elected to the state legislature after a hard and bitter fight, and doom lay on his brow and weariness.

"And so," he said, "Redlaw will kill me tomorrow, for I shall be unarmed. I'm tired of killing men. . . . Pass the wine Bayard. . . ."

And the next day he was dead.

There is this highly romantic passage about the family at the end of the novel: "For there is death in the sound of it (the name of Sartoris) and a glamorous fatality, like silver pennons downrushing at sunset, or a dying fall of horns along the road to Roncevaux." The view that the family is fated to suffer glamorous fatalities is developed at length in *Sartoris*, but the family's coming down in the world (the Falkner family did come down, although not drastically) is treated with a tone of great *gloom* in other places, especially, one must feel, when they are identified, or partially identified, with the twentieth-century Compsons. It is relevant that at an early point in his career Faulkner was commonly called Count No Count by his fellow townsmen.

As a place to live, Oxford is pleasant enough. Faulkner once wrote a letter in which he said he was sorry for all those millions of New Yorkers because they could not live in Oxford. Phil Stone, a lifelong friend of Faulkner's, has described it as a spot out of the contemporary mad rush, as a place for those who enjoy the savor of things. It is not far, he says, to any local landmark that recalls legendary days. It is, of course, the legendary side that has interested Faulkner. In Oxford one could also know gloom and terror. There was the gloom that had settled over a defeated people, and there was the terror of sudden violences, most frequently violence between white and black. There was the old jail, the courthouse, and a few ante-bellum houses (scratched on a pane of glass in one of them Faulkner has read: "U. S. Grant 1862"). For Faulkner all of this has held the same sort of interest that the Charter St. Burial Ground, Gallows Hill, and the Custom House held for Nathaniel Hawthorne.

There are undoubtedly many differences between the New England Puritans and the North Mississippi Presbyterians, but as the former are presented in *The Scarlet Letter* and the latter in *Light in August* they have at least one characteristic in common: their minds and imaginations are thoroughly moralized. In each novel, human weakness and the need to sympathize with and to forgive are played off against an iron-like rigidity and lack of sympathy. Presumably Hawthorne's reading about his Puritan forebears gave him his image of their society, and presumably Faulkner felt that there is (or was) enough truth in his view of the Calvinistic part of his society to justify examining it in relation to the Negro problem.

Harry Bamford Parkes, in an essay entitled "The Puritan Heresy" (*Hound and Horn*, v—1932—173-74), says that the Puritans were plain men with little capacity for mysticism and no talent for speculation:

> The sign of election was not an inner assurance; it was a sober decision to trust in Christ and obey God's law. Those who made this sober decision might feel reasonably confident that they had received God's grace; it was God, without human cooperation, who caused the sober decision to be made. But in actual practice this doctrine had the effect of unduly magnifying man's ability to save himself, as much as Calvin's conception had unduly minimized it; conversion was merely a choice to obey a certain code of rules, and did not imply any emotional change, any love of God, or for holiness, or any genuine religious experience; religion in other words was reduced to mere morality.

Parkes's comment gives sanction to Hawthorne's view that the Puritans were harsh and cold in their religion and their conduct. It does not account for the place, however slight, he gives to their belief in the mercy of God.

Hawthorne presents the Puritans as "iron men." At one point in the narrative he says the spiritual leaders "were fortified in themselves by an iron framework of reasoning." And in one of the most obviously symbolic scenes, when Hester goes to Governor Bellingham's house to beg him not to take Pearl away from her, the mother and child see themselves grotesquely mirrored in a steel breast-plate:

> Little Pearl—who was greatly pleased with the gleaming armor as she had been with the glittering frontispiece of the house—spent some time looking into the polished mirror of the breastplate.
> "Mother," cried she, "I see you here. Look! Look!
> Hester looked, by way of humoring the child and she saw that, owing to the peculiar effect of this convex mirror, the scarlet letter was represented in exaggerated and gigantic proportions, so as to be greatly the most prominent feature of her appearance. In truth, she seemed absolutely hidden behind it. Pearl pointed, also, at a similar picture in the headpiece; smiling at her mother, with the elfish intelligence that was so familiar an expression on her small physiognomy.

Hawthorne is implying that the treatment of Hester is itself grotesque and that the way she lives causes the elfin or unnatural ways of little Pearl.

Hawthorne also makes the point that Hester's exclusion from the society has given her a good understanding of it. From her perspective, the citizens of the colony, and especially its leaders, are far too rigid and unforgiving. She believes in the possibility of escape to Europe, for herself, for Dimmesdale, and for Pearl, and she almost communicates her hope to Dimmesdale. The following is an exchange between Hester and the minister:

> ". . . And what has thou to do with all these iron men and their opinions? They have kept thy better part in bondage too long already!"
> "It cannot be!" answered the minister, listening as if he were called upon to realize a dream. "I am powerless to go! Wretched and sinful as I am, I have no other thought than to drag out my earthly existence in the sphere where Providence hath placed me. Lost as my soul is, I would still do what I may for other human souls! I dare not quit my post, though an unfaithful sentinel, whose sure reward is death and dishonor, when his dreary watch shall come to an end."

For a moment, however, Dimmesdale is made to believe that escape is possible. But to escape, for him, means escape into sin—and on his way home from the forest meeting with Hester he sees himself as a member of the devil's party. Dimmesdale, a true Puritan, is unable until the very end of his life to believe that God could be merciful to him.

A major theme of *The Scarlet Letter* is that an excessive commitment to virtue, which was characteristic of the Puritans, gives rise to the spirit of persecution. There is a direct relationship between the rigid righteousness of the Puritans and the profound unhappiness and suffering in the lives of Hester Prynne and Arthur Dimmesdale. There was little or no place in the Puritan system for the idea of man as sinful and in need of forgiveness. On the contrary, they were obsessed with evil and with the need to suppress it.

Joe Christmas, the protagonist of *Light in August*, is also the victim of righteous zealots. Eupheus Hines, his grandfather, persecutes him out of a mad conviction that he, as God's agent, has been ordered to watch over him and to witness his destruction. Hines believes that God is preoccupied with bitchery and fornication and that the birth of Joe Christmas was His abomination. He is not unlike Roger Chillingworth in that he hovers at the edge of a human life relishing further and further signs of anguish and despair. Hines' own hatred of Negroes is insanely rationalized as a part of God's will. The terrible irony, of course, is that he persecutes in the name of Deity.

Simon McEachern, another of the zealots, unwittingly taught Joe Christmas to reject any human sympathy or impulse toward charity. A stern Presbyterian, he rejects any temptation to indulge the flesh. Even his gifts to the young Christmas are given in the form of opportunities to improve himself. When McEachern punishes him, as he did on one memorable occasion, for failure to learn his catechism, the punishment is given in a cold, implacable way. McEachern's "voice was not unkind. It was not human, personal, at all." Like Hines, he sees himself as God's agent. When he pursues Joe to a dance hall he is a "representative of a wrathful and retributive Throne." He is obsessed with the need to punish and to persecute— and always in the name of virtue.

Joanna Burden, New Englander by descent, is the daughter of Nathaniel Burden and the granddaughter of Calvin Burden. She too is incapable of sympathy. Christmas knows that her assistance to Negroes arises not out of charity or any acceptance of them as persons but out of a grim sense of duty. Her mind and imagination are fascinated by corruption, and when she fornicates with Christmas she feels herself in the very glare of "the fire of the New England biblical hell." Again, when she orders him to pray with her, she says it is God, not she, who is commanding him to pray. Even her attempt to murder him is God's doing. For her, like the others, religion offers neither solace nor forgiveness: It witnesses the filth and corruption of the human being.

Even the community, as Faulkner presents it, suffers from an inability to accept and forgive human weakness. Gail Hightower, separated like Hester from his fellow townsmen, says that their religion forbids them to forgive even themselves. Their pent up fury needs violent expression. But since they must act in the name of virtue, they will murder Christmas with a grim righteousness. "And they will do it gladly, gladly. . . . Since to pity him would be to admit self-doubt and to hope for and need pity themselves." (There is a moment in Hightower's life when he is a sort of Hawthorne character in that he is tempted to isolate himself from his fellows. Isolation is also one of the themes in *As I Lay Dying*.)

Both novels, *The Scarlet Letter* and *Light in August*, are concerned with the excesses of the thoroughly moralized imagination, and they are peopled, for the most part, by men and women committed to a vision of human conduct that is dark with a guilt that is not to be forgiven.

Henry James summarized what he conceived to be the intention behind *The House of the Seven Gables*: "Evidently, however, what Hawthorne designed to represent was not the struggle between an old society and a new, for in this case he would have given the old one a better

chance; but simply, as I have said, the shrinkage and ex-
tinction of a family." Possibly this remark tells us that
James was a little more inclined to reverence the past,
even the Puritan past, than was Hawthorne. *The House of
the Seven Gables* does describe the disintegration of a
family, but thematically it says, over and over again, that
the past lives on into the present. Maule's curse—that
God give the Pyncheons blood to drink—is merely a part
of the amusing paraphernalia of the novel; the real curse,
which is in the blood and bone of the Pyncheons, is their
desire for money, position, and "family." Clifford Pyncheon says that almost all men suffer from this obsession:
"What we call real estate—the solid ground to build a
house on—is the broad foundation on which nearly all
the guilt of this world rests. A man will commit almost
any wrong,—he will heap up an immense pile of wickedness, as hard as granite, and which will weigh as heavily
upon his soul, to eternal ages,—only to build a great
gloomy, dark chambered mansion, for himself to die in,
and his posterity to be miserable in." Even Holgrave,
the young radical, admits that this conservative impulse
is in him. When he proposes marriage to Phoebe she tells
him he is too unsettling for her. "You will lead me out
of my own quiet path." Holgrave denies that he will: "It
will be otherwise than you forbode. The world owes all
its onward impulses to men ill at ease. The happy man
inevitably confines himself within ancient limits. I have
a presentiment that, hereafter, it will be my lot to set out
trees, to make fences,—perhaps, even, in due time, to
build a house for another generation,—in a word to con-
form myself to laws, and the peaceful practice of society.
Your poise will be more powerful than any oscillating
tendency of mine." In his famous preface to the novel
Hawthorne spelled out his theme, saying the "moral" of
his tale is that the wrongdoing of one generation lives
on into succeeding generations, and, further, it is folly
for one generation to tumble down "an avalanche of ill-
gotten gold, or real estate on the heads of an unfortunate posterity." The point about the Pyncheon family
then is that they, at least the dominant male members of

it, are obsessively concerned with money and position, and that they brook no opposition.

A possible consequence of the family's sense of its position is that decay may set in, as it does in the case of Hebzibah. She is alone in the ruined old house and at the very end of her resources before she can bring herself to open a shop. When she says it is now necessary for her to give up her status as a lady, Holgrave tells her she is suffering no great loss:

> Let it go! You are the better without it. I speak frankly, my dear Miss Pyncheon! for are we not friends? I look upon this as one of the fortunate days of our life. It ends an epoch and begins one. Hitherto, the life-blood has been gradually chilling in your veins as you sat aloof, within your circle of gentility, while the rest of the world was fighting out its battle with one kind of necessity or another. Henceforth, you will at least have the sense of healthy and natural effort for a purpose, and of lending your strength—be it great or small—to the united struggle of mankind. This is success,—all the success that anybody meets with!

At one point in the novel, she is described as having spent so many years in the old house that "her very brain was impregnated with the dry-rot of its timbers." Her brother Clifford, with twenty years of prison life behind him, is also in an advanced state of decay. He is a sybarite with very few powers of self-discipline. Even the good fortune of their inheriting the estate of the villainous Judge Jaffrey Pyncheon, as they do at the novel's end, has a partially melancholy quality in that she and her brother are well advanced in years and the molds of their characters are set. Possibilities of health and vitality are suggested by the marriage of Phoebe and Holgrave. All four willingly depart from the seven gabled old house that had wittnessed so much evil, so much avarice and ambition.

In Faulkner's stories it is everywhere evident that he is concerned with the way the past lives on into the present. Two of the novels that show this, *Absalom, Absalom!* and *The Sound and the Fury*, bear some comparison with *The House of the Seven Gables*. In *Absalom, Absalom!*

Faulkner uses the word "iron" in the same way Hawthorne does, both of them using it to suggest the rigidity of their characters and of the mores by which they live; Hawthorne makes much of the Puritan heritage of the Pyncheons, and Faulkner makes much of the Mississippi Presbyterian heritage, which he frequently contrasts with New Orleans Catholicism. Thomas Sutpen is like the dominant male Pyncheons in his obsessive desire for a family line and for position in the community. No one could be more ruthless than he in using people, as he uses the Coldfields, and the Joneses, for his ends, and no one could be more tenacious. Sutpen leaves ruin everywhere, even on into the generations following him. But the Sutpen story has larger social implications than the story of the Pyncheons. The Pyncheon family is ingrown, but the Sutpens, in their rigid aversion to miscegenation, are guilty of spiritual incest. Quentin Compson, the narrator, knows this is more than Sutpen's story, that it is his own and his region's. If one will, he knows that slavery was a curse that is being slowly worked out and expiated. There is the passage, frequently quoted, in which Quentin answers Shreve McCaslin's question "why do you hate the South?" "I don't hate it . . . *I don't hate it* he thought, panting in the cold air, the iron New England dark; *I don't, I don't! I don't hate it! I don't hate it!*" Quentin Compson is a victim of his heritage. He knows that in having pieced together and understood Sutpen's story that he has learned something very important about the ambitions and family pride that are nurtured in his own Southern heritage. Both Hawthorne and Faulkner may be said to have ambiguous feelings, of liking and repugnance, for their heritages.

There are also certain connections between *The Sound and the Fury* and *The House of the Seven Gables* in that both have characters who, unhappy at the decline of their family from its once eminent position, live in genteel decay, and both have plots which are resolved when there is a repudiation of the decay. (For our purposes here, it is beside the point that Hawthorne's story may be said to have a "happy ending" and that Faulkner's does not, although to say that it has an "unhappy ending" would require some qualification.) The Compson family is narcissistic, a fact symbolized by Quentin Compson's relation to his sister Candace, of which more in a moment. Jason Compson III is an alcoholic lawyer who sits in his office writing satiric verses about his fellow townsmen and contemplating the gradual loss of Compson's Mile, the land owned by his eminent forebears. Unlike his son Quentin, who wants to retrieve some sense of purpose and honor, Jason believes in nothing at all. Mrs. Compson is a little like Hebzibah but much more egregiously committed to her gentility. She does not, for example, understand how God can allow indignities to be heaped upon one of her family origins, she is ashamed of her idiot son and changes his name from Maury (her brother's name) to Benjamin, and, because of her rationalizing about her dignity, she allows her son Jason IV to cheat her out of money sent to her by Candace. Jason IV, incidentally, is a vicious character who totally repudiates everything the family ever stood for. Finally the family disintegrates, their pride and ambitions ridiculed, ignored or forgotten. The strength that remains is with a servant, the Negress Aunt Dilsey. The Compson family suggest another theme common to both writers, incest.

The Marble Faun, though successful in much of its detail and in the way it evokes a sense of Rome, moves uneasily between the poles of reality and fantasy. One is never quite certain about Hawthorne's intentions. An important clue to them seems to lie in his references to the tragedy of Beatrice Cenci, the girl who assisted in the murder of her father after he had (or was said to have) committed incest with her. Hilda, the innocent young New England painter, sits before what is identified as Guido's *Beatrice Cenci* until she has thoroughly memorized the picture and is able to recreate it on her own canvas. In the chapter entitled "Beatrice" Miriam, the tragic young woman friend of Hilda, sits admiring the skill with which the picture has been transcribed, and Hilda is "startled to observe that her friend's expression had become almost exactly that of the portrait." During

the same visit Miriam asks that Hilda deliver a packet for
her to the Palazzo Cenci—and both of them discuss the
story of Beatrice Cenci. (Subsequently we are shown the
old palace of the Cenci as the "paternal abode of Beatrice.") In a later chapter, "Miriam and Hilda," there is
further discussion of the copy Hilda has made, and on this
occasion Hilda, seeing herself reflected in the mirror,
thinks that she too has taken on the expression of Beatrice. Hawthorne assures the reader that Hilda, purely innocent, is suffering from her knowledge of Miriam's
guilt: She had seen a look in Miriam's eyes—"a look of
hatred, triumph, vengeance, and, as it were, joy at some
unhoped for relief"—that asked Donatello to free her
from her pursuer and persecutor. In the postscript or conclusion that Hawthorne added to the novel, Kenyon is
asked what Miriam's last name was—and though the
question goes unanswered the implication seems to be
that she is a Cenci or at least related to them, and,
further, that she was betrothed to a man who was himself
either a Cenci or related to them. The most direct evidence for this inference is in the chapter entitled "The
Peasant and the Contadina." It is in this chapter too that
we are given various reasons why Miriam repudiated the
marriage that had been arranged for her. Among them is
this: "Moreover, the character of her destined husband
would have been a sufficient and insuperable objection;
for it betrayed traits so evil, so treacherous and vile, and
yet so strangely subtle, as could only be accounted for
by the insanity which often develops itself in old, close-
kept races of men, when long unmixed with newer
blood." (Possibly one may say that this theme was related in Hawthorne's mind to his condemnation of a man
cutting himself off from his fellows.) This quotation
would seem to suggest the point behind all these references to the Cenci family. The ingrown-ness of these old
Roman families is itself a kind of incest. And by identifying Miriam with the Cenci Hawthorne was able to draw
upon all the overtones of horror associated with that family. (Philip Young suggested the incest theme in relation
to Hawthorne and Faulkner and also that Melville's *Pierre*

—1852—suggested this use of the Cenci story in *The Marble Faun*—1860.)

Faulkner too uses incest as symbolic of ingrown-ness in two different novels, *The Sound and the Fury* and *Absalom, Absalom!* In *The Sound and the Fury* Quentin Compson is preoccupied with his sister's body, or, rather, as Faulkner put it in the appendix to *The Portable Faulkner*, he was preoccupied with the idea of incest. Most of the Compsons are sick with self-concern, their pride is empty pretentiousness, and they are unable to live vigorously. Quentin's preoccupation with incest (which Faulkner said Quentin did not actually want to commit) suggests a family that is narcissistic. The family's overinsistence upon its honor and dignity and upon no longer having its rightful eminence in the community is an extreme form of self love. Incest is the appropriate symbol for this diseased state of mind.

In *Absalom, Absalom!* Henry Sutpen's willingness to condone incest—to allow his half brother to marry his sister Judith—has a certain similarity to the incest theme in *The Sound and the Fury*. When Henry talks with his father Colonel Sutpen about Charles Bon's demand that he be allowed to marry Judith, he does not know that Charles is partly Negro, but he does know that the South is hovering on the brink of defeat, which he sees as shame and degradation. He says: "When you don't have God and honor and pride, nothing else matters except that you don't even care if it was defeat or victory." Henry condones incest as an ironic final mark of their shame and degradation. It is after he learns that Charles is colored that Henry shoots him to prevent the marriage. It was as Charles insisted, "the miscegenation, not the incest" which he could not bear. The reader then understands that the incest was not merely a bitter recognition of defeat but, further, though unwittingly on Henry's part, a symbol of a society that put its humanity above other humanity. Having set themselves above the Negroes, Henry and his kind had already committed spiritual incest.

It is clear that in all three novels, *The Marble Faun*, *The Sound and the Fury*, and *Absalom, Absalom!* that incest is used as a symbol of inward-turning. And Hawthorne and Faulkner have related it to evils that have their origins in a diseased sort of self-centeredness.

In *The Marble Faun* Hawthorne makes a number of observations about Catholicism, and perhaps one may say that Hilda's ambiguous attitude toward it, admiring and yet resisting it out of an allegiance to her Puritan heritage, is not unlike Hawthorne's. From her knowledge of the Roman churches and especially, as Hawthorne has it, of St. Peter's she found it "was impossible to doubt that multitudes of people found their spiritual advantage in it, who would find none at all in our own formless mode of worship." Hilda sees a young man before a shrine "writhing, wringing his hands," who finally kneels to weep and pray. Hawthorne's comment is this: "If this youth had been a Protestant, he would have kept all that torture pent up in his heart, and let it burn there till it seared him into indifference." After her visit to the confessional, Hilda tells Kenyon that the more she sees of Catholicism the more she wonders "at the exuberance that adapts itself to all the demands of human infirmity." But she adds that she is put off by the fallibility of the Church's ministers.

Faulkner, in *Absalom, Absalom!*, stresses Catholicism's acceptance of fallibility and human weakness, and contrasts its capacity for compromise with the Puritan's stern inflexibility. Young Henry Sutpen is seen thus in Catholic New Orleans: "I can imagine him, with his puritan heritage—that heritage peculiarly Anglo-Saxon—of fierce proud mysticism and that ability to be ashamed of ignorance and inexperience, in that city foreign at once feminine and steel-hard—this grim humorless yokel out of a granite heritage where even the houses, let alone clothing and conduct, are built in the image of a jealous and sadistic Jehovah, put suddenly down in a place whose denizens had created their All-Powerful and the supporting hierarchy—chorus of beautiful saints and handsome angels in the image of their houses and personal ornaments and voluptuous lives." Henry Sutpen is a stern literalist, almost as inflexible as his father, Thomas Sutpen. Most of the novel's tension is in terms of Sutpen's inflexibility and Charles Bon's needing and asking for human sympathy, acceptance and understanding. It is clear that Faulkner is saying that the Sutpen attitude and the Bon attitude have a great deal to do with their respective societies and religions.

One may point to these parallels or connections between Hawthorne's novels and Faulkner's novels without implying any very direct borrowings on the latter's part. And of course the tone of each novel is generated by its own subject matter and respective treatment. One may claim, however, both some similarity of temperament, and some knowledge on Faulkner's part of Hawthorne's work. Because of these factors and especially because of the similarity between Hawthorne's New England and Faulkner's Mississippi one can understand the very considerable similarities in their work. (Faulkner's first book was entitled *The Marble Faun*. Knowing that Phil Stone, the Oxford lawyer and friend of Faulkner, put up the money to publish it, I wrote to ask him what he thought about the connections between Faulkner and Hawthorne. The following is his reply: "Bill read some Hawthorne, but I don't think he is extremely well read in anything. I think I still have two copies of *The Marble Faun* but the title had nothing to do with Hawthorne at all. I know because I am the man that put this title on it.")

Perhaps one should add to all the above the observation that Hawthorne and Faulkner are both highly stylized writers. In each of them one finds a rhetorical style, the rigid selection proper to fiction as an art form, situations that are sparely and sharply dramatic, and characters that push away from commonplace reality toward the symbolic. Each as artist is properly respectful of the principle of aesthetic distance. It is true that Hawthorne is frequently deliberately allegorical, whereas Faulkner is not, and it is equally true that the latter writes a much more involuted style. On the other hand, both have what might be called the will to rhetoric, with the consequence that there are descriptive passages in the works of each writer that stick in a reader's memory. For example, this from "My Kinsman, Major Molineux":

> He was an elderly man, of large and majestic person, and strong, square features, betokening a steady soul; but steady as it was, his enemies had found means to shake it. His face was pale as death, and far more ghastly; the broad forehead was contracted in his agony, so that his eyebrows formed one grizzled line; his eyes were red and wild, and the foam hung white upon his quivering lip. His whole frame was agitated by a quick and continual tremor, which his pride strove to quell, even in those circumstances of overwhelming humiliation.

And this from "A Rose for Emily":

> Now and then we would see her in one of the downstairs windows—she had evidently shut up the top floor of the house—like the carven torso of an idol in a niche, looking or not looking at us, we could never tell which. Thus she passed from generation to generation—dear, inescapable, impervious, tranquil, and perverse.

Again, both writers are concerned with legendary and imaginative as much as with realistic materials, knowing that the imagined has its meanings and "tell[s] us something about the human heart." Thus Hawthorne can have the portrait of Colonel Pyncheon staring severely at generations of Pyncheons, can have a hidden panel behind the portrait, can have Alic Pyncheon mesmerized by a member of the Maule clan, and can have the very fowls in the Pyncheon garden become ingrown in spirit and rusty in movements. He is objectifying the spiritual weight of the Pyncheon heritage. And Faulkner can create idiots to suggest the decay of a family, can have a son talking to his father on an unrealistic twilight battlefield of the Civil War, or the great house that has symbolized ambition and family burn garishly to ashes in the night. Both writers respect the rights of the imagination and the rightness for fiction of the highly stylized and the dramatic. It may even be true as with *The Marble Faun* and *The Fable*, that the processes of stylization sometimes go so far that the reader finds an insufficient number of connections with the actual commonplace world.

In conclusion, one might say that of all the sections or areas of the United States, New England and the South are most "regional," both consciously possessing a heritage from their respective pasts. Perhaps a sense of the past invites not merely exploitation of legend but, at times, a sense of gloom. It is true at least that Hawthorne and Faulkner, the American writers who most exploit their own legendary pasts, are also preoccupied with "gloomy wrongs." (For another comparison see Randall Stewart, "Hawthorne and Faulkner," *College English*, xvii—1956—pp. 258-62. Our essays may be said to complement each other.)

**THE NARRATOR
AS DISTORTING MIRROR**

IN CRITICAL discussions of "point of view" a comment is usually made to the effect that the novelist has to establish the reliability and the intelligence of his narrator. In *The Great Gatsby*, for example, Scott Fitzgerald takes pains to tell us that Nick Carraway is a dependable moral mid-western type, with sound schooling behind him; he wants people to "stand at attention." When he tells us that Jay Gatsby is an essentially honest, honorable and admirable person, we believe him.

This is the usual way—to make the narrator a person whose judgment we can rely on. Yet there are examples of undependable narrators. A famous example is in Ring Lardner's "Haircut." Lardner uses as narrator a man who does not understand the full import of the story he is telling, and the irony develops as the reader perceives the difference between the actuality and what he is told. A considerable part of the meaning of the story derives from this seemingly odd method of narration. It is a method Lardner employed with regularity.

Harry T. Moore has reminded me that *H. M. Pulham, Esquire* and *The Late George Apley*, as well as *Catcher in the Rye* have such narrators. A less well known example is in Glenway Wescott's short novel, *The Pilgrim Hawk*. The action is presented by the narrator in such a way that one sympathizes with him, feeling him to be a sensitive observer of an insensitive middle aged couple. But near the end a young woman says to him, "You're no novelist." She tells him this because he has misunderstood the relationship between the couple. We come to see he is an outsider, perhaps a "homosexual," and incapable of understanding the struggle and the affection the two experience. They are "alive," but he is not. The reader cannot understand the fullness of their lives until he has understood the limited vision of the narrator. It is a Jamesian sort of story, and is perhaps indebted to James.

There has, of course, been a great deal of debate about the reliability of the governess, the narrator in James's *The Turn of the Screw*. James played a coy game about whether she was or was not a reliable observer. He speaks of the story as a piece of "cold artistic calculation" deliberately planned "to catch those not easily caught (the 'fun' of the capture of the merely witless being ever but small), the jaded, the disillusioned, the fastidious." He also speaks of the need of having the governess keep "crystalline her record of so many intense anomalies and obscurities"—then adding, "by which I don't of course mean her explanation of them, a different matter."

Leon Edel, one of our leading James scholars, makes three points about the story and the governess. One, it is a ghost story and psychological thriller with a maximum power to arouse horror. Too, James maneuvered the reader into believing the governess' story, despite its serious contradictions, and her own speculative theory about the nature and purpose of the ghosts, which she alone sees. Three, any reader who sees her as a "case" will find sufficient evidence to document his suspicions. There is serious question about her reliability as a witness. It is even possible to claim that she is mad. The horrors of *The Turn of the Screw* are intensified if one sees them arising from the disturbed mind of the governess. Ironically her well intended ministrations to the children drive one child to his death and the other to literal distraction. The house at Bly is not haunted. The ghosts live in the sick mind of the governess.

In James's "The Liar" the principal character, Oliver Lyon, a successful portrait painter, is not the narrator, but the point of view is his. In effect, he tells the story. As reader, one tends to sympathize with him, to agree with his interpretation of events. But when one looks more closely it becomes clear that what actually happens or, more precisely, the actual truth differs substantially from his accounts.

Lyon arrives as a house guest in Hertfordshire. He is to do a portrait of an elderly gentleman, Sir David Ashmore. Having arrived during a house party, he discovers that a young woman he had known years before, in Munich, whom he had asked to marry him, is there, with her husband, Colonel Clement Capadose. Before he is able to greet her, he sees, from across the room, that her eyes are lovingly attending to a handsome man. Lyon assumes correctly that this is her husband. He feels a twinge of envy or jealousy, but acknowledges to himself that he would have expected her to act so, and admits that there is an open, winning quality about Capadose.

In conversation with him, Lyon soon learns that Capadose is a great exaggerator. He wonders how she can suffer "a liar," and is later somewhat dismayed when he discovers she is not made uncomfortable by it. He is further dismayed to learn that people like Capadose and tolerate his "romancing" with the truth.

Back in London, Lyon cultivates Colonel and Mrs. Capadose. He does her portrait, and endeavors to become her confidante. He would like to believe that she realizes she made a mistake in choosing Capadose, rather than himself. Together they would share the sorrow of her mistaken choice. The Capadoses and Lyon remain on friendly terms, and he undertakes to do a portrait of Colonel Capadose. James states the desire in ambiguous terms: "The desire grew in him to paint the Colonel also—an operation from which he promised himself a rich private satisfaction. He would draw him out, he would set him in that rich totality about which he had talked with Sir David, and none but the initiated would know. [The portrait would be] a subtle characterization, of legitimate treachery."

He does the portrait, and greatly enjoys revealing the inner and true nature of his subject. He does not allow

Colonel Capadose to see it—but one day, returning to his studio, he discovers that both of them, husband and wife, are looking at it. Unseen, he hears Colonel Capadose repeatedly say, "damn! damn! damn!" and he sees her dissolve in tears. Next he sees her go out into the garden and wait as her husband cuts and stabs the portrait with a knife. Shortly thereafter the Capadoses travel on the Continent. Lyon does not see them until their return. When he does see them he tells them the picture has been destroyed, and they say they believe a woman, a former model (who has appeared briefly in the story) destroyed it. Lyon is not surprised that Colonel Capadose can tell such a whopper but he is amazed that Mrs. Capadose joins in telling it.

The reader too is somewhat amazed, since earlier she has been presented as a wholly truthful person. But one also suspects that the action is implying more than is openly stated. And upon thinking it through one realizes that Colonel Capadose is a gentle person and an inoffensive liar, not a malicious one, as Lyon has come to feel he is. The former model cannot be injured by his fabrication about her. (And perhaps he invented the tale to avoid an unpleasant scene with Lyon, perhaps even to avoid injuring his feelings.) But he and his family would have been greatly injured if the portrait, as Lyon had intended, had gone to the Academy. The real liar is Oliver Lyon, who has allowed envy and jealousy to distort his sense of fairness, and his judgment. The irony is that the open liar, Colonel Capadose, is harmless, whereas his righteous critic is a maleficent liar. There is a kind of peripety in which the promise of goodness coming from Lyon's actions turns into an evil and the evil seemingly resident in Colonel Capadose turns into a good.

Nathaniel Hawthorne's *The Blithedale Romance*, a criticism of New England culture at mid-century, employs a narrator who is not, at least not solely, the voice of the author. Most readers presumably are offended or shocked by the last line revelation that the narrator, Miles Coverdale, has been in love with Priscilla. At a number of points in the story they will, though sympathizing with him, have demurred at certain of Coverdale's actions and attitudes; they will have found him to be something less than a satisfactory hero. (It does not follow that they disapprove of all his actions and attitudes.) Coverdale's love has been kept for a moment of dramatic revelation, and Hawthorne, as though to make sure that we *see* what the story is about, has Coverdale say: "I perceive, moreover, that the confession, brief as it shall be, will throw a gleam of light over my behavior throughout the foregoing incidents, and is, indeed, essential to the full understanding of my story."

Briefly, or as briefly as possible, the action of *The Blithedale Romance* is this: Miles Coverdale meets Old Moodie, a down-at-heel character who, knowing that the former is going to take up residence at Blithedale, the community-living experiment, wants to ask a favor, but something Coverdale says deters him. The next day Coverdale goes to the farm, where he is enchanted by the exotic charm and physical beauty of Zenobia and by her intelligence, amused by the harshness (it had been snowing) of life in "Arcadia," and meets Hollingsworth, the reformer, Priscilla, a child of poverty, Silas Foster, the realistic Yankee farmer, and others. Coverdale is taken ill with a fever and he is nursed by Hollingsworth, who though a former blacksmith and a hulking man, seems the spirit of gentleness. Up and about again, he suspects that Hollingsworth took advantage of his illness to make him a convert to his system for rehabilitating criminals. Coverdale is somewhat disenchanted about the community, but believes it is justified especially because it has very obviously improved Priscilla's lot.

Old Moodie visits the farm, somewhat stealthily, to learn how Zenobia treats Priscilla, and deciding that Priscilla is patronized or treated as a servant (though this is not so to the degree he suspects) he leaves a curse on the community. Coverdale works conscientiously, but he also withdraws frequently to a little retreat in the woods where he contemplates his life and that of the community. During one of these withdrawals he meets Professor Westervelt, who wants information about Zenobia and Priscilla.

Coverdale strongly dislikes the artificiality of the man, believes him to be sinister, and refuses to aid him.

Next, there is a discussion about the problem of women's rights. Hollingsworth, it develops, is interested in no one's rights, but only in the successful outcome of his philanthropic project. Both women, however, are won by his dominant manner and fall in love with him. When Coverdale is asked to support the project, which he cannot believe in, he refuses, and Hollingsworth breaks with him. Hollingsworth also plans to take over the farm and use the community for his own purposes. Coverdale then returns to his earlier life as a gentleman author, a poet. From his hotel window one day he sees, in an apartment across the way, Zenobia, Priscilla, and Westervelt, and, suspecting that Priscilla may be in some difficulty or danger (Westervelt has some connection with Zenobia, or hold over her) Coverdale visits them. But he is unable to learn for certain that she is in any danger, and Priscilla does not indicate that she is.

Coverdale then seeks out Old Moodie and learns of his past. As Fauntleroy, he had been a man of wealth and position, and he tells Coverdale that Zenobia was the child of his first marriage. Having lost his wealth and reputation, Fauntleroy moved to Boston, where he was known as Moodie. There he remarries, and his second child is Priscilla. Priscilla is so delicate physically and so lacking in vitality that she seems half spirit. Professor Westervelt, who is a spiritualist quack, discovers her and uses her during his séances as the Veiled Lady, a medium. Fauntleroy has kept his identity a secret from Zenobia and allowed her to keep her inheritance from her uncle, Moodie's deceased brother, but he wants to be sure that Priscilla (who knows the relationship) is well treated by Zenobia. Westervelt, with the connivance of Hollingsworth, brings Priscilla back to the lyceum hall audience as the Veiled Lady. The performance is so degrading and cheap that Hollingsworth, partly at Coverdale's urging, interrupts it and takes Priscilla back to Blithedale.

Zenobia learns that she is in danger of losing, or perhaps already has lost, her fortune (presumably Old

Moodie has interfered). Hollingsworth, whom all had assumed would marry her, then rejects her in favor of Priscilla. Zenobia accuses him of having used Priscilla despite loving her, and says he would have married her, Zenobia, merely to get money for his philanthropic project. Priscilla identifies herself as Zenobia's sister, but Zenobia tells her to accept Hollingsworth, which she does. Then Zenobia drowns herself. Coverdale feels that a great brightness has gone from the world, and Hollingsworth, whom Zenobia had accused of monstrous egotism, is so guilt ridden that he is incapacitated, and leans on Priscilla's strength. Twenty years after the suicide Coverdale is writing the story of Blithedale. Finally, he informs the reader, who is quite unprepared for the fact, that he, Coverdale, now a genteel minor poet, had been and still was in love with Priscilla.

A glance at the *American Note-Books* makes it clear that Hawthorne made use of his Brook Farm experiences (1841) for materials, the "polar Paradise" that it seemed upon his arrival one wintry day, the sense of the farm being a little island of unreality in the New England countryside, an outdoor masquerade, and so on. Many of the passages describing the search for Zenobia's body he took from a later notebook record (1845) of his having assisted, in Concord, in probing a lake for a drowned body. The preface to *Blithedale* acknowledges the use of Brook Farm experiences because they offered "an available foothold between fiction and reality." Hawthorne insists, however, that the characters of the novel are fictitious: the "self concentrated Philanthropist; the high-spirited Woman, bruising herself against the narrow limitations of her sex; the weakly Maiden, whose tremulous nerves endow her with Sibylline attributes; the Minor Poet, beginning life with strenuous aspirations which die out with his youthful fervor." These, he said, might have been looked for at the actual Brook Farm, but they were not there. They are, we may add, highly symbolic characters.

There is in *The Blithedale Romance* a great deal of the sort of thing Hawthorne himself thought of as *romance* as opposed to *novel*. Probably no character at all is described merely to give a sense of reality and life to Blithedale. The symbolic characters are real enough, to the reader and to each other, but one hardly ever sees or hears the other members of the community. Old Moodie, alias Fauntleroy, is the poor outsider, hovering mysteriously on the edge of the action, and, near the end, turning into a *deus ex machina* by threatening to remove, or actually removing, Zenobia's fortune. The Silas Fosters are unimaginative Yankee farmers, in sharp contrast to the "visionary transcendentalists." Westervelt is pure villainy, a manipulator of lives and passions; he is also the contemporary type of quack doctor and lecturer. Hollingsworth is, until the denouément, pure egotism in the form of righteousness; he also is a manipulator of lives and brooks no opposition. Zenobia is womanhood at once natural and beautiful, defeated by a world that does not wish her to be what she is. Priscilla, except that she seems to have no desire for the forms of "cultivation," is the Victorian woman, without sensuality and with no sense of individuality or purpose, other than to worship and serve. Miles Coverdale is the uncommitted man, and, though gifted and perceptive, the victim of the New England mores. He is the genteel writer.

Blithedale itself is a symbolic setting: There the transcendental theory of human goodness is given a chance to prove itself in action. The legend of the Veiled Lady is developed frequently, until, finally, we understand that she is New England's idealized notion of womanhood. Hollingsworth's iron righteousness, which is like that of his Puritan forebears, is seen at its worst at Eliot's Pulpit, the place where the humane and holy apostle to the Indians had preached his gospel. An affectionate family living in rather elegant circumstances in a boarding house, seen from Coverdale's hotel room, becomes evidence that virtue is as common in the city as in the country. The dream of the Blithedale community is symbolized by a masquerade party. And so on. The characters and the actions function symbolically. It is quite likely that, for his purposes, Hawthorne left no loose ends, but the reader, accustomed to a more detailed examination of actions, sometimes wishes he knew whether so and so actually did thus and so. However, the major movement of the action and the motivations of the characters are clear.

The Blithedale Romance is not so much a satire on utopias—it is that too, but a mild satire—as it is an allegory about New England during its cultural heyday, its Renaissance or golden day. Shipping and the new factory system had brought a fair amount of prosperity to New England. Moreover, as the historians commonly see it, wealth and culture had wed in New England. (The Lowells, for example, founded both a manufacturing city and an institute for lectures and scholarly discussions.) Colleges flourished, each town had its library, and the lyceum platform brought such speakers as Emerson and Thoreau.

The lyceum as it is presented in *The Blithedale Romance* is not quite so golden. The occasion for the following description is Coverdale's visit to a lyceum hall to see a performance of the Veiled Lady:

> The scene was one of those lyceum-halls, of which almost every village has now its own, dedicated to that sober and pallid, or rather drab-colored, mode of winter-evening entertainment, the lecture. Of late years, this has come strangely into vogue, when the natural tendency of things would seem to be to substitute lettered for oral methods of addressing the public. But, in halls like this, besides the winter course of lectures, there is a rich and varied series of other exhibitions. Hither comes the ventriloquist, with all his mysterious tongues; the thaumaturgist, too, with his miraculous transformations of plates, doves, and rings, his pancakes smoking in your hat, and his cellar of choice liquors represented in one small bottle. Here, also, the itinerant professor instructs separate classes of ladies and gentlemen in physiology, and demonstrates his lessons by the aid of real skeletons, and manikins in wax, from Paris. Here is to be heard the choir of Ethiopian melodists, and to be seen the diorama of Moscow or Bunker Hill, or the moving panorama of the Chinese wall. Here is displayed the museum of wax figures, illustrating the wide catholicism of earthly renown, by mixing up heroes and statesmen, the pope and the Mormon prophet,

kings, queens, murderers, and beautiful ladies; every sort of person, in short, except authors, of whom I never beheld even the most famous done in wax. And here, in this many-purposed hall (unless the selectmen of the village chance to have more than their share of the Puritanism, which, however diversified with later patchwork, still gives its prevailing tint to New England character), here the company of strolling players sets up its little stage, and claims patronage for the legitimate drama.

But, on the autumnal evening which I speak of, a number of printed handbills—stuck up in the barroom, and on the sign-post of the hotel, and on the meeting-house porch, and distributed largely through the village—had promised the inhabitants an interview with that celebrated and hitherto inexplicable phenomenon, the Veiled Lady!

The hall was fitted up with an amphitheatrical descent of seats towards a platform, on which stood a desk, two lights, a stool, and a capacious antique chair. The audience was of a generally decent and respectable character: old farmers, in their Sunday black coats, with shrewd, hard, sun-dried faces, and a cynical humor, oftener than any other expression, in their eyes; pretty girls, in many-colored attire; pretty young men,—the schoolmaster, the lawyer, or student at law, the shop-keeper,—all looking rather suburban than rural. In these days, there is absolutely no rusticity, except when the actual labor of the soil leaves its earth-mould on the person. There was likewise a considerable proportion of young and middle-aged women, many of them stern in feature, with marked foreheads, and a very definite line of eyebrow; a type of womanhood in which a bold intellectual development seems to be keeping pace with the progressive delicacy of the physical constitution.

Westervelt speaks of a dawning era in which soul will be linked to soul, a great brotherhood. The Veiled Lady, who is Priscilla, is under his spell, and she is unable to hear the shouts and poundings of the country boys who go up on the stage for the purpose of testing Westervelt's power. The performance is degrading, and Coverdale sees it as a part of a downward movement "in the eternal march," unworthy of decent human beings. Hollingsworth, too, prodded by Coverdale, is moved by the spectacle of Priscilla's degradation and, holding a greater spell over her than does Westervelt, releases her.

But Hollingsworth, while still expecting to marry Zenobia, had bade Priscilla do what Westervelt desired of her. Exactly what part Zenobia plays in this is not clear. Although she is somehow dependent on Westervelt, she does not fear him, and in her legendizing about the Veiled Lady, seemingly as entertainment for the Blithedale community, she tells Priscilla that she knows all about her background, Old Moodie and Westervelt. Presumably Priscilla is free to do as she wishes—and, it develops, she chooses to do what Hollingsworth bids her do.

The major clue, presumably, to the theme of the story is to be found in what the two women are, and in the fact that both Hollingsworth and Coverdale choose Priscilla over Zenobia. In his preface Hawthorne calls Priscilla, as already noted, "the weakly Maiden," and Zenobia "the high spirited Woman [who bruised] herself against the narrow limitations of her sex." Of the two descriptions, the latter certainly seems more like praise. And in the novel itself Zenobia, named for the Palmyran queen, is persistently presented as spontaneous, natural and beautiful. She is capable of guile and quick temper, but she is also contemptuous of dishonesty. If Coverdale finds her a little too exotic and luxury loving, we must remember that he loved Priscilla. But even Coverdale is strongly attracted to Zenobia.

When Coverdale first sees her he is struck by the exotic flower in her hair. And responding to his twitting about the flower, she says: "As for the garb of Eden, I shall not assume it till after May-day!" Coverdale then thinks to himself: "Assuredly, Zenobia could not have intended it—the fault must have been entirely in my imagination. But these last words, together with something in her manner, irresistibly brought up a picture of that fine, perfectly developed figure, in Eve's earliest garment. Her free, careless, generous modes of expression often had this effect of creating images which though pure are hardly felt to be quite decorous." Coverdale then remarks that it is rare nowadays to see a woman who seems attractive as a woman. (Those who recall the *English Note-Books* will remember Hawthorne's grim distress and humor at the expense of middle-aged women beef-trusts.) "One felt an influence breathing out of her such as we might suppose to come from Eve, when she was just made, and her Creator brought her to Adam, saying: 'Behold! here is a woman!' Not that I would convey the idea of especial gentleness, grace, modesty, and shyness, but of a certain warmth and rich characteristic, which seems, for the most part, to have been refined away out of the feminine system." Throughout the story there are echoes of this description. Zenobia is presented as generous, intelligent, passionate, and, after quick bursts of anger, forgiving. Her view of Hollingsworth, before and after she is in love with him, is a fair one; she admires his capacities but deplores his obsession and egotism. Believing that life should offer variety, she could joke about "visionary transcendentalists" and yet give herself, partly at least, to the community experience.

The name Priscilla is described as "that quaint and prim cognomen," and the girl herself partakes of the characteristics attributed to the Veiled Lady: She is insulated "from the material world, from time and space. . . . [endowed] with many of the privileges of a disembodied spirit." She clings to Zenobia, and she clings to Hollingsworth. If Hollingsworth were successful in pursuing his plans for absolute reform, she would follow him, uncritically and admiringly. She would not interfere. When Hollingsworth, as the story has it, is unsuccessful, she is his unquestioning and faithful support. During the arguments that Hollingsworth and Zenobia have about the intellectual and cultural subjection of women, Priscilla unquestioningly sides with Hollingsworth.

Zenobia is not native to New England, but Priscilla, of course, is. Hollingsworth is the Puritan temper by midnineteenth century, and Priscilla is his faithful helpmate. Zenobia feels the power in Hollingsworth, and, married to her, he might have modified his excesses. More profitably to herself, as she says, she might have considered winning Coverdale, instead of Hollingsworth. "I think I should have succeeded, and many women would have deemed you the worthier conquest of the two. You are certainly much the handsomest man. But there is a fate in these things. And beauty, in a man, has been of little account with me, since my earliest girlhood, when, for once, it turned my head." But Coverdale, the genteel New England poet, loved Priscilla, because she was more nearly disembodied. If Zenobia is to be seen as a victim, if New England "killed" her, Coverdale's lot is also that of victim. His character is amply but not overly supplied with ironic awareness (he says, for example, that during his illness he "read interminably in Mr. Emerson's Essays"), and he can appreciate some of Zenobia's charm and power —but he has a fatal weakness for the Veiled Lady.

Hawthorne himself is certainly in his book, but he is not, in any full sense, Miles Coverdale, the Minor Poet who loves the weakly Maiden and who intrudes into private lives because of his interest in the way people feel, believe, and act. He intrudes also because he was in love with Priscilla and concerned about her fate. Hawthorne, as he says in the *Note-Books* was inclined to be the spectator—"whose nature it is to be a mere spectator both of sport and serious business." But he was troubled by his uninvolvement, his desire to live like an image shadowed in a mirror.

Malcolm Cowley, in "Hawthorne in the Looking Glass," makes this comment:

> Everywhere in his character one finds a sort of doubleness: thus, he was proud and humble, cold and sensuous, sluggish and active, conservative and radical, realistic and romantic; he was a recluse who became involved in party politics and a visionary with a touch of cynicism and a hard sense of money values. This doubleness, which led to struggles with his conscience and a sense of guilt, also led him to evolve a sort of theology.

If Miles Coverdale is Nathaniel Hawthorne, it is as a side of himself objectified and criticized.

One could be tempted to say the employment of a narrator as distorting mirror comes in a direct line from Hawthorne to James to Wescott. In a sense it does. On the other hand, James clearly failed to see that Hawthorne was employing a method he himself would use. One might also say that Browning's dramatic monologues employ narrators who twist and distort, who, out of their own maliciousness, fail to distinguish the reality from the appearance. Did James take the method from Browning? It has also been suggested that Poe's "Eleonora," Dostoevski's *Notes from the Underground,* and Mann's *Doctor Faustus* employ similar methods. Recently Peter Taylor employed the method in a story in *Happy Families Are Alike.*

Why should an author employ such a method? Surely James, for example, did not use it merely to entrap the unwary reader. Perhaps he used it, in "The Liar," to remind himself that *the* point-of-view is finally *a* point of view. No single vantage point is wholly reliable. And of course he was fascinated by the paradoxical situation in which the man exposing evil, lying, himself becomes a liar.

Hawthorne appears to have used it as a way of getting distance between himself as author and himself as man. He was trying to impersonalize his beliefs, the better to see them. Hawthorne belonged to his culture, but was trying to see it from outside himself. Miles Coverdale, the distorting mirror, helped him to do this. Probably he did not wholly resolve his ambiguous feelings about his culture, and perhaps Hawthorne even asks his reader to resolve them. This makes reading *The Blithedale Romance* both an engaging and sometimes an unsatisfying experience.

8 PLOTINUS PLINLIMMON AND THE PRINCIPLE OF NAME GIVING

NATHANIEL HAWTHORNE, Herman Melville, Henry James, and William Faulkner, have taken the principle of name giving in their novels and short stories with considerable seriousness. They see a character's name as a part of the characterization. Arthur Dimmesdale, Pearl, Hester Prynne, Roger Chillingworth, Miles Coverdale, Priscilla, Old Moodie, Westervelt, Judge Pyncheon—these and others suggest connotations that allow one to get at the thematic lines of a novel. Henry James uses such names as Mrs. Bread, Christopher Newman, Juliana Bordereau, Milly Theale, Dr. Sloper—sometimes almost allegorical, sometimes half elusive, subliminal, but usually right.

Faulkner went so far as to say he never named a character, the character named himself or went through the story unnamed, like the Reporter in *Pylon*. Flem Snopes, Ratliffe, Bobbie (Barbara) Allen, Joanna Burden, Joe Christmas, Gail Hightower, and all the others exhibit Faulkner's instinctive sense for appropriate names for character.

Melville had a pretty good feeling for the principle of name giving too. The tormented Spanish Captain is Benito Cereno, the innocent American Captain is Amasa Delano, and his ship is *Bachelor's Delight*. The cock in "Cock-a-doodle-do" is Benventano. Israel Potter is the wandering Jew, the homeless man, and his grave is Potter's field. The mad zealot, eye-for-an-eye, tooth-for-a-tooth Captain in *Moby Dick*, of course, is Ahab. Pierre Glendinning and his mother Mary live at Saddle Meadows, where their butler is named Dates. The servant girl is Delly, and Pierre's fiancée is Lucy Tartan. The very air seems innocent. Into this comes Isabel, and a muted yet deep sounding gong rends the air. And then Mr. Falsgrave, the sycophantic, hypocritical minister who serves neither charity nor justice but Mary Glendinning's malevolence.

As a name Mr. Falsgrave is a little too deliberate, a bit too abstract. It suggests a major defect of the novel itself, Melville's abstracting of the theme. Instead of an action, a sea to be crossed, a mountain to be climbed, a mystery to be solved, a lost son found, Melville obtrusively presents a thesis. The religious leader Plotinus Plinlimmon argues the thesis, and Pierre, we come to see, is the sad example of a failure to live in accordance with Plinlimmon's doctrine. The doctrine is explicitly stated in Chapter xiv, in the lecture on chronometricals and horologicals. Eternal truths, chronometricals, are Christ's truths. Whatever, Plinlimmon says, "is really peculiar in the wisdom of Christ seems precisely the same folly to-day as it did 1,850 years ago. Because, in all that interval his bequeathed chronometer has still preserved its original Heaven's time, and the general Jerusalem of this world has likewise carefully preserved its own." Man lives, and should live, by horological time. He cannot live by chronometrical time.

No, this conceit merely goes to show, that for the mass of men, the highest abstract heavenly righteousness is not only impossible, but would be entirely out of place, and positively wrong in a world like this. To turn the left cheek if the right be smitten, is chronometrical; hence, no average son of man ever did such a thing. To give *all* that thou hast to the poor, this too is chronometrical; hence no average son of man ever did such a thing. Nevertheless, if a man gives with a certain self-considerate generosity to the poor; abstains from doing downright ill to any man; does his convenient best in a general way to do good to his whole race; takes watchful loving care of his wife and children, relatives, and friends; is perfectly tolerant to all

other men's opinions, whatever they may be; is an honest
dealer, an honest citizen, and all that; and more especially
if he believe that there is a God for infidels, as well as for
believers, and acts upon that belief; then, though such a
man falls infinitely short of the chronometrical standard,
though all his actions are entirely horologic;—yet such a
man need never lastingly despond, because he is sometimes guilty of some minor offence:—hasty words, im-
pulsively returning a blow, fits of domestic petulance,
selfish enjoyment of a glass of wine while he knows there
are those around him who lack a loaf of bread. I say he
need never lastingly despond on account of his perpetual
liability to these things; because not to do them, and their
like, would be to be an angel, a chronometer; whereas, he
is a man and a horologe.

In trying to be a chronometer, poor Pierre, a horologic,
destroys himself.

Where did Melville get this name, Plotinus Plinlimmon,
for his voice-of-experience, his character-exemplification of
his thesis? From the philosopher Plotinus and from Mount
Plinlimmon or Plynlimmon in Wales. Together the names
spell out the implications of the thesis. Plotinus, of
course, is associated with Neo-Platonism. When he died
in 244 A.D. in Rome, he left behind fifty-four tractates.
He held that man is a soul, and that the arrangement of
inanimate compounds are evidence of a determining
Reason. Man is more than a vegetative soul; he is also
an imaginative and remembering soul, and, as such, in
contact with Reason. The Divine Mind is not, for Plotinus, the ultimate principle. Beyond it is a realm of Ideas,
the simple One. It is above the dualities of man, and
even above the dualities of the Divine Mind. It cannot
be known. Melville appears to be assigning *chronometrical*
time, truths beyond men's absolute comprehension, to the
supernatural, both the Divine Mind and the One. They
are beyond our understanding. *Horological* time is a prac-
ticable morality. It does not, and should not, try to super-
sede chronometrical time.

Thus far, so good. What about Plinlimmon? Melville
says it is a Welsh name, as indeed it is. He might have
read about Plinlimmon in Thomas Gray's "The Bard":

> Modred, whose magic song
> Made huge Plynlimmon bow his cloud-topped head.

Or more probably in some book on Welsh legend. Dylan Thomas in *Under Milk Wood* has Reverend Eli Jenkins, the poet, recite verses of his own, having to do with Welsh history and legend. One passage is—

> Plinlimmon old in story,
> By mountains where King Arthur dreams.

Neither Jay Leyda nor any other Melville scholar, so far as I can find out, mentions the source of Melville's knowledge of these legends. His choice of the name Plinlimmon indicates pretty clearly that he knew something about them.

In *Wild Wales* (1862), George Borrow describes Plinlimmon as the third largest mountain in Wales. In the tenth century the Danes and the Welsh fought a bloody battle on one of its five spurs. Early in the fifteenth century Plinlimmon saw Glendower lead the Welsh in another battle. More important however is the circumstance that the mountain is the source of three rivers, the Severn, the Wye, the Rheidol. Borrow presents a song translated from the Welsh of Lewis Glyn Cothi:

> From high Plynlimmon's shaggy side
> Three streams in three directions glide;
> To thousands at their mouths who tarry
> Honey, gold and mead they carry.
> Flow also from Plynlimmon high
> Three streams of generosity;
> The first, a noble stream indeed,
> Like rills of Mona runs with mead;
> The second bears from vineyards thick
> Wine to the feeble and the sick;
> The third, till time shall be no more,
> Mingled with gold shall silver pour.

The mead, wine, gold, and silver were gifts given by the lord of the castle, Dafydd ab Thomas Vychan. The mead was poured at banquets, wine from Gascony was carried to the sick and feeble in the village, and gold and silver were given to those like the bard who were willing to be tipped.

The streams of Plinlimmon suggest the doctrines of Plotinus Plinlimmon. When one of the latter's admirers gave him a set of books, he returned them and asked for a few bottles of wine. The wine would comfort his spirit more than books could. Plinlimmon would have agreed with Housman that

> *Malt does more than Milton can*
> *To justify the ways of God to man.*

This legend of Mount Plinlimmon says that man is a horologe, a creature of flesh and blood, who enjoys camaraderie, and charity.

Mount Plinlimmon implies a commentary on Pierre's Delectable Mountain, a mountain at Saddle Meadows. From a distance its "white amaranthine flowers" are beautiful, but they are distasteful to the cattle and destroy the herbs and catnip. "The catnip and the amaranth!" Melville says "—man's earthly household peace, and the ever-encroaching appetite for God." Here are horological and chronometrical time once more. In a dream Pierre sees the mountain from a distance, in a guise of great beauty. Seen close up its crags and crevices are ugly, justifying the name The Mount of Titans. As Enceladus, one of the Giants, Pierre turns "his unconquerable front toward the majestic mount," but soon is throwing himself wildly against the mountain. This is the consequence of Pierre trying to live chronometrically. Instead of dreaming of the delectable Mountain Pierre should have dreamed of Mountain Plinlimmon.

In art, the impropriety of the wrong sensation means failure, means, as Yeats once suggested, the will doing the work of the imagination. In Melville's case, it is a powerful conceptual mind trying to cover the failure of the intuitive-imaginative mind. Melville gets a lot of mileage out of the name Plotinus Plinlimmon, but even so it doesn't create the right sensation. The name is made-up, artificial. A name like Amasa Delano (and it makes no difference that Melville found it ready to hand—he had enough sense not to change it) is right. The subliminal, half echo of Massah, Massah is altogether appropriate. And Delano, ship captain of Dutch extraction, suggests the self-centered piety of Northern Europe; its inability to see that inside black skins were human beings. Bartleby, the Scrivener, is right too. He is closed in, beetle like, and shell-like; he is barnacle-like. It is also a Dickensian name, suggesting neither high nor low born but the class of clerks. Plotinus Plinlimmon isn't quite right. Like *Pierre* itself and some of Melville's other writing during a difficult period in his life it is a trifle counterfeit. It doesn't give the ring of a true Melvillean coin.

9 EMILY DICKINSON: THE DOMESTICATION OF TERROR

EMILY DICKINSON IS commonly seen as a strange, pixie-like little lady, dressed in white, who lowered verse messages in a small basket to neighborhood children, tended her flowers, and disappeared whenever a stranger appeared at the front door. As a girl she had been shy but witty, even writing humorous articles for the school paper. But as the years went by she became more and more isolated, except for her immediate family, her father, her sister Lavinia, and next door her brother Austin and his wife. She lived in a world of starched Sundays, dissenting churches, and the building of railroads, and usually she viewed it all with ironic detachment. For example, about the genteel female she wrote:

> What soft cherubic creatures
> These gentlewomen are
> One would as soon assault a plush
> Or violate a star.

There can be no question about the intensity of her feelings. Sometimes she probes with a long needle into the living quick of her subject, but sometimes her emotions are directly, harshly expressed, and one realizes how deeply anguished she could be. Here is a poem about her spinsterhood:

> Title divine is mine
> The Wife without
> The Sign.

Acute degree
Conferred on me—
Empress of Calvary.
Royal all but the
Crown—
Betrothed, without the swoon

God gives us women
When two hold
Garnet to garnet,
Gold to gold—
Born—Bridalled—
Shrouded
In a day
Tri-Victory—"My Husband"
Women say
Stroking the melody,
Is this the way?

Usually she managed a mask for her emotions, or, to use another figure, caught them in the elliptical and epigrammatic tensions of lines, rhythms and metaphors. Her poems and letters suggest a woman who saw herself as delicate, sensitive, feminine, and, however much a recluse, also saw herself "on stage." Late in her life she was in love with Judge Lord (about which more shortly). When he was recovering from what had been apparently a mortal illness, she wrote this to him:

To remind you of my own rapture at your return. . . . I enclose the Note I was fast writing, when the fear your Life had ceased, came, fresh, yet dim, like horrid Monsters fled from a dream . . . "Mr. Lord is very sick." I grasped at a passing Chair. My sight slipped and I thought I was freezing. While my smile was ending, I heard the Doorbell ring, and a strange voice said "I thought first of you." Tom had come, and I ran to his Blue Jacket and let my heart break there.

Judge Lord, with justification, might have replied, "But it was I who seemed to be dying, Emily." He must have known that in her letters she could bow, cry, mimic, be flirtatious, cover her heart, expressing her tormented imagination and indulging her wit.

Recent studies, such as Johnson's biography and his edition of the poems, Jay Leyda's day by day account of her life in Amherst, and Mrs. Todd's publication of certain letters, are making it easier to bring her life and poems into a sharper focus. Winfield Townely Scott in *Exiles and Fabrications* has put together an ingenious and fairly convincing account of her one-sided love affair with Samuel Bowles, editor of the Springfield *Republican*. One of her notes he believes she sent Bowles was accompanied by the second poem quoted above—"My Husband, Women say . . ." When Bowles appeared at Amherst she refused to see him—but would then send him letters both arch and full of repressed passion.

Emily Dickinson's contemporaries knew she was "queer," and at least one of them believed she was "insane." In *Emily Dickinson, a Revelation* Mrs. Millicent Todd Bingham tells of a visit made by a Mrs. Stockton to Abbie Farley West, the niece of Judge Lord. "Picking up a volume of Emily's poems, she made some innocuous remark about them. To that Mrs. West replied, picking the book up by one corner, 'Take it away. Little hussy— didn't I know her? I should say I did. Loose morals. She was crazy about men. Even tried to get Judge Lord. Insane, Too.' " Her letters and notes certainly suggest a neurotic woman, one who found release alternately in pixie-like gestures and in writing poems that subdued her visions of terror. Her letters are filled with self-conscious rhetoric: her mother "ceased," a correspondent is her "Donor," a friend in Philadelphia is "My Philadelphia," or she is a "little Simon Peter." Emily, dressed in white, hidden away in her room, was the Poet. Frightened recluse or not, she must have been a formidable lady, as this love letter to her Judge Lord, Associate Justice of the Supreme Judicial Court of Massachusetts, would seem to prove:

> The celestial Vacation of writing you after an interminable Term of *Four Days*, I can scarcely express. My Head was so sick when I woke this Morning that I feared I couldn't meet Tom, though how did I know that the dear necessity at that particular Moment existed? And more afraid, that should it, I couldn't respond tonight, and a Night is *so*

long, and it is snowing too, another barrier to Hearts that
overleap themselves. Emily "Jumbo"! Sweet Name, but I
know a sweeter—Emily Jumbo Lord. Have I your approval? Tom's suspicions however will be allayed, for I
have thinner Paper, which can elude the very Elect, if it
undertake.

This letter was written rather late in her life. Years earlier,
in 1862, she had been asked by Col. T. W. Higginson,
her literary mentor, to tell him something about herself,
and she had replied thus:

April 25, 1862

Mr. Higginson—Your kindness claimed earlier gratitude, but I was ill, and write today from my pillow. . . .
You asked how old I was? I made no verse, but one or
two until this winter, sir.

I had a terror since September, I could tell to none;
and so I sing, as the boy does of the burying ground, because I am afraid.

You inquire my books. For poets I have Keats, and Mr.
and Mrs. Browning. For prose, Mr. Ruskin, Sir Thomas
Browne, and the *Revelations*. I went to school, but in your
manner of the phrase had no education. When a little
girl, I had a friend who taught me Immortality; but
venturing too near, himself, he never returned. Soon after
my tutor died and for several years my lexicon was my
only companion. Then I found one more, but he was not
contented I be his scholar, so he left the land.

You ask of my companions. Hills, sir, and the sun-down
and a dog as large as myself, that my father brought me.
They are better than beings because they know, but do
not tell; and the noise in the pool at noon exceeds my
piano.

I have a brother and sister; my mother does not care
for thought, and father, too busy with briefs to notice
what we do. He buys me many books, but begs me not to
read them, because he fears they joggle the mind. They
are religious, except me, and address an eclipse, every
morning, whom they call their "Father."

But I fear my story fatigues you. . . .
Is this, sir, what you asked me to tell?

Your friend,
E. Dickinson

In a manner of speaking, a great deal of the biography of Emily Dickinson is there: In Higginson, a kindly but not over-perceptive editor and critic, she found a friend, and eventually, with Mrs. Mabel Loomis Todd, the editor of her first published volumes. Her age? She dates her life from that winter, 1862, when she began to write. (But Thomas H. Johnson in his fine biography says that at this time she was thirty-one and had written well over 300 poems.) The events of her life? She "had a terror since September." This is cryptic enough, but most of the biographers say this is a reference to the Reverend Charles Wadsworth, a well-known Presbyterian minister. Emily apparently had met him during her trip to Philadelphia and Washington in May, 1854, to visit her father, then a member of Congress. The two corresponded for a number of years, and in 1860 Reverend Wadsworth visited Emily in Amherst. In 1862, some weeks after the above letter was written, the Wadsworth family moved to California. The "terror," these biographers say, is Emily's knowledge of his imminent departure.

The skeptical reader may feel that two meetings in eight years (there was a third meeting in 1880) are hardly evidence of a consuming passion, even a one-sided passion. Certain of her letters at the time of his death seem to indicate that he no longer meant a great deal to her. Mr. Johnson refers to three "love letters" to Wadsworth that were found among Emily Dickinson's papers. The letters clearly indicate that the writer was in a highly disturbed state of mind, but they are not addressed to anyone by name, and there is no evidence that any of them was mailed. Mrs. Todd Bingham says that while Wadsworth may have been the object of her "fine frenzy" there is no direct evidence that he was. And she adds: "But whoever the man, or men—for all three letters may not be addressed to the same person—here is further evidence that for Emily Dickinson her own heart was her most insistent and baffling contendent." She was, to use our idiom, a highly neurotic woman, and at this point in her life her suffering, from whatever real or imagined cause, was intense; thus far no biographer or critic has been able to explain in a satisfactory way either the cause or the nature of her neurosis.

Emily's "terror" *may* have been the recognition that she, a woman with a haunted imagination, had already become a recluse and that she would spend a lifetime in her father's house, described by Mr. Higginson as "dark, cool, stiffish." There was terror enough in that. Or it may have been something far different.

The friend who taught her Immortality is thought to be Benjamin Franklin Newton, a law student in her father's office. Ben Newton had given her books to read and probably encouraged her desire to write poetry. In 1848, when Emily was eighteen, he returned to his own community, Worcester, Massachusetts, where he married. Two years later he was dead. Leonard Humphrey, one of Emily's actual teachers, is said to be the "tutor" who died.

The brother is Austin, who studied law at Harvard, and, like his father and grandfather before him, became a leading citizen in Amherst. He married Susan Gilbert, the daughter of a tavern keeper, and, as Emily said, frequently visited his sisters, who lived next door, to escape the "Vesuvius at home." The sister is Lavinia, who was younger than Emily. She too became a spinster and a somewhat cantankerous recluse who complained that their father, by discouraging the visits of young men, had kept Emily and her from marrying. The mother, long an invalid, did "not care for thought."

The father, lawyer Edward Dickinson, true to his heritage, was rather fearful of books—they might "joggle the mind." His own father had been one of the chief founders of Amherst College, and he himself was a trustee until he died in 1874. Edward Dickinson was the most successful lawyer in Amherst. Emily seems to have been both devoted to and in awe of him. Mr. Higginson, during his Amherst visit, wrote this to his wife: "I saw Mr. Dickinson this morning a little—thin, dry, and speechless. I saw what her life had been. . . . Her father was not severe, I should think, but remote. He did not wish them to read anything but the Bible." Her companions? The hills, the pond, the sun set . . . Were these replies what Mr. Higginson expected, or, better, would they suffice? They could hardly be what he expected, but their allusiveness is a part of the charm of Emily Dickinson, whether as biographical subject or poet.

Emily Dickinson died in 1886, and Lavinia, though without experience in the matter, determined to publish her sister's poems, more than one thousand of them. She obtained the assistance of Mrs. Mabel Loomis Todd, wife of an Amherst instructor, and Colonel Higginson. The manuscripts were undated and for the most part in disorder, and many, on scraps of paper, were written in a manner that defied comprehension. But Mrs. Todd and Higginson published two series, in 1890 and 1891, followed by *Letters of Emily Dickinson* in 1894, and a third volume of poems in 1896. The reception of the volumes was friendly, a few critics recognizing in her poetry a high degree of originality, even genius. That three volumes of poetry were published and further volumes planned seems evidence enough that the reception was looked upon as favorable. Suddenly, because of personal difficulties within the Dickinson family and with Mrs. Todd, publication ceased.

As told in *Ancestors Brocades*, by Mrs. Todd's daughter, Millicent Todd Bingham, this is what happened. Despite Mrs. Todd's many months of work with the manuscripts, Lavinia kept all of the royalties. Austin, feeling the injustice of this, caused Lavinia to join him in ceding a small piece of property to Mrs. Todd, but after his death in 1895, Lavinia, egged on by Austin's widow, Susan, sued to recover lost property. The suit, which divided Amherst into two camps, was decided in Lavinia's favor. Mrs. Todd promptly locked up the manuscripts remaining in her possession. They remained hidden for a good many years.

In 1914, Austin's daughter, Martha Dickinson Bianchi, published *The Single Hound*, in 1924 *Life and Letters* and *Complete Poems*. But *Complete Poems* was followed by *Further Poems*, 1929, and *Unpublished Poems*, 1936. When questions were raised about the authenticity of this latter volume, Mrs. Todd assured her daughter Millicent that they were genuine—and she took out the old manuscripts to prove it. After Mrs. Todd's death, her daughter published *Bolts of Melody*, 1945, which included several hundred poems that had escaped Mrs. Bianchi. At the present time the manuscripts held by the Dickinson family are in the possession of Harvard College and Thomas H. Johnson has edited a scholarly edition of three volumes (*The Poems of Emily Dickinson*, Harvard University Press, 1955; Mr. Johnson had access to the manuscripts still in the possession—although ownership is claimed by Harvard College—of Mrs. Bingham).

Mrs. Bingham has given additional biographical information in *Emily Dickinson, a Revelation*, a book written to provide a context for the love letters to Judge Lord, also left her by her mother to whom Austin had entrusted them. She believes that there were three loves in Emily's life, the youthful attachment for Wadsworth, then a love "beyond sentimentality" for Samuel Bowles, and lastly Judge Lord, her father's friend. Each of these relationships had a separate "apartment" in her mind. Mrs. Bingham writes that there was in Emily Dickinson "an intensity which terrified some people." Colonel Higginson, for whom she evidenced no romantic feelings, said, "I never was with anyone who drained my nerve power so much, without touching her she drew from me. I am glad not to live near her." Her intensity is certainly related both to the manner and characteristic themes of her poems.

Allen Tate in his well-known essay, "Emily Dickinson," said that she was fortunate in being born when and where she was, at a time when a "great idea was breaking up, and society was moving towards external uniformity." The "great idea," of course, was the grim Puritan tradition; it was giving way to the easy individualism of Emerson. For Miss Dickinson the world was filled with shadows. One of the frequent words in her poetry and letters is *immortality*, but one is never quite sure what it signifies to her.

> *It is an honorable Thought,*
> *And makes One lift One's Hat*
> *As One met sudden Gentlefolk*
> *Upon a daily Street*

> That We've immortal Place
> Though Pyramids decay
> And Kingdoms, like the Orchard
> Flit Russetly away

Death and eternity haunt her, but she seems ironic, unbelieving, in envisioning long centuries of twilight consciousness in the grave. She reduces God to the size of the human brain, and talks "New Englandy" about Him ("Heft them"):

> The Brain—is wider than the Sky—
> For—put them side by side—
> The one the other will include
> With ease—and You—beside—
>
> The Brain is deeper than the sea—
> For—hold them—Blue to Blue—
> The one the other will absorb—
> As Sponges—Buckets—do—
>
> The Brain is just the weight of God—
> For—Heft them—Pound for Pound—
> And they will differ—if they do—
> As Syllable from Sound—

Miss Dickinson's individualism also falls in between that of her forebears and that of Emerson or Whitman. Her ancestors saw man bearing the heavy guilt of original sin and therefore not readily given to thinking himself all-powerful. The primary relationship was between God and man. Emerson and Whitman did not see man as a "fallen creature," and they were much more confident about his power of controlling his own destiny. Their "religion" was man-centered, and they envisioned a great communion among mankind, a human brotherhood. Miss Dickinson, as it were, relieved man of his terrible guilt, but she was not able to believe in a great mystical brotherhood. Primarily the individual was alone.

> One need not be a Chamber—to be Haunted—
> One need not be a House—
> The Brain—has Corridors surpassing
> Material Place—

Far safer of a Midnight—meeting
External Ghost—
Than its Interior—Confronting—
That cooler—Host.

Far safer, through an Abbey—gallop—
The Stones a'chase—
Than Unarmed—One's A'self encounter—
In lonesome place—

Ourself—behind Ourself—Concealed—
Should startle—most—
Assassin—hid in our Apartment—
Be Horror's least—

The Body—borrows a Revolver—
He bolts the Door—
O'erlooking a Superior Spectre—
Or More—

And the occasions when, or the number of people with
whom, one has a true communion of spirit, love, or deep
understanding, were, she believed, infrequent and few.

In the letter to Higginson Emily Dickinson said she
wrote poetry, or sang, as a way of controlling her terror.
A fine instance of this is to be found in this poem:

Because I could not stop for Death—
He kindly stopped for me—
The Carriage held but just Ourselves—
And Immortality.

We slowly drove—He knew no haste
And I had put away
My labor and my leisure too,
For His Civility—

We passed the School, where Children strove
At Recess—in the Ring—
We passed the Fields of Gazing Grain—
We passed the Setting Sun—

Or rather—He passed Us—
The Dews drew quivering and chill—

For only Gossamer, my Gown—
My Tippet—only Tulle—

We paused before a House that seemed
A Swelling of the Ground—
The Roof was scarcely visible—
The Cornice—in the Ground—

Since then—'tis Centuries—and yet
Feels shorter than the Day
I first surmised the Horses Heads
Were toward Eternity—

She envisions death as the driver of the carriage, a gentleman escort. He is kindly, and his manners are irreproach-
able. She is also aware, as is the reader, of the immense
significance of the journey. Human time looms long or
short, depending on the experience one is having. The
poet is speaking of the experience of the last hours before death—a day scene is in her use of *immortality* and
eternity. Ordinarily *immortality* is one of the great words
associated with death. But in the imagery of the poem Immortality is made to ride in the carriage, another passen-
ger. Thus too the horses' heads are turned, not as they
ordinarily would be, toward a place up the road, but "toward Eternity."

In employing this mode of good manners she is examining the civilized mores, in which death is accepted with
dignity. Dignity in the face of death is one way of coming to terms with it. But decorum does not really hide
the awfulness of death. This contrast between the dignity
of our conduct in the face of death and the terrible feelings beneath it is caught in the tension of the imagery of
the fifth stanza. The carriage stops at a house, a
house that has a roof and a cornice but which is nonethe-
less a grave. The two realms are given at once, the familiar
domestic world, and the chill world of decay. What Emily
Dickinson tried to do in this poem, she tried to elsewhere:
to domesticate and to make beautiful a terrifying cosmos.

10   HUCKLEBERRY FINN AND
THE GREAT AMERICAN
NOVEL

FROM THE LATE nineteenth century to World War I, and
even after, there was much discussion of the great American novel. Eventually the idea died, apparently of its own
inanity. But in recent years the idea, though not the
phrase, has returned to life, for we are informed, from a
variety of critical positions, that *The Adventures of Huckleberry Finn* is the truly American novel.

A novel wants to be circumscribed, to live in its own
terms, to fulfill itself imaginatively. On the other hand,
it speaks to a people and to their beliefs about themselves.
Huck is said to live for us somewhat as Roland lives for
France or Arthur for England. If Huck is firmly enshrined
in myth it would be futile to try to dislodge him. But his
place in an American myth would not of itself be assurance that *Huckleberry Finn* is a great novel.

The following observations maintain that the book
owes much of its eminence to our mythologizing of the
West and, further, that the claim made for it as a source
book for all later "American" fiction is not a valid claim.
In making such observations it is helpful to refer to the
introductions of *Huckleberry Finn* written by T. S. Eliot
and Lionel Trilling. It is also necessary, on occasion, to
disagree with them. Mr. Eliot reads it—Twain's only masterpiece he says—as the story of the Boy and the River,
the former being the unconscious or all but unconscious
critic of civilization, its pursuits, wickedness, and vagaries,

and the latter the symbol of time that is timeless and of human affairs carried downstream, often capriciously. Lionel Trilling also writes of the unblinking honesty of the boy Huck, and of the river as a god. He finds it a central American document and one of the world's great books.

Both Eliot and Trilling suggest that there is only one flaw, and this not a very serious one, to be charged against the structure of the book: the overly elaborate scheme for Jim's escape engineered by Tom Sawyer in the closing section of the story. Trilling does say the episode is far too long but, like Eliot, he justifies it as a way of returning the reader to civilization, and of freeing Huck, allowing him to disappear. The Tom Sawyer episode is certainly *a* method for bringing off the dénouement, but involved with it is a serious anti-climax. Miss Watson's will had already freed Jim, and all the high jinks and genuine danger have been merely to satisfy Tom's desire to keep things hopping. Tom is the Practical Joker of American literature and Twain has a streak of it himself, which interferes with his true sense of comedy.

The critical acumen of Eliot and Trilling notwithstanding, there are a number of flaws in *Huckleberry Finn*, some of them attributable to Twain's refusal to respect the "work of art" and others attributable to his imperfect sense of tone. The downstream movement of the story (theme as well as action) runs counter to Jim's effort to escape. Life on the raft may indeed be read as implied criticism of civilization—but it doesn't get Jim any closer to freedom. One may also ask (it has been asked before) why it never occurred to Jim, or to Huck, to strike out for the Illinois shore and freedom. It is possible that Twain felt Tom's high jinks were necessary not merely to prepare for the disappearance of Huck but to shift attention away from his conflicting themes.

For the downward movement of the novel, of course, the picaresque form serves the subject very well, allowing for innumerable and rapid adventures, afloat and ashore, and for the sort of ponderings that are peculiar to Huck. The picaresque form is also a clue to the kind of unity the book does have, a melodramatic mixture of reality and

unreality and of comedy and horror. It is frequently theatrical in a good sense of the word. But the unity depends
on Huck's mind, and too often there are bits of action,
dialogue, and observation which are not appropriate to
him. There are two sorts of theatricality in the novel, melodrama and claptrap.

Huck's relationship with his father is melodrama. So
is the shooting of Boggs, or the tar and feathering of the
Duke and King. A proof of their being melodrama is
the ease with which one moves from a scene of violence
to a humorous dialogue. For example, the encounter of
Huck and Jim with the thieves and murderers aboard the
Walter Scott is followed by the minstrel show, end-men
sort of humor of "Was Solomon Wise?" Verisimilitude
offers no problem when reality merges with unreality or
horror dissolves innocently into comedy, but sometimes
Twain's sense of proper distance, the degree and nature
of the stylization he is employing, fails him and the action becomes gruesomely real. An instance of this is
Huck's telling of the murders in "Why Harney Rode
Away for His Hat." The starkness is too unrelieved. The
scene does not respect the premises nor the general tone
of the novel, and, even though it might work in another
novel, it does not work here.

A good deal is made, quite justly, of Huck's affection
for Jim, and the example commonly given is Huck's
apology to Jim after having tormented him with a lie
about there having been no storm. "It was fifteen minutes," Huck says, "before I could work myself up to go
and humble myself to a nigger, but I done it, and I warn't
sorry for it afterwards neither." But Twain sometimes loses
sight of Huck's moral sensitivity. An instance is in Chapters xvii and xviii.

Near the close of Chapter xvi the raft is run over by an
upstream steamboat. In the darkness, after he and Jim
have dived into the water, Huck cannot see Jim and his
calls go unanswered. Huck then strikes out for shore.
The following chapter, "The Grangerfords Take Me In,"
is a humorous introduction to the Grangerford family.
Huck stays with the Grangerfords for many days, perhaps

weeks, getting involved in their affairs, notably as courier between the lovers Miss Sophia Grangerford and Harney Shepherdson. No thought about Jim enters Huck's head! It doesn't occur to him to search for the old Negro. Jack, Huck's "nigger servant," finally invites him to see a "stack o' water-moccasins" in a swamp, a trick for leading him to the spot where Jim is hiding. "I poked into the place a ways and come to a little open patch as big as a bedroom all hung round with vines, and found a man lying there asleep—and, by jings, it was my old Jim!" There is not much indication that Huck is greatly relieved or moved at finding Jim alive: "I waked him up, and I reckoned it was going to be a grand surprise to him to see me again. . . . He nearly cried he was so glad." Huck says nothing about being glad himself. Perhaps we are to read this passage ironically, as an instance of a boy's self-centeredness and believe that true affection lies beneath it. This might be so, but it doesn't explain away Huck's absence of grief over Jim's "death," or his failure to search for him if alive, or his general indifference to Jim's fate.

Technically, too, the device for getting rid of Jim so that Huck can move into the Grangerford-Shepherdson world is awkward and unconvincing. Jim tells Huck he had heard him call for him when they were swimming toward shore but hadn't answered for fear of being detected. Presumably one reply would have quieted Huck and made detection much less likely. And if Huck had been allowed to help Jim hide, or even to maintain some awareness of him, he would be the Huck known to us in "Fooling Old Jim."

Huck's parody (Chapter XVII) of the activities of Emmeline Grangerford, poetess, is extremely amusing, but the "voice" is more nearly Twain's than Huck's. Many other things are put into the mouth of the twelve- or thirteen-year-old Huck that, sometimes only weakly humorous themselves, are Twain himself speaking. This, for example, from a boy with almost no schooling: "Look at Henry the Eight; this'n's a Sunday school Superintendent to *him*. And look at Charles Second, and Louis Fourteen, and Louis Fifteen, and James Second, and Edward

Second, and Richard Third, and forty more; besides all them Saxon heptarchies that used to rip around so in old times and raise Cain." There are other witticisms about kings, a theme appropriate enough to *Huckleberry Finn,* but Twain might have found some other way of introducing them. In "An Arkansas Difficulty," where Twain is giving a sense of life in a small river town, he makes Huck relate an observation on "chawing tobacker" that one would expect to find as "filler" in a nineteenth-century newspaper or magazine. Most incongruous of all, perhaps, is Huck's account of the Duke's rendition of Hamlet's soliloquy.

A more self-conscious artist would not have allowed such discrepancies to mar the tone of his novel. The truth is that Twain, however gifted a raconteur, however much genius he had as an improviser, was not, even in *Huckleberry Finn,* a great novelist.

A glance at Twain's biography reveals attitudes that, if they were related about another "major" writer, would appear highly damaging. In *My Mark Twain* William Dean Howells reported: "He once said to me, I suppose after he had been reading some of my unsparing praise of [Jane Austen]: 'You seem to think that woman could write,' and he forbore withering me with his scorn." Howells also wrote: "I fancy his pleasure in poetry was not great, and I do not believe he cared much for the conventionally accepted masterpieces of literature." And of Henry James, whose *The Bostonians* was serialized in the same magazine with *Huckleberry Finn,* Twain said, "I would rather be damned to John Bunyan's heaven than read that."

Huckleberry Finn is involved with the mystique of America. The chief symbols are the Boy and the River. Huck is the break not merely with Europe but with civilization, the westward push. Self-sufficient and yet dependable, he is the proper kind of individualist. He is also youth, a rugged Peter Pan who lives eternally. Huck belongs also with Cooper's Leatherstocking and Faulkner's Ike McCaslin, symbolic figures who reject the evils of civilization. (A weakness in all of them is that they do not acknowledge the virtues of civilization or try to live, as one must, inside it.) Huck is, finally, a sentimental figure, not in himself of course, since he is a boy, but in the minds of those who unduly admire his departure for the territory.

The River, as Eliot says, is time and timelessness, "a strong brown god" with his own thoughts about the machine, the hurry and fuss of cities, the illusions and struggles that make us lie, steal, or cheat. But the River is also the Mississippi as it borders the state of Missouri, the very heart of America. If Twain helped create a mythic river, the mythic river also helped Twain find his place as a legendary writer. Having such a place, he is sometimes, by sheer association, given more: he is made into the "Lincoln of American literature."

My Mark Twain concludes with Howells' account of seeing Twain in his coffin, the face "patient with the patience I had often seen in it; something of a puzzle, a great silent dignity, an assent to what must be from the depths of a nature whose tragical seriousness broke in the laughter which the universe took for the whole of him." Howells then adds: "Emerson, Longfellow, Lowell, Holmes—I knew them all and all the rest of our sages, poets, seers, critics, humorists; they were like one another and like other literary men; but Clemens was sole, incomparable, the Lincoln of our literature." Stuart Pratt Sherman in the *Cambridge History of American Literature* also compares Twain with Lincoln: "In the retrospect he looms for us with Whitman and Lincoln, recognizably his countrymen, out of the shadows of the Civil War, an unmistakable native son of an eager, westward moving people—unconventional, self-reliant, mirthful, profane, realistic, cynical, boisterous, popular, tenderhearted, touched with chivalry, and permeated to the marrow of his bones with the sentiment of a democratic society and with loyalty to American institutions."

The association of Lincoln and Twain may seem appropriate at first glance—but only at first glance. Presumably Howells meant that both men discovered their need for comedy in the pathos and tragedy of the human condition, that both men were sons of a frontier society. To a degree, then, the comparison holds. But to allow for a detailed comparison, Lincoln should have to have written novels, or Twain to have been a politician, statesman, or writer of speeches. Insofar as Lincoln the writer and Twain the writer can be compared, Lincoln is the greater. Lincoln's wit, also in a vernacular idiom, is frequently more subtle than Twain's and may be expected to be more lasting. Lincoln's ability in writing an analytical prose, flexible and closely reasoned, and his ability in writing a serious and, when the occasion required, solemn rhetoric were also greater than Twain's. The seriousness and solemnity in Twain are of innocence betrayed, as in the concluding paragraph of *The Mysterious Stranger*. Lincoln's seriousness is that of a man dealing with the world, in its own terms when forced to, but also above it, urging it to create its destiny in ways that make for the fullest sense of achievement and dignity. If Lincoln had written novels, he would, without doubt, have been a greater novelist than Twain. His virtues include Twain's and surpass them.

It was in *The Green Hills of Africa* that Hemingway made his now famous assertion that "All modern American literature comes from one book by Mark Twain called *Huckleberry Finn*." The genealogy, as commonly worked out, is as follows: *Huckleberry Finn* → Crane, Stein, Anderson → Hemingway → Modern American Fiction. Obviously there are other strands of American fiction. Writers like Willa Cather, Scott Fitzgerald, and Faulkner do not derive from Twain. Nor from Hemingway. Again, an English reader could undoubtedly point out much in the prose of Melville or Hawthorne or Poe that is "peculiarly American." In other words, several semiliterate Missouri idioms are not exclusively "pure American language." Perhaps one can say that these idioms bear the same relationship to general American English that the tall tale bears to American fiction as a whole. At any rate, the strand of language that Hemingway is concerned with is—though vigorous, vital, and concrete—unsuited to speculation or subtle distinctions. (Perhaps the best sum-

mary of the style Hemingway admires and employs is
Gertrude Stein's "How Writing is Written." There are
also good discussions of it in Frederick Hoffman's *The
Modern Novel in America* and Philip Young's *Ernest
Hemingway*.)

It is interesting to compare Hemingway's prose with
Lincoln's in "The Gettysburg Address." In the latter, one
finds not merely the simplicity and repetition of the
Hemingway prose but an ennobling rhetoric; Lincoln's
prose both meets the Hemingway aesthetic and tran-
scends it.

Probably it is a time and a place, with a language appropriate to them, that appeal to the followers of Twain.
In a series of letters addressed to Van Wyck Brooks,
Sherwood Anderson made many references to Twain, to
the midwest, and to *the* book. In Brooks's introduction to
the letters one reads:

> I can remember how struck I was by his [Anderson's]
> fresh healthy mind and his true Whitmanian feeling
> for comradeship, his beautiful humility, his lovely gen-
> erosity, and the "proud conscious innocence" of his na-
> ture. This was his own phrase for Mark Twain's mind
> at the time he was writing *Huckleberry Finn*; and it
> goes for Sherwood also. He was the most natural of men,
> as innocent as any animal or flowering tree.

This passage, in language reminiscent of Anderson's own,
of Hemingway's too, but a little thin and nostalgic to have
been Twain's, is obviously intended as wholly a compli-
ment. If one wonders why an American quality, innocence, and superior writing go together, there is Anderson's reasoning on the matter: "He [Twain] belonged
out here in the Middle West and was only incidentally
a writer." Presumably craftsmanship, wide experience, or
even thought in any complexity inhibit a truly American
writer. Innocence, that strange word in American life,
helps to account for Twain's place, and the place of
Huckleberry Finn, in the hierarchy of American literature.

Innocence, to pursue the subject a little further, also
helps account for the two writers who most clearly come

in the wake of Twain—Anderson and Hemingway. The protagonists in Anderson's stories, as Trilling points out, are ensnared or caught: in poverty (*Marching Men*), in marriage (*Many Marriages*), by inhibitions (*Dark Laughter*). Anderson's message is that we must be "free," economically, emotionally, intellectually, but in his stories to be free is to escape. Anderson did not accept the conditions of human existence and responsibility. The child, or the boy, is his chief protagonist, and the reader watches him confront and be offended by the adult world. In "I Want to Know Why," the point of which Hemingway borrowed and improved upon, Anderson has the young protagonist use one of Huck's phrases, "It gave me the fantods." In the context of Anderson's story the phrase sounds dated and ineffectual, but it may be a clue to what Anderson was attempting, to live in the nineteenth century, or, better, in the boy's world which Huck symbolized for him.

Nick Adams, the protagonist in *In Our Time* (1925), suffers, as Philip Young points out, a trauma, or to use the more literary word, a wound, the result of the anguish and evil he has experienced. He is the first of the Hemingway heroes. As Nick Adams this hero breaks with a pious and righteous mother. As Jake Barnes in *The Sun Also Rises* he is an expatriate in more senses than one. As Lieutenant Henry in *A Farewell to Arms* he makes a separate peace. As Harry Morgan in *To Have and Have Not* he is an outlaw. As Robert Jordan in *For Whom the Bell Tolls* he is a soldier adventurer. As Colonel Cantwell in *Across the River and into the Trees* he conducts a private war against stupid generals. As the old man in *The Old Man and the Sea* he fights his battle alone, except for a small boy admirer. The Hemingway hero, in addition to other characteristics, refuses the compromises all civilized people make. It is not fair to say he is Huck Finn grown up—but he is in part Huck Finn. Except for an occasional tribute to humanity as one, the Hemingway hero looks at civilization and says what Huck said: "I been there before."

Beyond the Huck aspect in Hemingway is the irony

that not even in the territory is there peace. In the simplest of his phrases there is a suggestion of terror. His protagonists would like to find innocence, and in a way they search for it. And perhaps this suggests a reasonable way of viewing *Huckleberry Finn*. It appeals to our desire for a condition of innocence. The difficulty we have in conceiving what Huck might be as an adult is an indication of the limited usefulness of Huck as a symbol. If we refuse to over-value him as a symbol, we may be less inclined to over-value the novel, or to over-value the language in which it is written.

IN THE EARLY 1850's, Bayard Taylor made a trip to Africa, traveling in Egypt, Soudan, and Ethiopia. He wrote a book about his travels entitled *A Journey to Central Africa, or, Life and Landscapes from Egypt to the Negro Kingdoms of the White Nile.* He also wrote a number of poems, including one called "Kilimanjaro." In the early 1930's, Ernest Hemingway was hunting in Africa. Out of his experiences came *The Green Hills of Africa,* as well as "The Short Happy Life of Francis McComber" and "The Snows of Kilimanjaro." It is merely fortuitous, of course, that two American writers, almost a century apart, chose to write about the great African mountain. The coincidence, however, affords an opportunity to examine two separate traditions in the American literary mind.

It so happens that Hemingway made a statement in *The Green Hills of Africa* about the "genteel tradition." He said the genteel writers were "good men with the small, dried, and excellent wisdom of the Unitarians. . . . They were all very respectable. They did not use the words that people always have used in speech, the words that survive in language. Nor would you gather that they had bodies. They had minds, yes. Nice, dry, clean minds." Presumably Hemingway would call Taylor's "Kilimanjaro" a genteel poem. And of course it is.

The opening lines of the poem are designed to humanize the great mountain, to bring it into a proper relationship with man and civilization:

> *Hail to thee, monarch of African mountains,*
> *Remote, inaccessible, silent, and lone,—*
> *Who, from the heart of the tropical fervors,*
> *Liftest to heaven thine alien snows,*
> *Feeding forever the fountains that make thee*
> *Father of Nile and Creator of Egypt.*

In the second stanza the mountain is clearly placed inside the orbit of civilized doings:

> *The years of the world are engraved on thy forehead;*
> *Time's morning blushed red on thy first fallen snows;*

On the other hand, there is an acknowledgment of the mountain's foreign otherness: once she was lost in the wilderness, unknown, unnamed. Even so, Taylor implies, nature is under *our* spell:

> *Knowledge alone is the being of Nature,*
> *Giving a soul to her manifold features,*
> *Lighting through paths of primitive darkness*
> *The footsteps of Truth and vision of Song*
> *Knowledge had born thee anew to Creation,*
> *And long-baffled Time at thy baptism rejoices.*

Taylor, as poet, relates how floating in a boat on the Nile he scoops up water, "a magical mirror," and sees therein a vision of the mountain "supreme in the midst of her co mates." He sees her as exhibiting, at various heights, the several seasons of the year:

> *There, in the wondering airs of the Tropics*
> *Shivers the Aspen, still dreaming of cold:*
> *There stretches the Oak, from the loftiest ledges,*
> *His arms to the far-away lands of his brothers,*
> *And the Pine-tree looks down on his rival, the Palm.*

If the mountain is a little mysterious, it is none the less as orderly as the coming of the seasons. Comparing Mont Blanc and other great mountains with Kilimanjaro, Taylor says thay were "baptized." In other words, and unlike a later American poet, Wallace Stevens, he could not conceive that the gods of Africa would be appropriate to Africa. In Taylor's mind Kilimanjaro is seen as having been reduced to the jurisdiction of the European community.

Taylor was willing to have Kilimanjaro exotic, strange,

and mysterious—but not too mysterious ("unseen but of God") and certainly not an object to contemplate with fear or terror. Taylor's own civilized order is interposed between himself and the great mountain rising from the hills and plains of central east Africa.

Near the end of December, 1933, Hemingway was in Tanganyika, where he fell ill with amoebic dysentery. He continued to hunt, but after a short period it was clear that he was too ill to remain. In mid-January a two-seater plane carried him 400 miles north for medical treatment, past Ngorongoro Crater and the Rift Escarpment to the town of Arusha and from there past the huge bulk of Kiliman-jaro to Nairobi in Kenya.

In his "The Snows of Kilimanjaro," a rather puzzling story, Hemingway makes use of the mountain as symbol. The oft debated epigraph to the story is this: "Kilimanjaro is a snow-covered mountain 19,710 feet high, and is said to be the highest mountain in Africa. Its western summit is called the Masai 'Ngaje Ngaji,' the House of God. Close to the western summit there is the dried and frozen carcass of a leopard. No one has explained what the leopard was seeking at that altitude."

The narrative itself recapitulates the life of Harry, a highly gifted writer. One learns that he has written a few good things, but mostly he has taken the easy way, even to marrying for money. Now, at the moment of the story's action, during a safari in Africa he is dying from gangrene. Half delirious, he picks quarrels with his wife, and he re-calls many of his experiences. Suspense is maintained by the promised arrival of a plane that will pick him up and carry him to a town where his leg can be treated. There are several quite startling images of death. Finally, he dies. In the moments before he dies he has a fantasy in which the night has passed, the plane arrives, and he is put aboard and carried out (the reader, for the moment, thinks this is actually happening, but then learns that it is still night, Harry's wife has awakened and sees that he is dead). A part of the fantasy is this:

And then instead of going on to Arusha they turned left, he [the pilot] evidently figured that they had the gas, and looking down he saw a pink sifting cloud, moving over the ground, and in the air, like the first snow in a blizzard, that comes from nowhere, and he knew the locusts were going to the East it seemed, and then it darkened and they were in a storm, the rain so thick it seemed like flying through a waterfall, and then they were out and Compie [the pilot] turned his head and grinned and pointed and there, ahead, all he could see, as wide as all the world, great, high, and unbelievably white in the sun, was the square top of Kilimanjaro. And then he knew that there was where he was going.

Man, like the leopard frozen near the western summit, pushes upward. As C. C. Walcutt has put it, all reason is against the leopard being found at that height and all reason is against Harry's ambition to rise above an "aimless materialism." Whatever it was that drove the leopard up there "is the same sort of mystery as the force that keeps idealism alive in Harry." But man is in material nature. The story tells us that Harry did capitulate. He had not written the true and beautiful stories it was in his power to write. He did not live to achieve what he might have achieved. Only in fantasy does he escape from the nature that has pulled him down. In his delirium, he believes he has escaped into the mysterious beauty that Kilimanjaro symbolizes—but he has not escaped. Among the final images in the story is one almost equally vivid with the white brilliance of the mountain: "She could see his bulk under the mosquito bar but somehow he had gotten his leg out and it hung down alongside the cot. The dressings had all come down and she could not look at it." Idealism does not always win. She has an implacable foe in physical decay which succeeds in winning major victories, perhaps the major victories.

Within Taylor's vision of civilization there is a far greater assurance of strength and abiding influence than there is in Hemingway's vision. Historically, it is that the affirmations of the "genteel tradition" gave way, as everyone knows, to affirmations of a more qualified sort. Taylor, the nineteenth-century visitor to Africa, was assured that the primitive could be civilized, whereas Hemingway, the twentieth-century visitor, feels or knows that the "primitive" is a part of civilization. To develop this point much further would entail an examination of the "genteel tradition" and certain of the reactions to it. Perhaps it is sufficient to observe, once more, that Taylor, the genteel poet, superimposed a civilized order of things on a nature that the twentieth-century man sees as alien or at least as apart from him. Taylor was in awe of the mountain, but not so profoundly in awe of it as Hemingway was.

Between Bayard Taylor and Hemingway lay the breakup of the genteel tradition. George Santayana, in his brilliant lecture, "The Genteel Tradition in American Philosophy," says "the three American writers whose personal endowment was perhaps the finest—Poe, Hawthorne and Emerson—had all a certain starved, abstract quality. They could not retail the genteel tradition; they were too keen for that. But life offered them little digestible material, nor were they naturally voracious." Santayana is saying that Poe, Emerson and Hawthorne tried to turn away from the genteel tradition, and in doing so had to become highly subjective writers.

James, he says, treated the matter differently. "Mr. Henry James has [freed himself] by turning the genteel American tradition as he turns everything else, into a subject-matter for analysis. For him it is a curious habit of mind, intimately comprehended, to be compared with other habits of mind, also well known to him. Thus he has overcome the genteel tradition in the classic way, by understanding it."

James's "The Madonna of the Future" (1873) is an excellent example of what Santayana means. James was only thirty when he wrote it—and obviously he had been thinking about his future as an American writer. His father's generation had aspired to create the Beautiful, and most of them managed to achieve little or nothing, because the Beautiful as a transcendental entity does not exist. Undoubtedly James feared this could happen to him. It was also, one would guess, a reason why he chose to live in Europe.

James invents a painter, an old man, an American exile.

The scene is Florence. The old painter dreams of the great madonna he will one day produce. He sits in a shabby room before a canvas, getting ready to paint it. Meanwhile his "beautiful" young subject has aged twenty years, becoming stout, coarse and vulgar. The painter "sees" her as she was. It would never occur to him to paint her as she is. When forced to see her as she actually is, he is shocked and shortly thereafter dies.

There is a second artist, a cynical Italian, who is the woman's lover. He does obscene statuettes of monkeys and cats in amorous relationships. He says, "The idea's bold; does it strike you as happy? Cats and monkeys— monkeys and cats—all human life is there! Human life, of course I mean, viewed with the eye of the satirist! To combine sculpture and satire, signore, has been my un-precedented ambition. I flatter myself I have not egregiously failed." The young American admits they are "strikingly clever and expressive."

James is saying that beauty must come fron lived experiences, and these may include the sordid and the ugly. Human life isn't all cats and monkeys—but they are a part of it. A dream of art separated from actuality is unnatural and doomed to failure. That is why, as James implies in "The Author of Beltraffio," the genteel tradition produced no serious art.

The genteel writers, and Taylor is an example, turned their backs on actuality. They separated love from sex, tried to separate the ideal from the forces of materialism and nature, and to create an art that ignored common-place and sometimes unpleasant or distressing human impulses or actions. Howells, Crane, Dreiser, Anderson and others struggled to free themselves from the genteel. One might almost say that for Hemingway in "The Snows of Kilimanjaro" the process is reversed: sex struggles to relate itself to love, and materialism and nature struggle to relate themselves to the ideal. Human impulses, pleasant and unpleasant, are the material of the art, and contribute to its beauty.

12 "GERONTION" AND
"THE DREAM OF GERONTIUS"

DESPITE the obvious similarity between their titles no one, apparently, has troubled to compare T. S. Eliot's "Gerontion" with Cardinal Newman's "Dream of Gerontius." The titles of both poems, of course, suggest a common subject matter, advanced age. A cursory reading of the poems shows that each is a religious or, more specifically, a Christian poem, Eliot's being concerned with an unbelieving world, a society indifferent to or unable to accept Christian beliefs, Newman's with the vision of a Christian's death and judgment. The themes of the two poems, then, have only a tangential relationship.

One would hardly expect to find that the whole of Eliot's poem was, in subject matter or in theme, written, as it were, *over* Newman's. Eliot's creative process frequently works with highly selective and disparate sources, ordering them into complex patterns and meanings of his own making. In a note in *American Renaissance*, F. O. Matthiessen has already pointed out two fragments which undoubtedly stimulated Eliot in writing "Gerontion." The first, a passage from A. C. Benson's biography of Edward Fitzgerald, describes an old man being read to by a boy, in language very close to that of Eliot's own in the opening lines of "Gerontion," and evokes a mood of frustration induced by impotent old age. The second is a passage from *The Education of Henry Adams* describing the "dogwood," the "judas tree," "the chestnut," the oppressive May weather, and making allusion to life-giving water. "Gerontion" as a whole is not a variant on either source. Eliot borrowed from the sermons of Lancelot Andrews. He also borrowed, as already suggested, from Newman's poem.

Newman's Gerontius is accompanied by his Guardian Angel to judgment. He says he has use of all his senses except sight. He asks if he is to be without sight during all of his "penance-time."

> *If so, how comes it then*
> *That I have hearing still, and taste, and touch,*
> *Yet not a glimmer of that princely sense*
> *Which binds ideas in one, and makes them live?*

Gerontius, in effect, has lost all his senses, because they are not bound together by passion.

> *I have lost my passion: why should I need to keep it*
> *Since what is kept must be adulterated?*
> *I have lost my sight, smell, hearing, taste and touch:*
> *How should I use them for your closer contact?*

In answering Gerontius' question about his sight, the Angel says

> *Thou livest in a world of signs and types,*
> *The presentations of most holy truths, . . .*

> *thou art wrapp'd and swathed around in dreams*

Until the Beatific Vision, the Angel continues, we see only through "symbols." Eliot's Gerontion states the same view, while apparently mocking modern skepticism, in strikingly similar phraseology.

> *Signs are taken for wonders. "We would see a sign!"*
> *The word within a word, unable to speak a word,*
> *Swaddled in darkness. In the juvescence of the year*
> *Came Christ the tiger,*

> *In depraved May, dogwood and chestnut . . .*

Eliot's first and third lines echo Newman's first and third lines. In his essay "Lancelot Andrews" Eliot gives us the source of the second line, in quoting a memorable passage from one of Bishop Andrews' sermons: "the word within a word, unable to speak a word." Eliot also quotes as memorable the line "Christ is no wild-cat," the obvious source of his own phrase "Christ the tiger." (In a quotation given just below these two Eliot also indicates a source for his "Journey of the Magi.") Incidentally, Eliot in this same essay compares the impersonal art of Andrews' sermons with that of Newman's sermons. It would seem that to the disparate passages from Benson and Adams should be added these from Newman and Lancelot Andrews.

Eliot may have found two further passages suggestive for his purposes. Gerontius finds that in the House of Judgment, "The sound is like the rushing of the wind . . ." Gerontion feels himself "an old man, A dull head among windy spaces." Secondly, as noted by Matthiessen, "dryness—'a dry month,' 'waiting for rain,' 'a dry brain in a dry season' "—is in "Geronion," as elsewhere in Eliot's poetry, a symbol of spiritual aridity while water, on the contrary, is life-giving. It would appear relevant that Gerontius, approaching confidently to the Deity to be judged, uses water as symbolic of his coming blessedness:

> a grand, mysterious harmony:
> It floods me like the deep and solemn sound
> Of many waters.

The two poems, one seventy-five lines, the other about nine hundred, are both concerned with the Christian mysteries and with salvation. Gerontius lives among believers. Their voices fade behind him as he approaches judgment. His faith is secure. Gerontion lives among non-believers. For his time there is no life-giving faith. It might also be noted that Newman's very elaborate and able employment of Church ritual in this poem may have suggested similar usages to Eliot.

13 WALLACE STEVENS:
IMAGINED REALITY

WALLACE STEVENS HAS come to be recognized as an American poet of the rank of Eliot. Actually Stevens and Eliot are comparable only in terms of their skill. Their idioms, themes and major interests are sufficiently dissimilar to discourage any explicit comparisons. Temperamentally the two men are different. Perhaps they are best characterized, providing neither term is used in any pejorative or absolute sense, as hedonist and as ascetic. Both poets are concerned with the nature of poetry and the role of the poet or artist. Both are concerned with belief, ideals and morality. But the major theme in Stevens by which these concerns are organized is the nature of imagination and its relation to "reality," while the major theme in Eliot is the need for a stable society, having traditional religious and cultural forms and values.

In "The Noble Rider and the Sound of Words," an excellent critical essay, Stevens says that we in the twentieth century are the victims of an obsession. We pride ourselves on being willing to face the facts. With Bertrand Russell, we, as free men, take a cold, ironic pleasure in living in an alien universe. If our "naturalistic" literature and our tendency to read "escapism" for imagination are indicative of the contemporary mind, we seem determined not to allow the imagination either to help reconcile us to the facts or to transform them. Stevens does not shy away at the mention of romanticism. Therein, he says, may lie our salvation.

Such statements as these necessarily offend many contemporary minds. When Stevens cries "jargon" or "cant" upon meeting indiscriminate use of terms like "escapist" or "realist," these same minds are likely to dismiss him with another label, "obscurantist," to dismiss him as a victim of the general failure of nerve. When we look more closely into his beliefs, however, we find that Stevens' concern that we recognize the place of the imagination does not have as its counterpart any admonition that we should deny the presence, nature or importance of "things-as-they-are."

In one of his earlier poems, "The Comedian as the Letter C," Stevens says he would see the world as the "stiffest realist" sees it. To those who remind him that man's life ends in darkness and dissolution, nothing more, he can point to these lines:

> *casual flocks of pigeons make*
> *Ambiguous undulations as they sink*
> *Downward to darkness, on extended wings.*

If he is reminded of the universe as mechanism he can note that he has observed for himself

> *the clanking mechanism*
> *Of machine within machine within machine.*

He admits, too, in "Theory," "Anecdote of Men by the Thousand," and "The Latest Freed Man," the awesome power of environment. Undoubtedly, if the theme had stirred him, there would be a proper acknowledgment of environment's twin, heredity. Again, he would acknowledge that man seems a chance phenomenon given life by the same impersonal forces that nourish the tree and allow species to become extinct. Stevens would deny no such bitter postulates, which many see as forced upon us by nineteenth-century science. But he would *add* that the mind is creative, that it struggles to control and dominate the world.

The modern mind, however, tends, to use Yeats's term, to be passive, to be in awe of objective fact. We do, for example, have a style but it tends to be skeptical, tentative and noncommittal. And sometimes it aspires to be photographic. We emphasize our sense of disruption and disorganization. We have come to mistrust the imagination itself. Stevens, by implication, reminds us that however dull the tones in which we see the world we are seeing it imaginatively. If we create such a somber style we are cheating ourselves. The imagination can serve us well if we grant it certain freedoms and learn how it creates. It can create a style, one informed by exuberance, aspiration and a resilient spirit, which at once sustains and expresses human dignity.

Every culture has a style, a way of expressing its motivating spirit. If that spirit is leaden and weighted down by a belief that the imagination should not be allowed to transform the surface of experience, the style of the culture will lack exuberance and resilience. It will exhibit the heavy spirit that is its informing power. Certainly the style of the Elizabethans is caught quite as distinctly in their pageantry, in their jeweled clothing and in their political maneuvers as in the rhetoric of their plays, just as the style of the Victorians is caught in their furniture, their clothing and their manners. It seems just, if somewhat ironic, that although the style of a culture exposes its informing spirit, the culture itself is responsible for the style through its control of and attitude toward the imagination. At the close of "Le Monocle de Mon Oncle," Stevens feigns surprise that "fluttering things"—the things of the imagination—"have so distinct a shade." The shade, in our terms, is the style of the culture. The degree of freedom for the imagination has its ultimate significance in the very character of the culture.

Again, more is involved than the externals—architecture, clothing or furniture—of a culture, important as these are. We as individuals, with styles, or, more fashionably, with personalities, create a part of the world in which we live. Our sense of the appropriate or of the beautiful dictates, as it were, the nature and the limitations of that style. In one poem, "Add This to Rhetoric," while noting the importance of individual style—

In the way you speak
You arrange, the thing is posed—

Stevens observes also that human expressions, style, will not keep the sun from rising. But we should not therefore neglect the importance of style.

Holding to his major theme, the relation between imagination and reality as coequals, Stevens has moved beyond a concern with aesthetics (although he was never, as he has been called, a "pure poet") to a concern with the relationship between imagination and humanistic ideals, morality and belief. Like many of the other moderns, as we have noted, Stevens finds the old beliefs "obsolete." Even though we have lost "the idea of god," we are free to substitute an "idea of man." We may still aspire. "The philosopher's man still walks in dew"—man may realize his "fictions." But Stevens is never naïve. He is not asking that the poet project filmy ideas and proceed to live within them. It is here, then, that his insistence upon the relationship between "things-as-they-are and the reality of the imagination" refers itself to the problem of belief. Together they form the "total reality." Ideals as well as an awareness of "things-as-they-are" can, or should, be kept before us through the agency of the imagination.

To deny freedom to the imagination is to deny a part of the total reality. In an untitled poem in *Notes toward a Supreme Fiction*, Stevens is saying, as he has said in "The Noble Rider and the Sound of Words," that the imagination is adding nothing to human nature that is not inherent in it.

The freshness of transformation is
The freshness of a world. It is our own,
It is ourselves, the freshness of ourselves,
And that necessity and that presentation

And rubbings of a glass in which we peer.
Of these beginnings, gay and green, propose
The suitable amours. Time will write them down.

To deny the imagination is to deny half of what we are. In "Poem with Rhythms," from *Parts of a World*, he further justifies the creations of the imagination. To the metaphor, first stated, of the hand between the candle and the wall, he adds:

> *It must be that the hand*
> *Has a will to grow larger on the wall,*
> *To grow larger and heavier and stronger than*
> *The wall; and that the mind*
> *Turns its own figurations and declares,*

> "This image, this love, I compose myself
> Of these. In these, I come forth outwardly.
> In these, I wear a vital cleanliness,
> Not as in air, bright blue-resembling air,
> But as in the powerful mirror of my wish and will."

Stevens' sense of irony is too keen to allow of his suggesting that the poet be the prophet of a new millennium. His proposal is more modest—that we accept the imagination, and therefore its capacity for helping us live, in aesthetic and in moral terms, more humanly. If man cannot be divine, he can be *human*.

The imagination, Stevens insists, leaps out from and plays over an actuality the most unimaginative could not deny. And the very fact that his poems are divisible into themes which taken together state many of the basic problems our society inherits would suggest, on the other hand, a kind of reality the most literal-minded intellectual could not deny. An eagerness to express the immediacy of nature is a characteristic of much modern poetry, including many lines by Stevens; but it is the reality of philosophical problems, particularly in his later work, which most interests him. The two realities are complementary. In them modern poetry has recovered some of the strength that was dissipated by the halfhearted illusion of some nineteenth-century poets that imagination could be kept alive by isolating it from unpleasant physical realities and from philosophical realities, which, it was thought, the scientific minded alone had the right to make authentic pronouncements about. For if the imagination is not mutually interdependent with reality it devolves into what we know as fancy.

In discussing a particular figure of speech employed in *Phaedrus*, Stevens explains its relative ineffectiveness by saying that Plato's "imagination does not adhere to what is real." From this instance he is led to a generalization: "The imagination loses vitality as it ceases to adhere to what is real. When it adheres to the unreal and intensifies what is unreal, while its first effect may be extraordinary, that effect is the maximum effect it will ever have." Plato envisioned the immortal soul as a winged horse and charioteer, then proceeded to develop his characterization of the soul in terms of the figure. Our first reaction, Stevens says, is to identify ourselves with the charioteer that we may fly through the heavens. "Then suddenly we remember, it may be, that the soul no longer exists and we droop in our flight and at last settle on solid ground. The figure becomes antiquated and rustic." The imaginative expression that moves out from something we know as real intensifies its reality, whereas that which moves out from something we know as unreal intensifies its unreality. Or, at least, it makes for the uneasy feeling that we are, at best, experiencing a dream-reality.

The first point that suggests itself relates to the elusive term *reality*. If love, for example, is accepted not as a spiritual reality but only as a delusion the senses exact, then any imaginative extension must be seen merely as intensification of an unreality. Again, if the ideal of nobility is held to be unreal, then the most imaginative statements can not make it real. In other words, the projections, in the forms of ideals and values, of the subjective world must be seen as real before the imagination is free to enlarge upon or to sustain them. Again, as with the style a culture allows itself to create, the agency, imagination, helping to create and sustain ideals and values, must not be merely tolerated or deplored as the human spirit's capacity to create illusions. If it is, then our constant bemoaning that we have been unable to reinstate values as universal factors in reality will be as self-contradictory as one bemoaning his inability to talk after he has torn out his own tongue.

To read Stevens with enjoyment and understanding it

is necessary to perceive that each subject, however commonplace or esoteric, becomes a variation upon the all-
controlling theme: the role of the human imagination.
In writing of the "death of Satan," Lenin, a city getting
ready for bed, a bowl of peaches, a lion roaring, modern
poetry, a sea voyage, love, war, or whatever, the basic
theme is always the same. Consequently in the body of
Stevens' poetry one lives in a world of related ideas, with
infinite variations and subtleties. The world of *Harmo-
nium* has the greatest density, perhaps, the most exquisite
and complex interdependencies of color, sound, symbol,
and theme. The language of the late books, *Parts of a
World* or *Transport to Summer*, is simpler, more direct,
more abstract. A part of this impression of an increasingly
simplified idiom is, however, illusory. The Stevens of
"Sunday Morning" believed that we should find in the

> comforts of the sun,
> In pungent fruit and bright, green wings, or else
> In any balm or beauty of the earth,
> Things to be cherished like the thought of heaven . . .

The Stevens of *Esthétique du Mal* believes that

> The greatest poverty is not to live
> In a physical world . . .

In order to live really in a physical world we have to slough
off the cliché forms, get rid of the habit of forcing all
knowledge into neatly rational patterns and admit the
transforming and ennobling power of the imagination.
We must create new forms, new metaphors, new myths
in order to experience without distortion the world as
Idea and the world as *body*.

> They will get it straight one day at the Sorbonne.
> We shall return at twilight from the lecture
> Pleased that the irrational is rational.

In order to help us understand and feel the world, the poet
creates these new forms, new metaphors, and new myths.
In reading Stevens it is helpful to know in advance that
he is employing a complex, ever enlarging symbolism, and

a dramatis personae. The abstractness of the later poetry is in part in the mind of the reader who fails to perceive the complexity and to feel the weight of meaning borne by the symbols and characters that live in his mythology.

A full examination of this mythology would require a very extensive study of individual images, symbols and figures recurring and growing by accretion from poem to poem over more than forty years. In a study of the symbolism one would find the sun, the moon, the sea, summer, autumn, geographical regions, color, and musical instruments. The sun in all of Stevens' poetry is the life force, physical existence, the unthinking source. To the sun and all that it symbolizes Stevens opposes "radiant reason" and "radiant will." The moon, the color blue, and musical instruments are constant symbols of the imagination.

> *Things as they are*
> *Are changed upon the blue guitar.*

The world sustained by the sun and made beautiful by the moon must be seen in its changing sad and comic colors. Sometimes all these symbols are brought together as in "Credences of Summer."

> *The personae of summer play the characters*
> *Of an inhuman author, who meditates*
> *With the gold bugs, in blue meadows, late at night.*
> *He does not hear his characters talk. He sees*
> *Them mottled, in the moodiest costumes.*
>
> *Of blue and yellow, sky and sun, belted*
> *And knotted, sashed and seamed, half pales of red,*
> *Half pales of green, appropriate habit for*
> *The huge decorum, the manner of the time,*
> *Part of the mottled mood of summer's whole . . .*

The dramatis personae, of course, are the human types who live among the "many blue phenomena" or who attempt to live solely with ideas. Among these characters are the ascetic, who attempts to see the sky without the blue; the poet, who helps us design and dominate the world; the musician or the singer, who like the poet *makes* and for the moment at least *controls* his world; the hero, who owes his existence to the willingness of people to conceive and respect heroism; the captain, who acts; the ephebi, who are the young requiring instruction; the Spaniard, who symbolizes the dark power of the imagination to give character to an entire people; the valet-comedian, who is the ironic, free intelligence; the puritan townspeople, who do not know the joys either of exuberance or imagination; the revolutionary, who is the fanatic ruled by a single "idea In a world of ideas"; the woman as summer, who is love, fecundity, and quite apart from sheer rationality; and the rationalist, who sees the whole truth in limited systems. The rationalists, like the revolutionists,

> *confine themselves*
> *To right-angle triangles.*
> *If they tried rhomboids,*
> *Cones, wavering lines, ellipses—*
> *As, for example, the ellipse of the halfmoon—*
> *Rationalists would wear sombreros.*

The rationalist and the revolutionary are examined, as are all the other figures in Stevens' mythology, against his constant awareness of the nature and function of imagination.

To examine Stevens' language adequately in order to place his work requires a fairly detailed study of his most persistent themes. No such examination can be very successful unless the examiner, knowing in detail the symbols of Stevens' mythology, appreciates and can give a sense of the accurate understanding and practiced ease behind Stevens' ability to separate incredible from credible imaginings and to state the latter so precisely that we seem to see an aspect of reality proliferate and grow luminous before us.

THE LITTLE CONTROVERSY generated by J. Donald Adams in the *New York Times* some time ago suggests that there is a good deal of misunderstanding about the nature of Robert Frost's poetry. Mr. Trilling, at a dinner honoring Mr. Frost, had observed that there is a considerable element of terror in Frost's poetry, as indeed there is. Mr. Adams protested, saying that Mr. Trilling was looking at Frost from out of the Freudian woods, and most of the letter writers who got into the controversy agreed with Mr. Adams. The common image of Mr. Frost is as a countryman, also a poet, who has gained his wisdom from nature; he is witty, shrewd, and serene. Commonly too he is said to be unlike most modern poets and fiction writers in that he is an optimist who also says clearly what he means. In other words, Frost is supposed to run against the drift of modern poetry. The extent to which these assumptions about Frost are true, untrue, or half true is the subject of this enquiry.

One way of getting at Robert Frost's general view of things is to compare "The Wood-Pile" with the passage in Herman Melville's *Israel Potter* which seems to have suggested it. Out for a walk on a cold winter's day, the poet comes upon a cord of maple, cut years earlier and forgotten. He describes the occasion and then adds:

> *I thought that only*
> *Someone who lived in turning to fresh thoughts*
> *Could so forget himself, the labour of his axe,*

And leave it there far from a useful fireplace
To warm the frozen swamp as best it could
With the slow smokeless burning of decay.

Frost does not make the point that all of man's purposes go awry or that everything he builds goes back into nature. Of course, he might say, intentions do go awry and human creations do decay, but the sensible thing to do is to accept what we cannot do anything to change.

Melville's Israel Potter, a forgotten hero of the Battle of Bunker Hill, returns as an old man to the site of his boyhood home. Only a few scattered bits of moss-covered masonry remain, and the family, its name forgotten, has disappeared. Israel does find one sign from these earlier years:

> Ere long, on the mountain side, he passed into an ancient natural wood, which seemed some way familiar and midway in it, paused to contemplate a sturdy beach. Though wherever touched by his staff, however lightly, this pile would crumble, yet here and there, even in powder, it preserved the exact look, each irregularly defined line, of what it has originally been—namely a half-cord of stout hemlock (one of the woods least affected by exposure to the air), in a foregoing generation chopped and stacked up on the spot, against sledging-time, but, as sometimes happens in such cases, by subsequent oversight, abandoned to obvious decay—type now, as it stood there, of forever arrested intentions, and a long life still rotting in early mishap.
>
> "Do I dream?" mused the bewildered old man, "or what is this vision that comes to me of a cold, cloudy morning, long, long ago, and I heaving yon elbowed log against the beach, then a sapling? Nay, nay, I cannot be so old."

The unused woodpile and its slow decay were to Melville a symbol of arrested intentions, of hopes dashed and of human frustration. He creates a romantic irony; great expectations collapse. Frost's irony works within a smaller orbit, as for example, the little joke about warming the outdoors. Though, of course, Frost realizes that his implicit advice that we reduce the cosmos to the realm of the everyday carries its own ironic overtones.

"The Wood-Pile" is from *North of Boston*, Frost's second book, but only a few poems in the first book, *A Boy's Will*, are very different in tone. "My November Guest" is the sort of nature poetry that William Cullen Bryant had written:

> *Her pleasure will not let me stay.*
> *   She talks and I am fain to list:*
> *She's glad the birds are gone away,*
> *She's glad her simple worsted grey*
> *   Is silver now with clinging mist.*

"Into My Own," "Ghost House," and "Love and a Question" might have been written by Wilfred Gibson, Lascelles Abercrombie or Edward Thomas, the Georgian poets with whom Frost associated during his several years' stay in England, but most of the poems in the first book, in theme if not always in manner, are pushing in the direction of "The Wood-Pile." "Storm Fear" describes a New England winter and says we must "save ourselves unaided." "Vantage Point" defines the circumference of man's world: houses on the opposite hill, cattle grazing, a few trees, a cemetery, the earth under his feet. And "The Demiurge's Laugh" presents Frost's view of what we can expect if we search in science or in metaphysics for ultimate answers:

> *It was far in the sameness of the wood;*
> *   I was running with joy on the Demon's trail,*
> *Though I knew what I hunted was no true god.*
> *   It was just as the light was beginning to fail*
> *That I suddenly heard—all I needed to hear:*
> *It has lasted me many and many a year.*
>
> *The sound was behind me instead of before,*
> *   A sleepy sound, but mocking half,*
> *As of one who utterly couldn't care.*
> *   The Demon arose from his wallow to laugh,*
> *Brushing the dirt from his eye as he went;*
> *   And well I knew what the Demon meant.*
>
> *I shall not forget how his laugh rang out.*
> *   I felt as a fool to have been so caught,*
> *And checked my steps to make pretence*

> *It was something among the leaves I sought*
> *(Though doubtful whether he stayed to see).*
> *Thereafter I sat me against a tree.*

Frost implies in "Reluctance," a Keatsian-sounding poem, that he casts his lot with reason, but by reason he means common sense, the plain mother-wit that can take us through a day and should tell us not to expect too much.

How unlike certain of his New England predecessors Frost is can be suggested by comparing him with Bryant or Ralph Waldo Emerson. For example, a passage from "To a Waterfowl":

> *All day thy wings have fanned,*
> *At that far height, the cold, thin atmosphere,*
> *Yet stoop not, weary, to the welcome land,*
> *Though the dark night is near.*
>
> *He who, from zone to zone,*
> *Guides through the boundless sky thy certain flight,*
> *In the long way that I must tread alone,*
> *Will lead my steps aright.*

Or this passage from Emerson's "Woodnotes":

> *The moss upon the forest bark*
> *Was pole-star when the night was dark;*
> *The purple berries in the wood*
> *Supplied me necessary food;*
> *For Nature ever faithful is*
> *To such as trust her faithfulness.*

Nature's intelligence, the ethical universe common to many nineteenth-century poets, is not to be found in Frost. "Stars," despite its idiom, presents the neutral universe of Stephen Crane or Ernest Hemingway:

> *How countlessly they congregate*
> *O'er our tumultuous snow,*
> *Which flows in shapes as tall as trees*
> *When wintry winds do blow!—*
>
> *As if with keenness for our fate,*
> *Our faltering few steps on*
> *To white rest, and a place of rest*
> *Invisible at dawn,—*

> *And yet with neither love nor hate,*
> *Those stars like some snow-white*
> *Minerva's snow-white marble eyes*
> *Without the gift of sight.*

Frost, commonly held to be in the line of nineteenth-century New England poetry, does not continue the tradition of romantic optimism.

At least three poems in his first volume are in a voice clearly that of the poet of the later books, and they investigate themes that will continue to hold his attention. "Mowing" advises us not to romanticize the world, but to find our pleasure in work and in commonplace experiences. If we idealize, as we must and should, it should be in relation to what we know to be so, to be a fact: "The fact is the sweetest dream that labor knows." And the manner of the poem, employing fourteen syllables to a line and rather irregular rhyme, is relaxed and conversational. "The Tuft of Flowers" is concerned with man's aloneless and his togetherness, and with one of the ways —the common experience of beauty—of assuaging our sense of loneliness. And "The Pasture" is about companionship in simple circumstances:

> *I'm going out to fetch the little calf*
> *That's standing by the mother. It's so young*
> *It totters when she licks it with her tongue.*
> *I shan't be gone long. —You come too.*

The Frost of *A Boy's Will*, despite the occasional reliance on a nineteenth-century idiom and a Georgian manner, is the essential Frost. This is not to say that the volume displays Frost's power at its best. Perhaps his achievement is most easily seen in looking into later treatments of these themes and examining, structurally, and rhetorically, the ways in which they are developed.

North of Boston took Frost deeply into his New England subject matter, and made clearer what were to be his most typical structures. Ignoring the regional characteristics for the moment, we may consider questions of structure. "Good Hours," seemingly only a description of a walk on a cold winter's evening, is a poem about one's inability to return to the habits and associations of former years:

> I had for my winter evening walk—
> No one at all with whom to talk,
> But I had the cottages in a row
> Up to their shining eyes in snow.
>
> And I thought I had the folk within:
> I had the sound of a violin;
> I had a glimpse through curtain laces
> Of youthful forms and youthful faces.
>
> I had such company outward bound.
> I went till there were no cottages found.
> I turned and repented, but coming back
> I saw no window but that was black.
>
> Over the snow my creaking feet
> Disturbed the slumbering village street
> Like profanation, by your leave,
> At ten o'clock of a winter eve.

The trip through life is a quick one, friends die or go away, and the joys once known cannot be re-experienced. The phrase "by your leave" provides the Frostian tone: that's the way things are but let us not worry the matter until we are morbid. "Good Hours," like many poems in later books ("The Runaway," "Stopping by Woods on a Snowy Evening," or "The Bear") is a self-contained symbol.

Some of the dramatic narratives are self-contained situations, with the reader being free to read in as much in the way of inference as he believes the poem will bear. (Like Browning, Frost cuts into the middle, *in medias res*, of his narratives, but, unlike Browning, Frost usually allows his second character more of a role than that of listener.) In "Mending Wall," for example, there are, if one wishes to press the implications, arguments for a conservative view of traditional modes of action and on the other hand arguments against rigidity of mind and unwillingness to question old habits. In "Home Burial" whose view, if either, is exclusively the right one? the man who rids him-

self of grief by going on with his daily jobs, even burying
their dead child himself, or the woman who wants grief
carried openly. The arguments, his and hers, are presented, but the poet does not take sides.

There are also poems, as in "The Wood-Pile," wherein
a situation is described or a symbol presented, in which the
poet furnishes an explication, saying this view or another
is thereby suggested to him. To take an example from a
later book, *A Further Range,* there is the fine poem "Un-
harvested":

> *A scent of ripeness from over a wall.*
> *And come to leave the routine road*
> *And look for what had made me stall,*
> *There sure enough was an apple tree*
> *That had eased itself of its summer load,*
> *And of all but its trivial foliage free,*
> *Now breathed as light as a lady's fan.*
> *For there had been an apple fall*
> *As complete as the apple had given man.*
> *The ground was one circle of solid red.*
>
> *May something go always unharvested!*
> *May much stay out of our stated plan,*
> *Apples or something forgotten and left,*
> *So smelling their sweetness would be no theft.*

Perhaps most often a poem is a mixture of metaphor,
explication, sly observations, and whimsical asides, as in
"October," from the first volume:

> *O hushed October morning mild,*
> *Thy leaves have ripened to the fall;*
> *To-morrow's wind, if it be wild,*
> *Should waste them all.*
> *The crows above the forest call;*
> *To-morrow they may form and go.*
> *O hushed October morning mild,*
> *Begin the hours of this day slow.*
> *Make the day seem to us less brief.*
> *Hearts not averse to being beguiled,*
> *Beguile us in the way you know.*
> *Release one leaf at break of day;*
> *At noon release another leaf;*

> One from our trees, one far away.
> Retard the sun with gentle mist;
> Enchant the land with amethyst.
> Slow, slow!
> For the grapes' sake, if they were all,
> Whose leaves already are burnt with frost,
> Whose clustered fruit must else be lost—
> For the grapes' sake along the wall.

Sometimes, as one would expect, the mixture of metaphor and observation does not quite come off. An observation is needed because the metaphor does not fully carry the meaning. A conspicuous example of this is in Frost's well known "Birches," from *Mountain Interval*, which seems *deliberately* poetic and *deliberately* significant. Deliberateness is particularly disturbing in a Frost poem because so much depends on the casual surface, the unsaid, the sly suggestion. When the theme has to be spelled out, the characteristic charm tends to evaporate.

This latter point is also involved in the rhetoric of a Frost poem. Poetry, after all, is the language of artifice, and there is artifice behind the seeming naturalness, as in the opening lines of "Blueberries":

> You ought to have seen what I saw on my way
> To the village, through Patterson's pasture to-day:
> Blueberries as big as the end of your thumb,
> Real sky-blue, and heavy, and ready to drum
> In the cavernous pail of the first one to come!
> And all ripe together, not one of them green
> And some of them ripe! You ought to have seen!

In this passage in "The Death of the Hired Man," there is the strong simple dignity of

> Among the harp-like morning glory strings,
> Taut with dew from garden bed to eaves,
> As if she played unheard some tenderness
> That wrought on him beside her in the night.

One goes from ordinary conversation into a language expressed in a slightly higher register. The passage gives a sense of sudden elevation, and the effect carries over into more prosaic lines that follow. All poetry needs language

that is apart from the ordinary, and the poet who manages
to see and isolate special qualities in the ordinary and the
slightly above ordinary is pursuing a difficult course. Occasionally he will over-reach himself, as Frost does when
he has Warren's wife say:

> He may not speak of it, and then he may.
> I'll sit and see if that small sailing cloud
> Will hit or miss the moon.
>> It hit the moon.

In another poet's work, the passage might seem rather
ineffectual rhetoric—in Frost's poem it seems deliberate
poeticizing. And in its context her epigram, "Home is the
place where, when you have to go there, they have to take
you in," seems forced, its having become a famous quotation notwithstanding. Again, in "Home Burial" the conversation is in vigorous language, spare and in focus
against its subject matter. In the middle of it, however,
one suddenly hears the wife use language more appropriate to a melodrama:

> I saw you from that very window there,
> Making the gravel leap and leap in air,
> Leap up, like that, like that, and land so lightly
> And roll back down the mound beside the hole.

The description is not in the idiom suitable to her sort of
grief or to her other language. Frost does have a genius
for catching the quality of livingness and naturalness in
ordinary daily affairs. But the ambience allowed thereby
is severely limited. When he writes a passage that does not
respect these restrictions there is a jarring effect, the intrusion of artificial lines.

Frost is, of course, the poet of New England, as Faulkner is the novelist of Mississippi, or Mark Twain was the
voice of Missouri and the Mississippi valley. *North of
Boston* and *New Hampshire* are more explicitly of New
England probably than any of the other volumes. Despite
its title, *Mountain Interval* is not especially regional. But
a parochially New England poem is likely to turn up in
any of the volumes, and attitudes commonly attributed to
New England are everywhere evident. "Two Tramps in

Mud Time," for example, one of his most explicitly regional poems, was published in A *Further Range*. The situation of the poem is commented on in such a way that the regional significances loom large. A New England spring is described and wryly enjoyed. The lumberjacks, outside the norms of respectability, are called tramps. The poet speaks for the spirit of individualism, self-control, and pride in workmanship, all of which are associated with the puritan heritage. "Two Tramps in Mud Time" also speaks in favor of a peculiar Frostian theme, the wisdom in doing well and in enjoying what we are obligated to do, that is, to make one's job or profession an art, not a burden to be endured for financial rewards.

Some of the images of New England which Frost presents can hardly be called flattering. Frost's New England is not, as already suggested, the prosperous, leather-bound culture one feels in Bryant, Emerson, Holmes, or Whittier. They saw New England as growing in wealth and wisdom, and their poetry, like their parlor furniture, suggested contentment and trust in the future. A New England port would be a new Rhodes or Carthage. Neither Hawthorne nor Melville was quite so committed to his contemporaries' sense of New England; they looked sharply at the effects on personality of a too straitened morality or at the effects on human optimism of farms that refused to prosper on the rock-strewn sides of mountains. Frost's poetry fulfills the full weight of their suspicions—but unlike his own contemporary, E. A. Robinson, Frost has refused to despair or even to be depressed by a twentieth-century New England that is considerably different from what the poets of her renaissance foresaw.

In Israel Potter Melville mentions the farms that refused to stay put on the mountains and the families that, hoping for better fortune, had disappeared westward. A few figures from a U. S. census report provide a good gloss on the rural world of Frost's poetry: Of the farm homes that existed in Massachusetts in 1890, eighteen per cent had been abandoned by 1930, in Vermont twenty-seven per cent, and in New Hampshire forty-five per cent.

"The Birthplace," from *West-Running Brook*, is about the houses that did not stay on the mountain:

> Here further up the mountain slope
> Than there was ever any hope,
> My father built, enclosed a spring,
> Strung chains of wall round everything,
> Subdued the growth of earth to grass,
> And brought our various lives to pass.
> A dozen girls and boys we were.
> The mountain seemed to like the stir,
> And made of us a little while—
> With always something in her smile.
> Today she wouldn't know our name.
> (No girl's, of course, has stayed the same.)
> The mountain pushed us off her knees.
> And now her lap is full of trees.

"A Fountain, a Bottle, a Donkey's Ears and Some Books," from *New Hampshire*, is even more explicit. Two young men visit the ruined and abandoned house of a nineteenth-century poetess, and in the attic they find volumes of her poems. Nature presses in on and has almost obliterated an older world and, with it, the culture that breathed security and trust in the future. And in "The Census Taker" there is a description of the census taker working in an area that is almost abandoned: The conclusion is

> The melancholy of having to count souls
> Where they grow fewer and fewer each year
> Is extreme where they shrink to none at all.
> It must be I want life to go on living.

Frost presents, then, a sense of rural New England in decay. A tough, resisting spirit opposes the decay, sometimes the poet himself and sometimes a symbolic New England farmer, but the decay is there, in physical and mental manifestations.

Several poems in *North of Boston* are concerned with lives that have been warped to the point of eccentricity, neurosis or even madness. "The Housekeeper," presented in dialogue, is about this situation: Estelle, the house-keeper, has become the common-law wife of a farmer named John. The mother of Estelle, who relates the story to a neighbor, says that her daughter has brooded over his refusal to marry her—and to even the score with him has gone off and married someone she did not really want to marry. John had no reason for not marrying her, other than human perversity. The mother, as her character is disclosed in her conversation, has become quite fatalistic about sheer perversity in conduct. "The Fear" has as its central subject a situation not too dissimilar from that in "The Housekeeper," it being about a woman who has gone off with someone not her husband and who lives in terrible fear of his finding her. "A Servant to Servant" is the story of a woman who, inheriting a streak of insanity from her father's family has such a difficult life as a farmer's wife that she is frequently near the edge of in-sanity and was once committed to the state asylum. She believes the insane should be in an asylum and not at home. Her reason is that her insane uncle, though before her birth, had been kept caged in an upper room and her mother, as a young bride, had had to listen at night to his mad and obscene screams. The woman has no hope that her own life will ever be any easier. *Mountain Interval* provides at least two further instances of strangeness; in the egotistical minister of a strange sect whose rejection by the community forces him to bizarre conduct ("Snow"), and lyrics devoted to a woman whom lone-liness drives insane ("The Hill Wife").

A word also on the culture of New England as it ap-pears in one poem, "A Hundred Collars," from *North of Boston*. Doctor Magoon, a university professor and "great scholar," returns occasionally to the small town of his boyhood, but there is no longer an easy relationship between the townspeople and himself. Unable to get a train through to his destination one night, he finds him-self in Woodsville, where he is obliged to share a room with a traveling salesman or, rather, agent for a weekly newspaper. There is no genuine communication between the two men—and the point of the poem is that there is no interrelationship between the official or "high" culture, which in Doctor Magoon seems pretty dessicated, and the everyday life of the people. And there is no awareness in the people of their forebears, who pursued culture avidly and had such great hopes for the future.

On the other hand, there are many poems in which Frost acknowledges a wiry sort of strength in his rural folk. One of the more explicit characterizations of the New England Yankee is "Brown's Descent," from *Mountain Interval*, a humorously fantastic account of Farmer Brown, whose house and barns were high on a mountain. One evening in winter, when the ground was cased hard in snow, he was caught in a mighty wind which sent him kiting and sliding, lantern in hand, all the way down the mountain. At the bottom of his descent he is two miles from home, straight up the mountainside. Looking at him, Frost then comments on Brown as Yankee stock:

> *Yankees are what they always were.*
> *Don't think Brown ever gave up hope*
> *Of getting home again because*
> *He couldn't climb that slippery slope;*
>
> *Or even thought of standing there*
> *Until the January thaw*
> *Should take the polish off the crust.*
> *He bowed with grace to natural law,*
>
> *And then went round it on his feet,*
> *After the manner of our stock;*
> *Not much concerned for those to whom,*
> *At that particular time o'clock,*
>
> *It must have looked as if the course*
> *He steered was really straight away*
> *From that which he was headed for—*
> *Not much concerned for them, I say;*
>
> *No more so than became a man—*
> *And politician at odd seasons.*
> *I've kept Brown standing in the cold*
> *While I invested him with reasons;*

But now he snapped his eyes three times;
Then shook his lantern, saying, 'Ile's
'Bout out!' and took the long way home
By road, a matter of several miles.

This rural stock, as it appears in Frost's poetry at least, are a little queer (and sometimes worse than that), but still hardy, resisting both the weather and economic difficulties.

To take a few poems in somewhat random fashion. "The Code," from *North of Boston*, explains how a hired man buried his employer under a load of hay because the latter was "bulling" him, that is, making remarks about working harder and faster. A self-respecting farm hand, who knows he is working conscientiously, will not accept such treatment, and, in this poem, the farmer himself, though angry, accepts his being buried as well deserved. His interlocutor asks the farm hand, "Did he discharge you?" "Discharge me? No! He knew I did just right." The title poem in *New Hampshire* is a fairly amusing essay on a people who having little or nothing to sell need not soil themselves with commerce. "The Axe Helve" also develops the theme of anticommercialism, with one Baptiste, of French or French-Canadian stock, explaining that machine-made axe helves are dangerous to use, that only hickory should be used, and so on. "Paul's Wife," a mockheroic Bunyan tale, gives a New England twist to the fabulous lumberjack. Frost gives him an exaggerated sense of privacy and personal possession, making him, in the language of the region, "a terrible possessor."

The philosophical and political conservatism evident in Frost, especially in the later volumes, *West-Running Brook* and *A Further Range*, also has a New England coloring. The traditional opposition to romantic and sentimental humanitarianism is evident, sometimes all too evident. The title poem of the former book presents two lovers studying the backward movement in a stream. Symbolically the westward running brook means westward expansionism, money making, progress, and democratic humanitarianism. In the rapids the water flows backward, against the current—and the lovers approve of those who go against the current of their times. "Build Soil" is a statement in favor of laissez-faire economics, and "Departmental" compares a socialistic society to an ant hill. It may be going too far to say that New England accounts for Frost's politics, but at least the politics are not in forthright contradiction to the region. Probably rural New England is closer in spirit to the nineteenth century than is any other section in the United States. Again, Frost has chosen to exclude from his poetry even what there is of urbanism, industrialism, and finance capital in his region. Therefore his doctrine of individualism, seeming to exist in a nineteenth-century world, has an air of being purer in virtue than, in a twentieth-century world, it really is. In certain contexts Frost's views are "reactionary," but in others they are vigorously healthy and affirmative. An instance of the latter is to be found in "Good-bye and Keep Cold," from *New Hampshire*, an address to a young orchard that will have to endure the harsh winter, but having endured it will be stronger. The concluding lines—

> *I wish I could promise to lie in the night*
> *And think of an orchard's arboreal plight*
> *When slowly (and nobody comes with a light)*
> *Its heart sinks lower under the sod.*
> *But something has to be left to God.*

Finally all of us are, and should be, on our own.

A few poems in the Frost canon deal directly, or almost directly, with the subject of poetry itself. An examination of them makes it possible to recapitulate a few of Frost's favorite themes and to see in what way the themes influence the poetry itself. There is, for example, a passage in "New Hampshire" in which Frost criticizes the effort to withdraw from nature into intellect. Frost says he knew a man whose fear of nature took the form of hating trees—

> *The only decent tree had been to mill*
> *And educated into boards, he said.*

The Frost doctrine, which appears in "Stopping by Woods on a Snowy Evening," "After Apple Picking," and elsewhere, is that man is half in nature and half out. He feels the pull of nature in instinct and in the desire to participate in the processes of nature—and on the other side he feels the pull toward reason, duty, idealization. He is neither pure animal nor pure mind, and it is as grievous an error to live by mind alone as by instinct alone. In "New Hampshire" he is being critical of those who attempt to live outside of nature, which Frost calls "Matthew Arnoldism." The man afraid of trees

> *knew too well for any earthly use*
> *The line where man leaves off and nature starts,*
> *And never over-stepped it save in dreams.*

In "To Earthward," also in *New Hampshire*, Frost recalls that as a young man he viewed the world through the eyes of an aesthete—

> *The petal of the rose*
> *It was that stung.*

But as he grew older he desired experiences that were bitter and harsh:

> *The hurt is not enough:*
> *I long for weight and strength*
> *To feel the earth as rough*
> *To all my length.*

The poet should therefore make his poetry out of rigor and difficulty. Presumably Frost would say that the value in a poem is involved in the sense it gives of the emotional impact life made. "The Aim Was Song," more explicitly about poetry than "New Hampshire" or "To Earthward," says that man is artificer, that is, he subdues or controls nature. The poet takes the wind and turns it into song:

> *He took a little in his mouth,*
> * And held it long enough for north*
> *To be converted into south,*
> * And then by measure blew it forth.*

North is nature in its raw forms, and south is nature after man has brought it under control, idealizing and loving it in the process.

"On a Bird Singing in Its Sleep," from A *Further Range*, is the poet Frost asking what is the relationship of art to nature and to human life. The poem describes a bird singing in the night—and by bird he means poet:

> *A bird half wakened in the lunar noon*
> *Sang halfway through its little inborn tune.*
> *Partly because it sang but once all night*
> *And that from no especial bush's height;*
> *Partly because it sang ventriloquist*
> *And had the inspiration to desist*
> *Almost before the prick of hostile ears,*
> *It ventured less in peril than appears.*
> *It could not have come down to us so far*
> *Through the interstices of things ajar*
> *On the long bead chain of repeated birth*
> *To be a bird while we are men on earth*
> *If singing out of sleep and dream that way*
> *Had made it much more easily a prey.*

Does art belong in the world, in a world that finally we do not understand? Frost replies that art, like the bird's song, has belonged to our kind immemorially. A certain kind of art, he also says, the kind that attempts to lift us into romantic idealism, could make us vulnerable at many points. The poet should take human life for what it is, with one foot in nature, and the other lifted a little bit above it.

Frost is sometimes held up, in contrast with T. S. Eliot or James Joyce, as an optimistic poet. If he is more optimistic than either it is in a special sense of the word. A close look at "Birches," in contrast to "Ash Wednesday," will show that Frost has no expectations of another world, and a close look at "The Demiurge," in contrast with "The Four Quartets," will show that he puts little stock in metaphysical speculations. Again, a poem such as "An Old Man's Winter Night," from *Mountain Interval*, is certainly as disenchanted as any poem one is likely to find in Eliot. There is a deep and profound sense of comedy in Joyce. There is comedy in Frost too, but it seems to have its source in whimsy, an ironic playfulness, rather than in a deep *joie de vivre*. He has contemplated the world in all its variety and decided that, all things considered, it is better to be an optimist.

15 SOME NOTES ON MODERN LITERARY CRITICISM

AMONG other things that our contemporary critical movement has brought to the study of literature are enthusiasm
and common sense evaluations of literary situations. As
an example we can point to a recent article by Yvor Winters, "Problems for the Modern Critic," published in the
fall 1956 issue of the *Hudson Review*. Mr. Winters is a
man altogether willing to pass judgment on any number
of things. In this essay he ranges over a great number of
topics and up and down the centuries. I want to single
out two comments. The first of these is concerned with
the dragon in the first book of *The Faerie Queene*. This is
what Mr. Winters says about the dragon:

> The gentle knight encounters the dragon, and after many
> Spenserian stanzas he slays it. We eventually learn that
> the dragon represents Error. But the dragon in general and
> in all its details, and merely as dragon, is a very dull affair;
> it is poorly described and poorly characterized. I do not,
> frankly, know what one might do to make a dragon more
> interesting, but it seems to me that unless one can do
> better than this one had better not use a dragon. In its
> capacity as Error, the dragon spews up a number of books
> and papers (along with other items), and of course the
> dragon is ugly, but little is done in this way to further our
> understanding of error; There is no functional relationship
> between the dragon, either in general or in detail, and
> that which it represents. The relationship is arbitrary,
> and we have to be told explicitly what the relationship is.
> . . . The gentle knight himself suffers from the same de-

fects as the dragon, and to understand him and his actions
we have to read him with a chart at our elbow, and even
then the significance remains on the chart and is never
functional in the poem. The poem has other defects:
the clumsy and tyrannical stanza, the primitive and un-
varied use of the iambic pentameter line, and an habitual
redundancy; but at present I am concerned only with the
incurable flaws in the method.

If I may be autobiographical here, I'd like to say that this
paragraph pleased me very much, largely I think because
it recalled and scored off for me a very dull semester
course I once took in Spenser. I still have Jones' *A
Spenser Handbook*, which we used in that course, and I
took it down to see what was said about the dragon. This
is what it says:

> The monster encountered by the Red Cross Knight and
> Una in the Wandering Wood is, for Ruskin, "Error in her
> universal form, the first enemy of Reverence and Holiness;
> and more especially Error as founded upon Learning; for
> when Holiness strangles her,
>
> > *Her vomit full of books and papers was,*
> > *With loathly frogs and toades, which eyes did lacke.*
>
> Having vanquished this first open and palpable form of
> Error, as Reverence and Religion must always vanquish it,
> the knight encounters hypocrisy, or "Archimagus." Unequal
> to the machinations of this new enemy, Holiness is sepa-
> rated from Truth, and then, first of all, quite naturally
> meets Infidelity and Falsehood.

And on the passage goes, with never a word about whether
the dragon is successfully conceived or not. The Jones
handbook belonged to a tradition which required the
scholar or the student to explain what Spenser, or whoever, meant; one was not asked to say how successful or
unsuccessful it was.

Mr. Winters also has a few things to say about Pound's
Cantos:

> The details, especially in the early *Cantos*, are frequently
> very lovely, but since there is neither structure nor very
> much in the way of meaning, the details are details and

nothing more, and what we have is the ghost of poetry, though I am willing to admit that it is often the ghost of great poetry. . . . A number of young scholars at the University of California and at Northwestern University are now engaged in running these references down, and the voluminous notes which they have provided for a few of the *Cantos* are very helpful; but the notes are almost as voluminous as the *Cantos* and can scarcely be held in the head—so that we shall eventually have to read the *Cantos* with a guide more awkward than anything required by Spenser or Dante.

It may well be true that the *Cantos* are a white elephant; certainly it is true that many parts of that elephant are monumentally lacking in any real significance.

Modern critical writing has made great inroads in English departments. *Understanding Poetry* (1938) began a revolution—and now about half of our textbooks are in the analytical mode. Dissertations are now written on the theories and critical practice of T. E. Hulme, T. S. Eliot, Allen Tate or John Crowe Ransom, and professors lecture about the "dissociation of sensibility," the "objective correlative," "the intentional fallacy" or "form as achieved content." University professors also write critical essays of a sort that twenty years ago could have been found only in advance guard magazines, and rather frequently they collect their essays in book form. Notable recent examples of such books are William York Tindall's *Literary Symbol* (1956) and Leonard Unger's *The Man in the Name* (1956). Students and teachers alike keep an eye out for critical articles being published in *Kenyon Review, Sewanee Review, Hudson Review, Western Review, Accent, Partisan Review, Essay in Criticism* and the other "little magazines." It is no exaggeration then to say that criticism flourishes in English departments.

But modern literary criticism—at least the criticism of poetry—did not originate in English departments. It began with Ezra Pound and T. E. Hulme, both of whom influenced Eliot. Again, there may be no great point in identifying the original source or sources of the movement, for it is clear that many of the preoccupations found in modern criticism have their antecedents in Coleridge, in Henry James, in Remy de Gourmont, or in Benedetto Croce. An easier matter is the listing of the critics who have written books that have proved seminal or in other ways significant.

The close critical examination of fiction did have academic beginnings, the first significant study being Joseph Warren Beach's *The Method of Henry James* (1918). Beach wrote a similar volume on George Meredith, but his major contribution came with *The Twentieth Century Novel: Studies in Technique* (1932). Percy Lubbock's *The Craft of Fiction* had appeared several years earlier (1929), and it is sometimes held to be a landmark in the criticism of the novel. Brilliant though it is, Lubbock's book lacks the catholicity of taste and the critical range of Beach's *The Twentieth Century Novel*.

R. P. Blackmur's *The Double Agent* (1935) and *The Expense of Greatness* (1940) are fairly early examples of the close reading of poems and novels. Blackmur has not developed a literary theory, or at least he has not published a theoretical book. His value as a critic, despite occasional involuted sentences and awkward phrases, has been in the acuteness and subtlety of his explications. Cleanth Brooks is perhaps the most "academic" of the new critics. His *Modern Poetry and the Tradition* (1939) is indebted to Richards, Eliot, Ransom, Tate, Leavis, and probably to Robert Penn Warren. In this book Brooks helped to formulate the break with Victorian standards and to point up connections between seventeenth-century poetry and modern poetry. In *The Well Wrought Urn* (1947) Brooks developed his theory of the structure of poetry. He holds that the nature of poetry is essentially the same generation after generation, and he develops in great detail the thesis that poetry employs a language of indirection.

Kenneth Burke in *Counter-statement* (1931), *The Philosophy of Literary Form* (1941) and *A Grammar of Motives* (1945) showed himself possessed of a wide-ranging mind. Perhaps his primary interest is in the rhetorical aspects of language and in the structural aspects of a literary work. William Empson, a student of Richards, published his influential *Seven Types of Ambiguity* in 1930. A more precise term than ambiguity is Wheelwright's "plurisignification," meaning that a word in a given context may have two or more meanings and that these meanings in some way complement each other or one another. It is quite possible that Empson was indebted to Freud for such concepts as *latent* meaning and *over-determination*. He is explicit about his indebtedness to Robert Graves and Laura Riding's A *Survey of Modernist Poetry* (1929).

John Crowe Ransom's *The World's Body* (1938) is an admirable defense of the needs and requirements of the sentiments, of the life of feeling, against the encroachments and restrictions of scientism. *The New Criticism* (1941) is Ransom's interpretation of what Richards, Eliot, Winters, and certain other critics are trying to say. Allen Tate, once Ransom's student, has been a vigorous defender of literature as knowledge. "It [poetry] is neither the world of verifiable science nor a projection of ourselves; yet it is complete. And because it is complete knowledge we may, I think, claim for it a unique kind of responsibility, and see in it at times an irresponsibility equally distinct." Tate's books include *Reactionary Essays* (1936), *Reason in Madness* (1941), and *On the Limits of Poetry* (1948).

Lionel Trilling's *The Liberal Imagination* (1950) occupies a unique position in modern criticism. It grew out of the liberal tradition, a tradition that tended to minimize the nature of the work of art and to emphasize its social uses. Trilling does not deny the social consequences of a work of art, but he shows that the liberal's sense of urgency in bringing about social reforms frequently made for a too simplified point of view. Having recognized this, he re-examined the writers whom liberals have glorified, and pointed to virtues in writers whom liberals were suspicious or disapproving of. Edmund Wilson has also been identified with the liberal tradition. His books from *Axel's Castle* (1931) on tend to mirror the interests of each decade. He is not so much an original critic as a highly intelligent interpreter of books and movements.

Perhaps the major lines that have emerged from the work of all of these critics can be called Eliotic preoccupations and Richardian preoccupations. By this I mean Eliot's interest in tradition, in the impersonality of art, and in the "dissociation of sensibility," and Richards' interest in the poetry of synthesis (tension) and in myth. A large body of commentary has grown up around each subject, and much of it has been assimilated into contemporary critical consciousness.

Yvor Winters on the other hand is original even though often wrong-headed. His *In Defense of Reason* (1947) collects two earlier books and an essay. Winters insists that each element in a poem should be under the rational control of the poet, and that a work of literature, whether poetry or fiction, is explicitly a presentation and evaluation of a subject in moral terms. F. R. Leavis, the editor of *Scrutiny*, should be mentioned in conjunction with Winters. Leavis' theory of poetry, unlike Winters', is indebted to Eliot, but the manner and tone of the two men are alike insofar as both are intensely moralistic.

On the jacket of Wellek and Warren's *Theory of Literature* (1950), the publishers claim that "This book will mark an important mile-stone in the study of literature. It crystallizes a movement that has been under way for two decades in this country, to focus literary criticism and literary study in general on literature itself, rather than on historical backgrounds, the psychological mechanisms, the political and social currents that influence literary creation." This statement certainly implies that we have reached a point of summing up, evaluation and recapitulation. A fine recapitulation of a great many themes is Solomon Fishman's *The Disinherited of Art* (1953): the modern writer is alienated, the importance of tradition to the writer, the regional element in literature, and so on. Another volume largely indebted to modern criticism at the same time that it is a history of it is Frederick Hoffman's *The Twenties* (1955). What is new in Hoffman's method is that first he summarizes various movements, for example, Freudian theory, or the idea of a "usable past," and then demonstrates how each of them functioned or operated in a literary work of major importance; in other words, he writes literary history in the older ways but adds to this closely written analytical studies of poems and novels. Another volume that falls into our recapitulation category is Murray Krieger's *The New Apologist for Poetry* (1956). Krieger, with a good knowledge of aesthetics and considerable training in philosophy, sets out to clarify the positions of a number of contemporary critics, ranging from T. E. Hulme to the Chicago Aristotelians. He examines them in the light of the history of certain critical concepts as well as certain general principles of his own, and in the process he demonstrates inconsistencies in and the partialness of the systems of all of them.

One could point to a great many books that draw upon the concepts developed and the terminology coined by one or another of the new critics. There is, for instance, Charles Feidelson's *Symbolism and American Literature* (1953). Feidelson makes good use of the theory of the impersonal nature of art in his discussion of *Moby Dick*. What I am trying to say is that we may have reached a plateau. We now have a great many useful concepts and terms: patterns of imagery, analogous actions, epiphanies, key word, ambiguity, unified tone, tension, foreshortening, *ficelles*, reflectors, intentional fallacy, affective fallacy, and so on. There is God's plenty in the way of aids for getting inside a work of literature. Judiciously employed, they help us to see what is going on in a novel or play or poem and to talk more easily about what we see there. Models of critical explication are R. P. Warren's essay on Hemingway's *A Farewell to Arms*, L. C. Knight's "Restoration Comedy: the Reality and the Myth," and Francis Fergusson's chapter on *Hamlet* in his *The Idea of a Theater*. In such works, the new criticism has made an important contribution to the humanistic study of literature.

In reading through volumes of the *English Institute Annual*, a remarkably useful and intelligent series of essays, one may observe a preoccupation with rhetoric and myth. The study of rhetoric is certainly useful, but it seems merely a further extension of the interest we have had in the verbal aspects of literature, another tool. There have been many books and essays on myth too, but there are grounds for assuming that we have had very little in proportion to what is ahead for us.

To talk about myth, one needs at least a working definition. In *The Greek Myths* (1955) Robert Graves says this: "True myth may be defined as the reduction to narrative shorthand of ritual mime performed on public festivals, and in many cases recorded pictorially on temple walls, vases, seals, mirrors, chests, shields, tapestries, and the like." Mr. Graves seems to be saying that truly mythical stories dramatize, partially through the use of established rituals and partially through the appeal of iconography of various sorts, the beliefs held by a society. Presumably Spenser's *Epithalamium* and Shakespeare's *A Midsummer Night's Dream*—both of which have the ritual of blessing the marriage bed, hoping for fecundity, spiritual unity, and mutual happiness, and even invoking the aid of supernatural or preternatural creatures in this hope—are mythic in Mr. Graves' sense. The contemporary reader may feel uneasy with this definition because Mr. Graves apparently insists on the relationship between public festivals and myths. Also the Greek world is a long, long way behind us, and our trying to get at an understanding of myth through its literature has obvious hazards.

A definition that is at once closer to home and a little looser can be found in Mark Schorer's *William Blake: The Politics of Vision* (1946):

> Myths are the instruments by which we continually struggle to make our experience intelligible to ourselves. A myth is a large, controlling image that gives philosophical meaning to the facts of ordinary life. . . . Without such images, experience is chaotic, fragmentary and merely phenomenal. It is the chaos of experience that creates them, and they are intended to rectify it. All real convictions involve a mythology, either in its usual, broad sense or in a private sense. In the first case it is embodied in literature or in ritual or in both, in which it has application to the whole of society and tends to be religious. In the second, it remains in the realm of fantasy, in which it tends to be obsessive and fanatical. . . . [Myths] unify experience in a way that is satisfactory to the whole culture and to the whole personality.

Schorer makes other useful points: The term myth does not mean a falsehood, nor is an acceptance of myth necessarily a form of anti-intellectualism or obscurantism; myths in our time tend to be political in character; and we live in a period of multiple and conflicting myths. Again, there is the relationship of myth to literature: "Literature ceases to be perceptual and tends to degenerate into mere description without adequate myth . . . when we feel that we are no longer in a position to say what life means, we must be content with telling how it looks." In contrast we have the Shakespearean or Elizabethan myths: that of divine and earthly governance, with the accompanying belief in man's dignity and potential nobility, and that of the transcendent importance and power of love, with the accompanying belief in plentitude and ripeness. On the other hand, as all students of modern literature know, the modern writer has faced the necessity of trying to create a myth, the very substance necessary before he can discover, imagine, or give order to his images: Eliot made his excursions into anthropology and various religions, Joyce, with a comic glint in his eye, made his into the psychology of human organisms, whereas Yeats and Stevens made theirs into various realms of the aesthetic. As Schorer says, "The hunt for the essential image goes on everywhere today— but the problem is hardly new."

A philosopher and critic who has been writing about poetic language and about myth for a number of years is Philip Wheelwright. In 1954 he published an extremely suggestive book, *The Burning Fountain*. Wheelwright has a subtle and far-ranging mind. For example, there is a chapter entitled "Four Ways of Imagination" in which he complains, with justice, that the new criticism has overemphasized the esemplastic, the synthesizing power of the imagination. Wheelwright lists and elaborates upon four general ways in which the active mind responds to and integrates its sense of the world:

> There is the Confrontative Imagination, which acts upon its object by particularizing and intensifying it. There is the Stylistic Imagination, which acts upon its object by stylizing and distancing it. There is the Archetypal Imagination, which sees the particular object as embodying and

adumbrating suggestions of universality. And there is the Metaphoric Imagination, which fuses heterogeneous elements into some kind of unity.

In this first category Wheelwright is isolating what Joyce, following Aquinas, called *integritas*, one's awareness of radical individuality in an object or situation. Discussing the second category, Wheelwright says: "Imagination, even in its stylizing and distancing aspect, is more than a play of fancy; it is subtly but effectively a real contributor to the very nature and significance of our world." Oddly, this problem, which would seem to be the very center of the study of imaginative literature, has received little attention. Possibly there may be many attempts to characterize it in the next few years. In his third category, Wheelwright discusses certain particulars which have "more of an archetypal content than others"—"they enclose in themselves a certain totality, arranged in a certain way, stirring in the soul something at once familiar and strange, and thus outwardly as well as inwardly they lay claim to a certain unity and generality." In his fourth class, Wheelwright discusses the esemplastic imagination: "It is present in all art that is anything more than purely formal or purely decorative; for an artist's characteristic attempt, in its semantic aspect, is to express and communicate an experience comprising some grouping of perceived and imaginative here-nows for which there is no publicly accepted word, formula, or other symbol already available." In another place, he says, "metaphor is a medium of fuller, riper knowing; not merely a prettification of the already given." Among other chapters that could be useful to students of literature are "The Mythic World-View," "The Semantic of Ritual," and "Dramatic Action and Mythic Imagery."

A recent detailed examination of Wheelwright's third category, that on Archetypes, is James Baird's *Ishmael* (1956). Baird says he is dealing with primitivism, which he defines as follows:

In this study, the mode of feeling which exchanges for traditional Christian symbols a new symbolic idiom referring to Oriental cultures of Oceania and Asia is ad-

mitted as genuine primitivism, even with the closer quali-
fications that most of the authors [he is primarily concerned with Melville] involved, certainly the major ones,
should have travelled in the Orient and that they should
have derived from direct physical experience a medium
of feeling to inform the symbols which their art presents.

Baird believes that Melville captured in at least certain
provinces of his imagination "the sentience of archaic
man." Baird has written a lengthy book, and the correct-
ness of his interpretations probably should be left to
Melville scholars and to those who know a good deal
about archetypes. Even the general reader, however, can
observe that Melville, like so many other American writers,
was in pursuit of innocence. For example, he was greatly
taken by the nakedness of the Polynesians, or, more specifically, the Marquesans. He celebrates, as Baird says, "the
nakedness of the Polynesian body and the innocence in
which it was displayed." Baird also has a chapter entitled
"Puer Aeternus: Eternal Innocence," which centers
around the Polynesian word *tayo*, which means friendship
on a high plane of idealism and selflessness, and around
the ideal of acceptance. "As the archetype of the primor-
dial whale becomes the avatar of God the unknowable in
Moby-Dick," Baird says, "so the archetype of *puer
aeternus* becomes in *Billy Budd* the avatar of God the
knowable through the communion of fraternal love, innocent, free of self-consciousness, carelessly enduring."

It seems fairly clear that the "American experience" has
been such that as a nation we desire virtuous conduct,
freedom from difficulty, and that many of us like to believe
that our motives are purer than the motives of people in
other countries. This is a big subject, and one can merely
point at it. John Sisk wrote an article (1952) in *Thought*
which he called "American Pastoral." The common characteristic of the literature he examines is a desire to escape
from complexity. He shows how frequently pastoral heroes
turn up in our novels. Behind all this, he says, "is the
whole business of a young, hearty, clean-blooded, freedom-
seeking, wilderness-encircled band finding a physical and
spiritual vigor in its primitive environment and asserting

itself boldly and successfully against an effeter, over-sophisticated father-land." Quite a full discussion of inno-cence in nineteenth-century American literature is to be found in *The American Adam* (1955) by R. W. B. Lewis. Lewis centers his study around the American as a new Adam. "It was not surprising, in a Bible reading genera-tion, that the new hero (in praise or disapproval) was most easily identified with Adam before the Fall. His moral position was prior to experience, and in his very newness he was fundamentally innocent. The world and history lay all before him." It is easy enough to see how Emerson, Thoreau, Whitman and certain others properly fall inside Lewis' study. Other books that are related to this subject of innocence are Philip Young's *Ernest Hemingway* (1952), Leslie Fiedler's *An End of Innocence* (1955), and Frederick Carpenter's *American Literature and the American Dream* (1956). This desire for innocence is obviously a two-sided medal, and undoubtedly the investi-gation of it that is currently under way tells us something about our capacity for self-scrutiny.

A work-in-progress which seems to deserve attention here is being written by Philip Young of Penn State Uni-versity. Mr. Young, who expects to call his book Studies in Classic American Myth, describes his subject this way:

> I propose to examine certain American traditions which have worked their way through our literature, particularly, and our culture generally, chiefly by having been used and re-used by several hands. For instance; the stories of Poca-hontas, Rip Van Winkle, the Kentucky Tragedy, and the Angel of Hadley. The purpose is primarily an interpreta-tion of these themes in the hope of appreciating the sig-nificance for our civilization of this sort of American "literary mythology." The idea is that the meaning of the themes, if known, might throw a good deal of light both on the myths themselves and on the audiences, the gen-erations of people of the United States, which have re-peatedly found them compelling.

A good many scholars and critics are undoubtedly thinking and writing about literature in similar ways, and it seems likely a large number of articles and books having to do with belief and myth will be published in the next few years.

A postscript:

Literary Criticism, a Short History (1957) by William K. Wimsatt, Jr., and Cleanth Brooks may prove to be a volume that ended an era of literary criticism. The histories of literary criticism written by Saintsbury or Atkins, their usefulness aside, are dull, and the reason for this is that they provide summaries of critical theories and critical quarrels that in large part are dead. Whether the epic or tragedy, for example, is (or was) the ultimate in literary achievement no longer strikes us as being a very significant question. It was, however, a significant question in its own day. As scholars, students or practicing critics, we should know the history of Western criticism. We should also be able to distinguish between the questions that are dead and the questions that are of radical significance for our own period. Wimsatt and Brooks tell us the history of criticism, but they are selective, trying to emphasize the issues that are alive for us, or at least to recast the way in which ancient literary theories or arguments were put, to the end of making them more available for us. Nor does their volume suffer from a common characteristic of literary histories: opinions and evaluations seeming to come from on high, from some ineffable realm where the gods have established a hierarchy of received opinion. Wimsatt and Brooks argue from a position, *their* position, which emerges clearly as chapter follows chapter, and which is stated explicitly in the epilogue. Theirs is an analytical history. And this is a good word with which to close our little survey. The study of literature during the past twenty years or so has been largely in the *analytical* mode.

CAROLINE GORDON belongs to the generation of writers who spent at least a part of their youth in Paris. The gods of the nineteenth century had fallen, but these young people found another, *ART*. Like most gods, Art had many guises, and was sometimes called Poetry, sometimes the Novel, and sometimes Modernism. Art had innumerable prophets, but in its guise as the Novel the chief of these prophets were Flaubert, James, and Ford Madox Ford. Miss Gordon has expressed great reverence and respect for each of them, and was fortunate enough to be personally acquainted with the third, Ford.

Several intervening generations, younger than Miss Gordon by ten or fifteen or twenty years, also believed in Art. Anyone who aspired to write knew that it was impious not to believe in Art. In the years between the two wars, the poets, and the novelists and the critics who amounted to anything in the eyes of their fellows were true believers. Art was, well, sacred. A great many sermons or homilies were given about technique and structure and point of view, and occasionally someone protested that the fervor was leading toward heresy, or at least an excess of scrupulosity.

After World War II, Art continued to be respected, but some of the young writers occasionally protested. When drunk they might even say, "Let's get off this crap about Art—ya gotta have something to say!" or "Look, kid, if you can't invent you can't write," or "This technique stuff, stow it!"

The older writers, like Miss Gordon, knew the pendulum swung back and forth, toward Art, then toward Life, and they would try patiently to explain that they were not opposed to life getting into literature; there was no other way of serving Art. But Art had to be served. And the younger writers, rather shamefacedly would admit, "Yeah, ya gotta serve It." Despite the seeming unanimity a schism had begun, although a rather lax theologian might say, "The differences are merely matters of emphasis. Nothing is wrong provided each of us serves Art in our own way."

Miss Gordon, the author of many articles and books on fiction, and a writer's writer the way Katherine Anne Porter is a writer's writer, has served Art faithfully. She has been to school under the masters. In one of her textbooks she makes this comment:

> Chekhov presented difficulties to his first English readers. Imaginations "conditioned" by the Victorian novelists' leisurely pace were not athletic enough for the collaboration he demanded. And, indeed, his achievements surpassed anything the Victorians had imagined. He may well be compared to the great Pointillist painter, Seurat, on whose canvas every fleck of paint, when viewed in the proper perspective, united with a neighboring fleck of paint to make the color the artist had in mind. There are no "dead" spots on Chekhov's canvases. Each detail not only vibrates with a life of its own but "acts" upon the neighboring detail. The result is a scene of extraordinary animation. The actors' speeches and gestures are lifelike in the extreme and they move through their roles with consistent boldness, but in addition, the whole scene seems to be bathed in a living air. Reading a Chekhov story one feels often as one does on an early autumn day when fields, woods, mountains, lakes and rivers show more brilliantly for the luminous light which shimmers between us and them.

The best of Miss Gordon's stories are like that; the details are vibrant. "The Brilliant Leaves" is a good example. A boy watches the girl he loves fall to her death from a ledge they had been climbing. The two had arranged a tryst in the woods. She insists on climbing high into the rocks near a waterfall, called Bridal Veil. She slips on a rock and falls. In the hands of certain writers the horror would be the story. Miss Gordon does much more. The wood are life and adventure, the waiting future; and the dazzlingly brilliant leaves are passion and also death. Human lives are in Nature, and to live well is to live adventuresomely, aware of love against death, for death is the mother of beauty.

In the same story there is also the "death" of the women who sit gossiping, almost ghostlike, apart from love. They live in the little white houses that seem staid and permanent and secure. Perhaps the young man should run away with his girl—we are not told. But the women on the porch had gossiped about Sally Mainwaring, now a bitter old spinster, whose young man, fearing her father, had failed her. The boy had often heard the story, but it had not upset his sense of the equilibrium of the world. The death of his beloved shows him how precarious that equilibrium had been.

> He ran slower now, lurching sometimes from side to side, but he ran on. He ran and the brilliant, the wine-colored leaves crackled and broke under his feet. His mouth, a taut square, drew in, released whining breaths. His starting eyes fixed the ground, but he did not see the leaves that he ran over. He saw only the white houses that no matter how fast he ran kept always just ahead of him. If he did not hurry they would slide off the hill, slide off and leave him running forever through these woods, over these dead leaves.

"The Forest of the South" and "Old Red" are also excellent examples of Miss Gordon's willingness to describe essentially inert situations, to create what Joyce called "mere literature." She wants not merely for the reader to look into the eyes of the characters—she wants the characters to look back at the reader; to have a light radiating from the page.

"The Forest of the South" describes the destruction of a Southern household, Clifton, in the Civil War, its total destruction. The Yankee victor, Lieutenant Mumford, has fallen in love with the daughter, Eugenie. There is a mysterious, yet beautiful light in the girl's eyes, and Mumford, still loving her, realizes she is mad, and the reader realizes that her madness is the madness of the destruction itself.

Even more skillful is the whole texture of details in "Old Red," undoubtedly one of the finest short stories written in our time. Alec Maury, who appears prominently in a number of Miss Gordon's stories, is a man who tries to unveil nature's secrets. He looks into the burning eyes of a possum, and he studies the soft colors in streams and lakes with the quiet intensity of a Buddhist monk. He is a scholar, and he learns to respect classic simplicity—but he loves life, not death, and hunting and fishing become the center of his pursuits. He refuses the blandishments of the ghostly ladies who sit on the porches of the white houses. In the process he alienates his wife, and she dies after having kept her illness secret from him.

The central symbol in "Old Red" is the fox, a wily creature. Maury, trying to get off to sleep one night, finally realizes that he and Old Red are being pursued, and will eventually be caught. But when he is caught, it will be because he can no longer run. The identification of fox and man comes gracefully and unexpectedly into the story, like an ancient tale of metamorphosis:

> If he allowed his mind to get active, really active, he would never get any sleep. He was fighting an inclination now to get up and find a cigarette. . . . The young men would hold back till Uncle James had wheeled Old Filly, then they would all be off pell-mell across the plain. He himself would be mounted on Jonesboro. Almost blind, but she would take anything you put her at. That first thicket on the edge of the woods. They would break there, one half of them going around, the other half streaking it through the woods. He was always of those going around to try to cut the fox off on the other side. No, he was down off his horse. He was coursing with the fox through the trees. He could hear the sharp, pointed feet padding on the dead leaves, see the quick head turned now and then over the shoulder. The trees kept flashing by, one black trunk after another. And now it was a ragged

mountain field and the sage grass running before them in waves to where a narrow stream curved in between the ridges. The fox's feet were light in the water. He moved forward steadily, head down. The hounds' baying grew louder. Old Mag knew the trick. She had stopped to give tongue by that big rock and now they had all leaped the gulch and were scrambling up through the pines. But the fox's feet were already hard on the mountain path. He ran slowly, past the big boulder, past the blasted pine to where the shadow of the Pinnacle Rock was black across the path. He ran on and the shadow swayed and rose to meet him. Its cool touch was on his hot tongue, his heaving flanks. He had slipped in under it. He was sinking down, panting, in black dark, on moist earth while the hounds' baying filled the valley and reverberated from the mountainside.

Miss Gordon has a fine ear for conversation, even to the shifts one hears in the speech of an educated Southerner. For example, when Alec Maury is talking to his daughter, his language is formal: " 'Well,' he said, 'I'd better be starting.' " In the woods, thinking to himself, he says: "Aint it funny now? Niggers always live in the good places." Miss Gordon's own prose has a simplicity in keeping with good taste. There is nothing pretentious, and when occasionally it does rise toward rhetoric the rhetoric is always justified by the action itself.

Her subject matter, too, is essentially simple. For the most part, she writes about the relationships of men and women. Ideally, she seems to say, a woman should give herself to a man, wholly and without question, and he should not betray her faith. The stories frequently have to do with betrayal, by the man, the sudden intrusion of nature (violence or death), or the breakdown of the society (the Civil War). Sometimes the failures are the woman's. By and large, Miss Gordon's subject is not a complicated one, and the grave simplicity of her style is in accord with the subject.

The Women on the Porch is in treatment and subject a typical Gordon novel. A young stallion provides the central symbolism, and there is a clearly discernible pattern of water and cloud and leaves imagery. The writing, quietly beautiful, hardly calls attention to itself. Theme and subject have to do with masculine failures and with women's frustrations. Because of accident, weakness of character, or possibly the period in history in which we find ourselves, men fail to satisfy the female need for loyal, courageous, and forthright action, for love. As a form, the novel has that firmness of surface, the impersonality to which Miss Gordon's writing aspires. The story opens:

> The sugar tree's round shadow was moving past the store. At five o'clock when the first leaves were withering on the burning macadam the storekeeper raised his eyes to the fields across the road and those distant woods. Always at this hour he looked, expecting to see it rise out of that far cornfield and always when he looked it was there. Only a light shimmer now above the green, but the shimmer would deepen as the field brimmed over. In a few minutes the first waves would beat against the porch. He got up and, walking to the end of the porch, lifted the lid of the red metal ice-chest.
> "How about you, Ed?" he asked.
> The man at the other end of the porch leaned forward, felt in his trousers pocket until he found a nickel, and pitched it to the storekeeper.

This description, immediately involving the reader in the action, as though the author, Joyce-like, had dissolved into the atmosphere, is reminiscent of the opening paragraphs of *The Red Badge of Courage* and *A Farewell to Arms.* Miss Gordon's is equally skillful. The atmosphere, of dust and heat and ennui, with occasional relief, is maintained throughout the novel.

There is lore or learning of various sorts, about flowers, mushrooms, horses, painting, local history, even architecture and literature. For the most part all of it functions unobtrusively. The story itself, of course, is about the search for love. A male reader, incidentally, might easily feel that Miss Gordon's idyll of peace deep in the forest of time, death and danger is a woman writer's dream. She seems to ask a lot of the male, more understanding, courage and tenacity than most mortals, male or female, possess. And the same reader, especially if he does not share

Miss Gordon's respect for the "cold pastoral," for Art, might feel that something is being put over on him. The "cold pastoral" on an urn is the right place for cold, eternal truths. The poor male, with all his weaknesses, could wish that the artist, like an ancient genie, had not dissolved into the atmosphere. There are a couple of questions, in all fairness, he would like to put to her.

Being, for the moment, a little hard on Miss Gordon, we ought to take a look at yet another novel, *None Shall Look Back*, in which ironically her very artistry seems to have deadened the subject. There are many beautiful, skillfully evoked scenes, but they are so numerous that one finishes the book feeling one has seen too many pictures, all of them exquisitely wrought, of forts, cannon, gun boats, staring corpses, gutted houses, handsome young soldiers tall on their sturdy horses, and young women crying in their darkened rooms. One gives *None Shall Look Back* a sort of credence, but the sort given to an excellent book of Civil War pictures. Miss Gordon's Southern piety may also have interfered with the dramatic possibilities of the subject. There is not, in other words, enough in it about the human heart in conflict with itself. Faulkner quarreled with his heritage and produced *Absalom, Absalom!* Miss Gordon brought too much respect and too little skepticism to her Civil War novel.

But Miss Gordon deserves to be judged by her best work. At least two of her novels, *Penhally* and *Alec Maury, Sportsman* are first-rate. Of the former, Ford Madox Ford said, "I think it is the best novel that has been produced in modern America." This may be, and probably is, too great praise. *Penhally* is, none the less, a very fine novel. *Alec Maury, Sportsman* is probably that very rare thing, a masterpiece.

Both novels deal with trying to stay the hand of time. *Penhally* has what *None Shall Look Back* lacks, an inner life growing out of two ideas in conflict. In *Penhally* nostalgia about the old ways, the ante-bellum world, is in conflict with Change, and the latter inevitably had the victory, ironic and bitter though it turns out to be. *Alec Maury, Sportsman* is individual man, fully aware that his

enemy is Time. Day after day, Maury increases his art
and skill as a fisherman and his artfulness in dodging those
who would waste his time. His drama is not less poignant
for being quiet. For seventy years, his head has been filled
with the sound of clocks, stilled only when he is standing
in a stream casting, or sitting peacefully on a smooth lake.
The reader comes to share his every success, his every failure. Miss Gordon's style, touched with a detached and
loving irony, has never been in the service of a happier
subject matter. In Alec Maury skillful, thoughtful, and
sensitive men win at least temporary victory, all they have
ever hoped to win.

Most of the critics who have written about Miss Gordon
have discussed her as a Southern writer—and of course she
is. Certain of her characters are deracinated Southerners or
Midwesterners, usually intellectuals who have left the
home place. They are invariably unhappy types, trailing
trouble and disorder along their foreign paths or bringing
it with them when they occasionally return home. There
are also many passages, even whole novels, about the land,
its moral power, healing and giving one a sense of belonging. Miss Gordon especially likes the land that has not
given up its fruits and rewards too easily; one appreciates
what one has sweated to achieve.

Is Miss Gordon's preoccupation with Art also Southern?
Possibly so. Her style however is closer to Willa Cather's
than it is to Southern rhetoric, even to the quiet rhetoric of
Katherine Anne Porter. The respect for form itself is in
part Southern—in manners for example, covering and
even controlling personal likes, dislikes, drives and ambitions, possibly too in a fairly general disregard for scientific
principles and a preference for the arts that bear on personal relationships, and in a more open respect and liking
for "elegance." But change comes on apace, and the
Southern world of Miss Gordon's youth is no longer what
it was. North and South grow more alike, not less, and at
least one or two of her novels seem to acknowledge that
this is so.

Miss Gordon's art too, as we suggested at the beginning,
is related to the nineteenth-century European heritage.

There was Flaubert, James, Ford, Chekhov, Crane, Joyce, Hemingway, and others. In her fiction and explicitly in her many critical discussions of the novel and the short story she has clearly identified herself with it.

Did she, in choosing to be a part of this literary heritage, choose well? It is presumptuous to answer such an Olympian and possibly impertinent question. But having posed it, we must answer. Chekhov in one of his many letters says, "One must write about simple things: how Peter Semionovich married Maria Invanovna. That is all." When Miss Gordon writes about American Marias and Peters, she can be, and often is, an excellent fiction writer. She is always excellent in writing about the Alec Maurys. She is at her best when the subject matter arouses her sympathy and humor—rather than when subjects arouse her anger or lead her into large theoretical conclusions about men and women or about the social order.

Miss Gordon has written enough good stories—at least two novels of a very high order and a half dozen excellent short stories—to have won a permanent place for herself in the hierarchy of American letters. Recognition has come slowly but it has come, and it continues to grow. Miss Gordon has served Art well, and, by and large, it has not betrayed her.

17 THE WRITER
AND THE UNIVERSITY

DURING THE PAST twenty years there has been an increasing
identification of the writer with the university, particularly in English departments. Since World War II, many
writers have been taken on as part-time and full-time staff
members. Most of them have not had Ph.D.'s. Often they
have taught only "writing courses," but some have joined
the graduate faculty and taken a hand in preparing students for the M.A. and the Ph.D. More significant for
the future is the fact that a large number of graduate
students are now taking the Ph.D. with the intention of
becoming professional writers, dramatists, poets, fiction
writers, biographers, or essayists of one kind or another.

The subscription lists of philological journals have
dwindled or merely held their own despite hundreds of
new Ph.D.'s in English and American literature. But the
"little magazines," or literary quarterlies, most of them
subsidized by a university, have multiplied. The contribu-
tors to these magazines are aspiring writers. They have
learned to write "critical pieces" whereas their counter-
parts a generation ago learned to prepare research articles
for *PMLA* or *The Journal of English and Germanic
Philology*. Many of them also write poetry and fiction. A
small handful of university-connected writers have won a
Pulitzer Prize or a National Book Award—and one can be
sure that many of the others have an eye on these prizes.

In some universities, the writing program, as lamb, lies
down next to the academic program, the lion. But the

lamb occasionally appears to have the heart of a lion, and
the lion sometimes backs away when the lamb growls. To
put it less fancifully, often there is no great difference
between what the programs are trying to achieve, and no
great difference between the writer and the academic.
Sometimes he is the same person. In Mencken's day,
the writer lived in New York or Paris, and the scholar
hoped one day to live in Cambridge, Mass. The former
was experimenting wildly with the English sentence. The
latter rejoiced that Milton and his kind did not have to
resort to novelty. If, by chance, the writer strayed onto a
campus, he was not likely to remain there very long.

The career of Joel Spingarn is instructive to anyone
looking into this shift. In his lectures and essays back there
in 1910 or 1915 or 1920, one finds Spingarn attacking
literary journalists—they lack learning and do not understand critical principles. He also attacked his colleagues.
Most of them, he said, thought an iamb or a trochee
could be measured with the metronome, and that a "re-
venge tragedy" or a "tragi-comedy" could be defined and
the definition put into a handbook. According to Spingarn,
they believed the study of literature was the study of fixed,
measurable, and inert facts. Neither the literary journalists
nor his colleagues welcomed what he was saying. Spingarn
retreated to Amenia, New York, sold his library, and
raised flowers. Spingarn's book on Renaissance literary
criticism and his anthologies of seventeenth-century criticism were recognized as scholarly achievements of a high
order—but Spingarn's heart was in a theory of literature.

His one later venture into criticism was an unhappy
affair. He gave three lectures on literary theory at the New
School for Social Research. One of his points was that
"economic determinism" as a primary factor in literary
creation was, in his opinion, a simple-minded doctrine. He
said this in the 1930's, and most of his audience, the
younger ones certainly, thought Spingarn an old fogey,
and he went back to Amenia and his flowers. Probably if
Spingarn were in an English department today he would
be publishing critical articles and poetry, and exerting a
strong influence on his students and younger colleagues.

To be the kind of academic and writer Spingarn wanted to be is far easier today than it was in his generation.

It goes almost without saying that a critic lurks behind every other office door in most English departments. But poets, and dramatists, and fiction writers are there too. The following is a list of the living poets represented in *Modern Verse in English*, recently edited by Allen Tate and Lord David Cecil: Williams, Eliot, Pound, Jeffers, Marianne Moore, Ransom, Aiken, MacLeish, Van Doren, Cummings, Louise Bogan, Tate, Winters, Ghiselin, Blackmur, Eberhart, Warren, Roethke, Fitzgerald, Bishop, Cunningham, Nims, Schwartz, Shapiro, Berryman, Lowell, Jean Garrigue, Barbara Hawes, Coxe, Smith, Meredith, Whittemore, Nemerov, and Wilbur. Among those poets over seventy, only Ransom has had an academic career. Among those over sixty, only Van Doren has had a lifetime academic career; MacLeish, of course, has in recent years been Boylston Professor at Harvard. But beginning with Tate, now in his early sixties, down to Wilbur, in his thirties, almost without exception these poets have spent all or a considerable part of their adult lives on campuses.

A similar list of short story writers, compiled from the Best Short Stories or the O'Brien anthologies, would show that a majority of short story writers are on campuses. The editor of one of these annual collections teaches at the University of Iowa, the other at Columbia. Mona Van Duyn, co-editor of one of the literary quarterlies, *Perspective*, wrote this several years ago:

> To our post office box comes a steady stream of manuscripts, accompanied by self-addressed, stamped envelopes, and the address on the return envelope, nine times out of ten, is that of a college or a university. One revelation, in fact, among the many revelations which come to a little magazine editor, is how many such institutions exist in the U.S. And at every one of them, or so it seems to us, there is at least one who, after correcting his stacks of freshman themes and research papers, or after conducting his seminar on Milton, or after attending a committee meeting on how to cope with cheating, or the staff meeting on whether sophomores should learn reading skills

or the history of literature, goes home and begins work
on a short story or a novel or a piece of criticism or a poem.

For a variety of reasons, there may be proportionately
fewer novelists on campuses than poets or short story
writers. Writing a novel may require more extended application than writing a series of poems or a group of short
stories, and in some cases the novelist may feel that
academic duties interfere too much with his writing. There
is also the American tradition that the campus is the
wrong place for the novelist. Even so, a number of names
come to mind: George Stewart, Wallace Stegner, Hudson
Strode, Walter Van Tilburg Clark, Andrew Lytle, Allan
Seager, Albert Guerard, Lloyd Wimberly, Bernard Mala-
mud, Peter Taylor, Mark Schorer, Howard Nemerov,
Robie Macauley, Virgil Scott, Robert Bowen, Charles
Angoff, Walter Sullivan, George P. Elliott, and such one
shot novelists as Paul Engel, Carlos Baker, Theodore
Morrison, and Randall Jarrell. Robert Penn Warren, of
course, gave up teaching only recently.

In his symposium, *The Living Novel*, Granville Hicks
published articles by ten young novelists: Saul Bellow,
Paul Darcy Boles, John Brooks, Ralph Ellison, Herbert
Gold, Mark Harris, Wright Morris, Flannery O'Connor,
Harvey Swados, and Jessamyn West. Five of them have
permanent or more or less permanent connections with a
college or university.

In England too the writer appears to be increasingly
identified with the university. The group sometimes labeled the New University Wits will serve as an example.
Iris Murdoch, who has been called the best of the British
novelists to emerge since the War, is a tutor in philosophy
at Oxford. In her fiction, she has drawn on her academic
background for characters and situations, although by no
means exclusively, and she has used, with admirable skill,
her knowledge of modern philosophy, especially in its
French existentialists manifestations. Kingsley Amis' *Lucky
Jim*, an extremely funny satire on certain academic types,
is directed against what Amis calls "Oxford accented culture." Amis is an able poet and his critical pieces and

reviews are witty and shrewd. Amis has taught at Swansea. Philip Larkin, a close friend of Amis, is a fine poet, and the author of two novels, one of them a skillful evocation of war-time England. Larkin, however, is a librarian, not a lecturer in English. Dennis Enright has written half a dozen volumes, fiction, poetry, and criticism. Enright was a student of F. R. Leavis. He has taught in various parts of the Commonwealth, with only temporary posts in England. Donald Davie and John Holloway have published scholarly criticism, the former on eighteenth-century poetic conventions and the latter mostly on the Victorian greats. Both men are good poets. John Wain, whose novel *Hurry on Down* is usually labeled, incorrectly, the first of the angry-young-men novels, formerly taught at Reading. He left academic life for journalism and free-lance writing. There is no mistaking the academic training, or, if one wishes, the academic tone of these writers. But one ought not to leap to the conclusion that this is unfortunate.

To return to the American scene. The fact that criticism flourishes on American campuses is probably responsible for the fact, if it is a fact, that literature is taught more imaginatively than it was a generation ago. But criticism itself, except in a very special sense, is not creative writing. Many critics, academic or otherwise, are poets and fiction writers *manqué*. It would be a misrepresentation to say that each American English department is now a nest of singing birds or singing typewriters. There is, however, a quite different atmosphere. It is also true that there are many more writers in English departments than there used to be—and there will be even more in the future.

There appear to be two causes for the writer's increasing identification with academic life. One is economic and the other the change in academic life itself, or, more specifically, in the nature of the English department. Charles Fenton, in a piece called "The Writer as Professor," put the economic factor this way:

> It is an economic impulse which is primarily responsible for the infiltration of the university faculties by writers. The relatively flush times of thirty years ago have vanished in the arts. Advances are wrung from harassed publishers

with difficulty. Even when they are extracted, they're likely to be small and demanding. Publishing costs are up, book-buying is down, and the writer's royalties, for the majority, are meager. The advertising agencies, which briefly supported so many young writers during the early 1920's—Sherwood Anderson, Fitzgerald, J. P. Marquand, Stephen Vincent Benet—have become highly organized and professional. The casual, easily broken and easily resumed relationship between writer and agency is no longer possible. Journalism, too, has become formal and regularized: it recruits young men for a lifetime, and the boomer, looking for rent money while he finishes his novel, is no longer welcome.

In *The Literary Situation* (1954), Malcolm Cowley spelled out the economic woes of the writer in pitiful detail. The writer had to turn somewhere for assistance. He turned to the campus.

And he was welcomed there. His acceptance has been a gradual process—it is still developing—and some writers may have had experiences of a kind they find hard to reconcile with the statement that the writer has been welcomed. Generally speaking, though, the writer has been welcomed. Behind his welcome, to put it simply, was the Brooks and Warren revolution.

This revolution began in the late 1930's at Louisiana State University and gradually spread. Since World War II almost all undergraduates have been taught the analytical method of studying literature. This method moved into the graduate school and there joined other critical methods and learned how to adjust itself to the long established historical scholarship. The revolutionaries of a generation ago, R. P. Blackmur, Allen Tate, Cleanth Brooks, and others, are now highly respected professors of English literature. They are all the proof graduate students need that one can be both an academic and a writer.

In the 1920's and 1930's professors of English used to say that their research into church records, into biography, in establishing texts, discovering sources, and so on, was a preparation for the study of literature *as* literature, for criticism. Some of the then young men who had gone into graduate work with the mistaken assumption that an English department was a proper place for a novelist or poet tended not to believe them. The young men suspected that most of their professors believed that literary criticism was centered in one man, Matthew Arnold. And of course some of their professors did believe exactly that. But the principle they enunciated, or sometimes simply mouthed, has proven true. This of course is not to say that research old style, or new style, has ceased. But there is less of it, and what is done is often seen as having a different end.

Prior to World War II, the study of literature was allied to the study of history, whereas it is now, much of it anyway, closer to the study of philosophy. This simply means that the instructor, or the student, sets up his critical premises, which can be of quite different kinds, and examines the play, or novel, or poem in the light of them. If the premises are valid, the work of literature lights up, as though it had been brought into an electric field. Historical information of one sort or another is usually involved in the premises, and thus gradually the old quarrel between "new critic" and "historical scholar" has ceased. Which brings us to the point: English departments nowadays look at literature pretty much as writers do.

The acceptance of literary criticism on the campus has inevitably influenced the process of selecting teaching staff, and the setting up of new courses. There has been a lessening of the old emphasis on historical periods. One is more likely to ask nowadays whether a man knows the drama or the novel or the lyric than to ask whether he knows the scholarship in a given field, the Elizabethan drama or the Romantic period. The practicing poet, a Karl Shapiro, can teach the Tudor lyric; a dramatist, a Robert Chapman, can teach Restoration drama; a short story writer, a Wallace Stegner, the American short story; and a novelist, a Saul Bellow, either the history of the novel or the technique of the novel. The critic and the literary historian have adjusted their differences and even learned to borrow from each other. Now both of them are being asked to share the platform or the texts with novelists, short story writers, and poets.

Meanwhile, a new breed is emerging: the Ph.D.'s who want to be writers. They will have studied the history of the language, up to and including its twentieth-century manifestations. And they will know English and American literary traditions. There may seem to be nothing new in such a program—but there is. These students will be studying the language and the literature partly as historians and as critics but also as journeymen, prospective practitioners, and, if they have the talent, as artists. If this group proves at all numerous, at least a few should deepen and extend our knowledge and understanding of literature as an academic study.

These young men and women have, or will have, the credentials, and if they are not willingly accepted they will do what all groups do, band together. They will prove a hungry generation treading their elders down. But as Mr. Fenton says, there is "a lumbering integrity in the academic world," and a place will be found for them. They will be judged, as their elders were, on their ability as teachers and with the typewriter.

We have been discussing the influence of the writer on English departments. What about the influence of English departments, or, more generally, of academic life on the writer? Mr. Fenton tells about hearing a professor say, "Writers must not become academics. They must never become teachers. A writer, a creative writer, that is, should never have to be both creator and judge. They are separate functions and should not be practised together." Surely, if the professor, whoever he was, had stopped to think about it, he would have realized that the creative act and the critical act are inseparable. And of course writers make judgments about other writers, just as the rest of us do.

A more common criticism is that the groves of academe are an ivory tower, or the closest we can come to one nowadays, and that the writer living on a campus has separated himself from "real life." The cult of experience is part of the American literary scene. Hemingway shoots lions, and Faulkner says he is a writer, not a literary man. A writer is supposed to gather experience, as a pearl diver gathers pearls. The writer gathers black pearls. He fills his head with memories of raids behind enemy lines, or fights in a hobo jungle, love affairs with dark-skinned lasses in a Texas border town, and philosophical chats with the madams of bawdy houses in New Orleans or Joplin, Missouri. Most commonly, experience is taken to mean noise, violence, the bizarre or the offbeat.

But one does not have to be a stoker in the boiler room of a liner to be involved in "real life." Anyone who has been graduate student, teaching assistant, instructor and has become or failed to become an assistant, associate or full professor should have learned something about his fellow mortals and himself. He should understand the dedicated man; the methods of the "operator." He should have experienced the muted joys of scholarly investigation and explication, of testing his own insights. He should have learned something about power, and the exertion of pressure, direct and oblique; and something about "quiet desperation." Chekhov would have found plenty of subjects to write about if fortune had put him down on an American campus.

Henry James complained that American life was insufficiently complicated for the novelist: no Ascot, no ancient castles, no stratified society to provide contrasts in manners and morals. The American campus is a little hierarchical society. There are various academic ranks, chairmen, deans and associate deans, various colleges, the graduate school, the chancellor, and that mysterious body with star-chamber powers, the regents. It is a world with plenty of contrasts for the student of manners and morals. If no one has written a really good novel about academic life the blame should not be placed on the subject matter. A Trollope or a Joyce Cary could have brought off such a novel.

Of course, the writer living on a campus does not have to write about academic life. Robert Penn Warren, during his years as an academic, stuck mostly with nineteenth-century subjects. Saul Bellow, Walter Van Tilburg Clark, Peter Taylor, Andrew Lytle, and Wallace Stegner do not write about campuses—they have their own subjects.

Mark Harris and Saul Bellow have had their say about

the writer on the campus. Harris, in an article called
"Home Is Where We Backed Into," says he took a Ph.D.
as job security. He thinks the discipline of course work
and of writing a thesis were good for him. He likes to
teach—or, as he says, to talk about literary matters with
students. If he were not a teacher, he would have to seek
out people to talk with. His basic point is that the university community provides a good critical audience for the
writer: "Trained in the logical disciplines, conversant with
centuries and places not the writer's own, the best people
on any good campus in the United States provide a writer
with a critical forum unsurpassed in knowledge and understanding by a non-academic community anywhere."

Bellow, in "The University as Villain," is concerned
with the experience doctrine. He opens with a question,
"Are writers greatly harmed by teaching in universities?"
He answers, "The first reply that comes to mind is that a
man may make a damn fool of himself anywhere." He
tells about an accidental meeting he had with a Madison
Avenue executive, formerly an assistant to Hutchins at
Chicago, where he and Bellow had known each other. The
executive could understand society's supporting scholars—
but the writer, to write, needed the experience of the
gutter, of "life." Bellow says:

> It seemed crazy to explain to the executive of a large
> corporation how powerfully pervasive life could be; and I
> didn't think it would be suitable to tell the chancellor's
> former assistant that his implied view of professors was
> not flattering. Were they fat, tame and lazy, or did they
> take no harm from the special protection of society? Were
> they too good for the gutter, or not good enough for it?
> How is it that a philosopher might live in the *tour d'ivoire*
> whereas a writer belonged out in the *marais de merde* by
> which Flaubert thought his tower to be surrounded?

Bellow also says this:

> It is not easy to find the right way. You must learn to
> govern yourself, you must learn autonomy, you must man-
> age your freedom or drown in it. You may strain the will
> after Experience because you need it for books. Or you
> may perish under the heavy weight of Culture. You may

make a fool of yourself anywhere. You may find illumination anywhere—in the gutter, in the college, in the corporation, in a submarine, in the library. No one holds a patent on it.

No one can say where a writer is to find his subject. No one really knows why James wrote so frequently about the virtues and the limitations of innocence, Conrad about skepticism as opposed to such simple virtues as loyalty and hard work, or why Robert Penn Warren is preoccupied with the rationalizations and often the viciousness of men who strive to be honorable. Why was Joyce obsessed with the city and the culture and the religion he rejected? There are plenty of theories—each has a psychic wound, or he is "shedding a sickness" in writing his novels, or he is trying to work out a theory of morality. No one knows why one writer spends a lifetime reconstructing his childhood, whereas another writes only out of his adult experience. Nor, for the most part, does anyone know why a theme dies out, a subject dries up. E. M. Forster wrote a half dozen brilliant novels as a very young man and then stopped writing novels altogether. John Crowe Ransom's poetry was written in his middle years. Asked why he stopped writing poetry, he said, "It's a free country, isn't it?"

In Joyce's *Finnegans Wake* there is a dramatic illustration of the drying-up process. Wright Morris in "The Territory Ahead" tries to account for it:

> Joyce was left with no alternative to grinding up his own work and starting over, since nothing of importance, except his work, had happened to him. The consequential events of his life were those of his adolescence and young manhood—in his exile, in his withdrawal, he withdrew from the world. Dublin *was* his life, and in *Ulysses* he processed it. *Finnegans Wake* is less an example of the inscrutable ways of genius than an instance of genius having run out of raw material.

Mr. Morris goes on to say that Joyce, perhaps intentionally, sacrificed life to art. *Finnegans Wake*, he says, is the proof that technique is not enough. But this does not explain why Joyce ran out of material. He had lived in Trieste, Zurich, and in Paris. Apparently the sources of one's art can dry up anywhere, even in Paris. Had Joyce been a language professor in Dublin, we would be saying that academic life cut him off from real life!

Another question: Does the kind of thinking the academic does professionally interfere with the spontaneity, vigor, and imagination necessary to literary creation? And related questions: Are the professor's poems or novels going to be too "intellectual" or too genteel? Probably there are different answers for all of these questions. Among them, these: Knowledge need not always express itself conceptually, in abstractions. Intuition can lead to imagination, to art. The conceptual and the intuitive-imaginative mind need not be mutually exclusive. And, considering the society we live in, the academic is unlikely to find himself unable to utter the word *spit*.

Modern writing is consciously intellectual, Carlyle complained about this in his day, and Yeats called it "Alexandrianism." Joyce was almost a parody of the professor. Only chance kept Ezra Pound and T. S. Eliot from being professors. Wallace Stevens in his heart of hearts was an academic. He even kept up on university-press books. Wily old Robert Frost merely pretends he is a farmer. Reviewers frequently say that too many of our poets and fiction writers are strong on technique and short on having something to say. Possibly modern criticism is at fault, or the age, or the individual writer. But this accusation is no more applicable to writers connected with universities than to nonacademic writers. It seems clear, for good as well as bad, that the spirit and the conventions of modern writing invite an academic alliance.

Whether the metaphors *demonic writer* and *visceral writer* make any sense is an open question. Rimbaud and Hart Crane have been called demonic writers, and a few critics have said Faulkner writes out of his viscera. Lacking adequate knowledge of these phenomena, we probably should assume that these writers would have found academic life distressing and disturbing. It might have destroyed them.

Hemingway's very subject involves a prior rejection of what the campus stands for, and therefore he was probably well advised to stay away from it. It is altogether likely, on the other hand, that John O'Hara, James Farrell, James Gould Cozzens, and others would be better writers if they had experienced the direct and personal criticism of men who respected their talents but refused to tolerate their pretentiousness. O'Hara, for one, might have discovered that there are more things to write about than the art of getting someone else's wife into bed. It is unlikely that a campus would harm Norman Mailer or James Jones; it might help them.

But not everyone will agree that certain writers can or should become academics. John Aldridge, in *In Search of Heresy* (1956), says the writer should stay away from campuses. He is also sharply critical of what he calls "the development which has made the university the seat of literary politics and power in our time and which has transformed so many of our younger intellectuals into university apologists and literary politicians." Aldridge says the writer nowadays accepts the middle class world, or, as he puts it, refuses "to leave the warm protection of the bourgeois womb." The writers in the 1920's preferred Bohemia and "the possibility of the free creative life." Aldridge does not say that the young expatriates in Paris were able to stay there indulging the free creative life because the money sent them by their families could be trebled or quadrupled when exchanged into francs. When Hitler started to rant, they came home. Bohemia not only has no seacoast, it has no geography. It is a state of mind, or, perhaps better, the part of the mind that is looking for a free ride.

Many of the young or relatively young university writers spent several years in the Army, in Europe, North Africa, New Guinea, the Philippines or Korea. They have seen enough of the big world to recognize that life in Paris or Manila is not so very different from life in New York, Minneapolis, or Peoria, Illinois. Also, a continual carping about crass middle class values can be very tiresome and not, at this date, very illuminating. Writers have been complaining about it for over a century and a half. The writer will continue to protest—that is his nature—but now he has a different record to put on his long playing set. He will write about suburbia, or what it is like to grow middle-aged, and a hundred other things. Frederick Henry resigned from Society—resigning from Society was the thing to do in the 1920's. Joining up is the thing now.

Aldridge also makes the point that the writer teaching literature on a campus is likely to let his talents atrophy. He can write an occasional review or engage in literary politics, and think of himself as a literary man. Undoubtedly there is something to this. But the temptations are not peculiar to the writer on a campus. All writing, especially after one reaches forty, depends on personal discipline. Life is easier if one gets himself appointed to the dean's steering committee—but writers living off campus develop rackets too. On or off campus, the writer's problem is the same: to keep that little self-propelling machine in his chest wound up.

Aldridge's final point is that the university writer is "part of a vast and complex social organization which very largely *is* the literary-intellectual life of America today. The academic world and the literary world are, for all practical purposes, synonymous in this country at the present time. The universities control literature, its agencies, and its functions." This all sounds very ominous—but less ominous if one suggests that it is still the readers and editors at Scribners, Macmillan, or Viking who decide what fiction is to be published. A letter from the chairman of the English department won't do the trick.

And one other thing. There is always diversity of opinion on a campus. Partial proof of this is the fact that Aldridge is himself an academic. He has had his share of awards, and not because he has written fiction or poetry or even criticism but because he has taken on the role of saying there's something rotten in more places than Denmark.

Anyone who has been teaching a decade or longer will have seen English Literature sharing more and more credit hours, its part of the curriculum, with World Literature,

Modern Literature, and American Literature. Occasionally someone predicts the day when English Literature will be a series of several courses in the Department of American Literature, or even American Civilization. In that dark day, when the rough beast rises, its hour come round at last, those who are genuinely interested in literature should be able to trust the writer, as an ally, to face the part of the beast that has a head like a man's and talk intelligently to it about the nature of literature, its civilizing power, etc. Perhaps it will listen.

Not so very many years ago, the ordinary English professor's sense of history was much more orderly, more fixed, than it could possibly be today. Events like St. Bartholomew's Day, Guy Fawkes Day, or Sidney dying on the battlefield at Sutpen stood out like the cherished pictures in one's own family album. But history no longer seems static. One has a greater sense of the variousness of the peoples of the world, their histories, and the rapidity with which history is made. For Conrad, the Congo was still the heart of darkness. Twenty years ago the Vale of Kashmir was only a song title, Outer Mongolia was a dark land, out of which Attila and his horsemen had come, and Lhasa was the rarely seen city of the mysterious llamas. Today electrical impulses bring these lands and their peoples into our living room on a Sunday afternoon. History has become kaleidoscopic. In a sense, it has exploded.

If our minds tried to hold in a fixed or static way all the History now available, or with which we are constantly bombarded, something would click in our heads and allow us to retire into a protective darkness. It may not be wholly fanciful to suggest that the analytical method we have seen develop and whatever it is that the professional writer will bring to the study of literature are ways of responding to this bombardment. As Wallace Stevens used to say, the writer is a shaper, constantly trying to bring order out of disorder.

The relationship of the university to the outside world has also changed. The physicists who worked in the Chicago football stadium are dramatic proof. But the change is not limited to scientists and economists. The humanities are involved in it. The university, in a more complicated way than ever before, has involved itself with the living arts, music, painting, literature. Possibly the writer, or the aspiring writer, has been listening with his inner ear to some appeal from the time spirit, and has heard it say that the university is now one of the *creators* as well as custodians of culture.

This is why so many writers now live on a campus rather than on the Left Bank or in Greenwich Village.

> Travelers on roads outside of Boston sometimes en-
> counter a harassed stranger in an old-fashioned great coat.
> He is accompanied by a small girl. "I beseech you, sir," he
> says, "what is the way to Boston?" Some times the travel-
> ers learn he had once, during a thunderstorm, made a vow:
> "I will see home tonight, or may I never see home!"
>
>   "Peter Rugg, the Missing Man" (1824)
>   by William Austin

> Nathaniel Hawthorne gave Peter Rugg a place in "A
> Virtuoso's Collection." It has been said that Peter Rugg
> berated Hawthorne for not devising a tale to get him back
> to Boston and restored to his home and family. Hawthorne
> half in anger, but speaking the truth, answered, "I put you
> in the Museum. That's all the security any of us can
> achieve." I cannot vouch for the authenticity of this, but I
> believe it to be true.
>
>   The Author

THE MUSEUM was like almost any museum one has visited.
There was a marble staircase, and rooms filled with portraits and statues. The rooms seemed empty and very
quiet. When I entered late in the afternoon, near dinner-
time, I saw the moderately tall, not quite plump figure
moving along the balustrade toward the top of the stairs.
I knew at once it was Nathaniel Hawthorne. He had a
bushy white mustache, leonine hair, and dark half-smiling
eyes. He waited as I climbed the stairs.

"Mr. Hawthorne," I said, extending my hand. He shook
it solemnly. His eyes, I saw, had a yellowish cast.

"Your name?" he asked. When I told him, he seemed
not to hear.

"What is down that way?" I asked, pointing to a long, narrow corridor, at the end of which was a lighted room.

"That's the Virtuoso's Collection. Have you visited it?" His voice was resonant and heavy, with a slightly ironic edge.

"No, but I read your account of it. I believe there are many strange, perhaps bizarre items to be seen, Spenser's 'milk-white lamb' in the company of Una, Rosinante, and Dr. Johnson's cat Hodge. If I may say so, it sounds more like a menagerie than a museum collection."

"Well, one doesn't always write at the top of his bent," he said, apparently not offended. "That always surprised me—the way the pen seemed to move as it were without my control. Sometimes I affirmed doctrines I did not feel sure about. Sometimes I seemed to be speaking from the pit itself!"

"Especially when your nongenteel self was trying to tell the truth. That's where the ambiguity resides. Really, Mr. Hawthorne, if you had given your dark haired women half a chance, given their voluptuous . . ."

"Sir!" he said.

Then, more gently, he asked if I would like to visit the Virtuoso's Collection. Together we walked slowly along the balustrade and down the corridor. Mr. Hawthorne's body exuded a strange coldness, but he walked easily, in a strong gliding movement. He seemed not wholly aware that he had a companion.

"Do you write?" he asked as we approached the room, and after my elbow had accidentally touched his.

"A little," I said.

"It is a sickness, like not being able to resist breathing a poison flower. Eventually one eats the flower, petal by petal, and dies."

"Better I suppose than dying after eating a box of bromides."

Mr. Hawthorne regarded me through half-opened eyes.

There in front of us, inside the door, was Peter Rugg, the Missing Man. He wore an old-fashioned great coat, a faded blue, and threadbare. At first I thought he was made of wax, but there was a twitch of his cheek. His body was able to fill less than half of the coat, and the collar set off his hawk-like, weather-burned, and anxious face. He extended his hand to me, but his gaze went past both of us, down the empty corridor. The hand was thin and cold, and it shook despite my effort to hold it firmly. "Have you come from Boston?" he asked plaintively.

"Not recently," I said.

"Ah," he answered, dropping my hand.

"Where is his daughter, Mr. Hawthorne?" I asked as we passed on. "Has she gone back to Boston?"

"No, one must see that she could not be long separated from her father."

"Yet you have the wolf here that suckled Romulus and Remus, but not the boys themselves." I said, pointing.

"The wolf is believable," he said sharply, "but not those damned twins! Besides," he added, "I'm not the curator. There are any number of ridiculous items in this collection. Pegasus over there," he said, motioning with his great head, "he never seemed wholly credible to me. Pan does, especially when he's very good on the flute."

"Those dark ladies again," I said.

"You, sir, appear to have a slight obsession about dark haired ladies."

"Well, scholars have repeatedly discussed your dark haired ladies."

"None of their damned business," he said, walking on.

"There's Shelley's skylark!" I said, pointing. "It's stuffed!"

"Your generation has lifted that young man, Shelley, to eminence, I'm told."

"My father's generation, perhaps."

"His pursuit of wenches—what was he trying to learn from them, do you suppose? He must have read Lord Chesterfield—in the dark all cats are gray."

"You don't believe that, do you, Mr. Hawthorne?"

"Sir, your questions tend to be rather blunt," he said, lifting his head. "That friend of Shelley's, Byron," he added slowly, "he is engaging. What wench worth pinching would not have pitied and loved him for his club foot and his poor wretched handsome face?"

"Why should they love him for his club foot?"

"Oh, come now. Why does Pan have a cloven hoof? Look, there's Aladdin's lamp. Give it a rub. Do you expect to see the cave and the jewels?"

"No, but I would like to see the lamp. Have you rubbed it, sir?"

"Only until I could see the beginnings of a scene in the dark silver. That damned genie business I never could abide."

"If you could add a few items to this collection, what would they be? Quickly, before you've had time to ponder," I said, stopping him in front of Cowper's sofa.

Frowning he put his hand firmly on my shoulder. "Your manners, sir," he said. Then the yellow eyes darkened. After a full minute, he said, "I should like to see the shadow cast by Cleopatra in the late afternoon as she bade Antony good-bye. A jade reproduction of Helen's nose. And the wig worn by Shakespeare's dark lady!"

"Shadows and wigs, but we listen too. Should there be a museum of sounds, the sounds that were caught in the wind and echo forever through space?"

"Yes," he answered at once and firmly. "I'd like to hear Roland's horn in the pass, the glutinous self-congratulating voice of Luther, and the cry of the first woman settler who saw a raised tomahawk in her doorway, and . . . There should, as you say, be a museum of sounds."

"The sounds you prefer are those that chill the blood."

"Those are the sounds one remembers."

"Mr. Hawthorne," I said, "did you ever hear about a museum of dreams?"

"What is that?" he asked, raising one bushy eyebrow.

"I read about such a museum in a story by Howard Nemerov."

"One of your writers?"

"Yes, a writer you'd like."

"I don't read any more," he said abruptly. "What about the museum?"

"The man who keeps the museum records all of his dreams. Fearful that one might be lost he describes each and files it in the cabinet. Dream after dream, like old documents or letters, is put away in the archives. Like saving old letters."

Mr. Hawthorne's lips were drawn together in disdain. "Morbid," he said, "morbid."

"Today we call it 'sick,' " I said.

Seeming not to hear me, he said, "Why not collect all the hair cut from one's head? Or the parings from one's fingernails!" He looked at me disdainfully.

"There would be good symbolic possibilities in both, especially the former, the hair. Did you know hair continues to grow after one's death?"

"Yes, indeed," he said sharply.

"Don't dreams interest you at all?"

"On reconsideration," he said, "I sympathize with your collector. I wonder what he learned." He paused. "So many hills, caves, meadows, the ocean and forests, what are they finally but the ancient shadows—reflecting what? The forest," he added, his chest swelling, "that is a fine symbol for a writer."

"That's what Mr. Freud has told us. The depths of the forest, the dark soft mystery, the now-I-lay-me-down-to-sleep at the forbidden edge of it. Even mother, he said . . ."

At the word *mother* Mr. Hawthorne's eyes narrowed.

"Mr. Freud," he said, regarding me closely, "who is he?"

"He came along later than you, but he was interested in many of your symbols."

"Hmm," he said, "that part about mother and the forest. It sounds sacrilegious."

"You sensed right away what he had in mind. It might," I added, "depend on whose mother was being talked about."

"Sir," he said, "I have detected a calculated irreverence in certain of your remarks."

"Forgive me," I said. "What more is to be seen in the Virtuoso's Collection?"

Mr. Hawthorne stood surveying various objects in the room. Raising his hand, he pointed toward a stag's head. "The one Shakespeare shot. And there's Bryant's water-fowl," he added, pointing to it. "Beyond is Coleridge's albatross. And over there," he said, moving his arm to the right, "is Robinson Crusoe's parrot."

"An object I'd like to see is the wine vat in which Richard drowned Clarence. That would have been a heady exit, if you follow me."

"Too clearly," he said, eyeing me rather severely. "It's not here. But we do have Bloody Mary's heart—with the word Calis worn into its diseased substance."

"You New Englanders are much too hard on Mary. By the way, nowadays, a Bloody Mary is tomato juice with gin."

"My, my, what impudence."

"Mr. Hawthorne," I said, again abruptly changing the subject, "there are other rooms. Over there is the Nineteenth-Century American Room. Some of your friends are represented in it. Could you tell me about them, please."

"Curiosity about writers—it's an intrusion into their private lives!" he said, with some disdain.

"Sir, if I may say so, they are dead. Besides, a writer invites public interest in himself, like an actor or a politician."

Pursing his lips, Mr. Hawthorne said, "Yes, I suppose such is the case. Here, give me your arm. This marble floor is slippery. One should not fall here among these strange fancies."

Leaving the room we passed Peter Rugg once more.

"You are not perchance going to Boston?" he directed to our backs.

"Not this evening, Mr. Rugg," Mr. Hawthorne answered.

As we went down the hall together, I said, "Reading 'The Hall of Fantasy' I detected a contradiction in your sentiments. You suggest that businessmen are subject to more foolish fancies than poets, and that the latter are less likely to make fools of themselves in real life. Incidentally, is that room here?"

"Yes," he said, "down this corridor and to the right. But back to your question. I assume you are wondering what I felt about certain of my literary contemporaries.

Were they fools?" There was a slightly malicious light in his left eye. The other was almost closed.

"You phrased the question," I said. "Here they are," I added as we entered a room full of statuary and busts.

"Ah," he said, "the mortal immortals."

"In school we were told you were the New England greybeards."

"Not I," he said sharply. "Never wore a beard. Nor for that matter did Ralph Waldo nor David Thoreau."

"Excuse me," I said, adding suddenly, "Look, there's Edgar Allan Poe looking at us from out those unseeing marble eyes."

"Precisely," he said, "the man was dead. Besides," he added, irrelevantly, "he was a critic."

"Our psychologists believe he suffered from necrophilia, that Poe was obsessed by the body of someone dead."

"He was from the pit," Mr. Hawthorne said, drawing himself up.

"He was 'sick,' " I said.

"He was evil," Mr. Hawthorne said.

"He didn't lust after his sister, as . . ."

"Stop," Mr. Hawthorne said, raising his white hand. "Stop!"

"Excuse me, I was merely pointing out that certain characters in your stories . . ."

"No," he said, "no. Some matters need never be gone into in this manner."

"Why not?" I asked.

"Because," he replied with even greater severity.

"Earlier you implied that a writer ought to look at the world as it is, not add to the number of veils between us and what is."

"Perhaps I was wrong," he said, rather quietly.

"Perhaps you were right."

"Are the people in your time as quarrelsome as you?"

"Worse," I said, "really much worse."

Mr. Hawthorne sighed.

"Whittier and Bryant," I said, pointing, "were they greybeards?"

"Indeed," he answered. "Soporific, like *The Dial*."

"But you'll hear nothing against Mr. Longfellow, your Bowdoin chum?"

"No, nothing against Henry. A man apart from the world."

"Did you say he was a good poet?"

"He was my friend."

"He did write a few good poems. Our generation has decided. Over there," I said, "over there is Ralph Waldo, the great Magoo of nineteenth-century letters." In the gloom Emerson seemed to be listening.

"Sir, Emerson's conversation flowed on and on, and I rarely could see either what was resting on the surface or carried in its depths. When I could see what it was I could not isolate it from his self-concern and egotism."

"Emerson liked you and felt you showed promise—but he found nothing to praise in your work. It's all there in his Journals."

"So I've been told."

"Is it true he had ice-water in his veins? Is this what caused him to pretend he loved the universe and all pulsing creatures?"

"Perhaps, if one accounts for writers by explaining what runs counter to what they claim to believe. His vogue, I assume, is not what it once was."

"No."

"And David's? Look at him," he said, pointing. "He was a saint, like Simon Stylites, sitting atop his pole. Ralph Waldo tried to love his fellows. David did not try. He was an awkward country boy."

"Incidentally, there's a committee trying to keep Walden out of the hands of building contractors."

"The poor pond," he sighed.

"Your Henry David Thoreau, Mr. Hawthorne, did not like girls, and was revolted by the domestic situation. Is that what a saint is? Thoreau wasn't aware that sex is pervasive in human life. This is all clear if one reads *Walden* at all carefully. We had a poet, or the Irish had, who knew how pervasive it is:

Bodily decrepitude is wisdom; young
We loved each other and were ignorant.

That's William Butler Yeats."

"Your thesis is that the pull of the flesh is the negation of *Walden*. And the thesis of your Irish bard."

"Yes, *Walden* gives a possible answer only for the unsexed. Thoreau descanting on chastity in marriage sounds like an eleven year old virgin who's been reading the Sunday school *Messenger*. Neither knows what he or she is talking about. Thoreau is your Priscilla."

"In Blithedale?" he asked, his interest rising.

"Yes, the Veiled Lady. Miss Prim Pants."

"My dear sir," he said with severity.

"You really did prefer Zenobia, didn't you?"

"One part of my mind did, I'm afraid," he said, his mouth still a little grim. "One could imagine her naked in the Garden listening to ripe pears slithering through the leaves. Dear, dear Zenobia."

"In the printed version of *Blithedale* you excised a sentence. After describing the scene with Zenobia in Eve's earliest garment you wrote, 'I almost fancied myself actually beholding it.' Why didn't you keep the sentence?"

"Did I excise the sentence?" he asked, clearly evading the question.

"Sir, may I ask you to consider a generalization?"

"We have the time," he said pensively.

"Well, you wrote a great deal about love. And you recognized the pull of the flesh. You didn't pretend the flesh was spirit. Our century has seen man as a biological creature. We struggle to define ourselves as physical creatures. Man is not trying to transcend his flesh—he is trying to understand it. Clearly it is there in our writers, in Yeats, in Joyce, in Lawrence, in Faulkner, in Camus."

"These are unknown names, except for your Irish bard, Yeats, was it? Rhymes with Keats?"

"No," I said, "it rhymes with Bates."

"Later perhaps you could tell me something about your contemporaries. You have no hesitation inquiring about mine."

"Be most pleased," I said, "especially those I've met or known, or feel I know something about."

"Very well," he said. "Let us stand beneath the bust of Margaret Fuller."

Walking slowly toward the middle of the room he seemed to be a part of the shadows. His white hands caught what little light there was, and as it was caught by the marble figures.

"In your *Journals*," I said, catching up with him, "you are pretty hard on her and Ossoli."

"He, Ossoli, was an ignorant young lout, and the instrument of Margaret's lust. The latter, the lust, is understandable. Her downfall proved her a weak creature after all." He was looking up at Miss Fuller's heavy jowls and thick lips. "Her sin was pride, intellectual pride and arrogance."

"You're sure you did not dislike her because she was ugly? Your age really invited intellectual arrogance. All that talk about spirituality wasn't good for a woman. Your Hester Prynne knew what nonsense it was. Dimmesdale was an ass, if I may say so."

"Sir, you may not say so," he said severely. "Reverend Dimmesdale was a virtuous man. The fire in his chest cleansed the evil that resided in his heart."

"It isn't a topic we ought to discuss," I answered. "Let us try another. Your friend, Herman Melville. You haven't mentioned him. Was there a fire in his chest?"

"Herman," he said softly. "Perhaps Herman belonged with the generation you have described. He was a seeker, but not after the things of our Lord."

"Probably not one of us. He did not seek definitions within his physical, his biological limitations. He wanted the secret to the universe. The secret is that there is no secret. He couldn't accept that."

Mr. Hawthorne, for the first time, gazed directly at me. Finally he said in a muted, solemn voice, "So it has come to that."

Slowly he turned and moved toward the bust of Melville. I followed. The white eyes of Herman Melville looked over our heads, into the darkness.

"When Herman and I were neighbors in the Berkshires, in western Massachusetts, he was preoccupied with the mystery at the center of the universe, the play of lights in the jewel. Again in England, when we sat on the dunes talking—he was enroute to the Holy Land—it was the same. He did not let the Lord seek him out. He was too restless."

"The years of his great silence apparently were not restless. Year after year in New York he lived with the knowledge that his genius was unrecognized."

"So I've been told by earlier visitors. Herman had a touch of nobility. I always knew that."

"Do you happen to know whether he ever met Whitman? They were practically neighbors for many years."

"Whitman? The name has a familiar ring. Wasn't it Waldo who had some interest in him?"

"Yes, he recognized the great genius as the American bard."

"You seem not wholly convinced that Waldo embraced a true poet. How does his poetry strike you?"

"Like a great bundle of wet wash!"

" 'Wet wash?' The phrase seems redundant. I can't help you about Mr. Whitman."

"Say, Mr. Hawthorne," I said, as a dark figure passed the open doorway, "wasn't he standing among the wax figures in the Virtuoso's Collection. I thought . . ."

"The Wandering Jew," he answered dreamily. "Sometimes he stands among the wax figures, as you observed, trying, one supposes, to experience death."

"Why is he in here, to speak with you?"

"No, he does not speak to me, at least only rarely. Occasionally he stands in front of Herman's bust, addressing him questions about Israel Potter. Once he asked whether I thought Israel Potter might be a member of his own family."

"What did you tell him?"

"That Herman never discussed the matter with me."

As the figure went by us, toward the Melville bust, the air was suddenly very warm. The eyes were bright, as though a fire were playing through cold frosted glass.

"He can never die. That's the horror—he can never die."

"The poor man, does he ever speak with Peter Rugg?"

"Not so far as I know. Their obsessions are too unlike. Mr. Rugg wants to find his home. The Wandering Jew is in search of his brethren throughout the world."

"Mr. Hawthorne," I said, taking him by the arm, "would you agree to accompany me through the Twentieth-Century American Room. Some of the busts in there are of writers still living. That is more comforting. To me, at least," I added lamely.

Mr. Hawthorne nodded. "There is time," he said.

Together we went out into the long corridor. There was a series of small dim, greenish lights along the ceiling, and we followed them. At the far end of the corridor we entered the Twentieth-Century Room.

"Instruct me," Mr. Hawthorne said, in a tone I took to be mildly ironic.

"That is very kind of you," I replied.

Standing in the doorway we surveyed the room. There were innumerable busts, and along the walls a few full length statues.

"What a lot of scribbling has been going on of late." Mr. Hawthorne said, obviously pleased with himself.

"I'm afraid so. We have had few geniuses, no more than the nineteenth century, but we have many more writers of distinction."

"Interesting, my dear sir, and now if you will separate the sheep from the goats. The geniuses first, and the distinguished scribblers second."

"I wouldn't dare, Mr. Hawthorne. One or another of the living figures might go out of his way to get me!"

" 'To get me!' That is a curious phrase. But some of these," he said, moving his arm in a slow sweep over the room, "some of them must be dead."

"Very well," I said, "Wallace Stevens was a genius. Furthermore, he was the most gifted of American poets, none excepted."

"That's better," he said. "Show him to me."

Looking about I saw Stevens' large head with the slightly full cheeks. He was smiling. There was appropriately a full length statue of him. "There he is," I said. "Come."

Mr. Hawthorne followed me and together we stood looking up at Mr. Stevens.

"Why was he the best poet?"

"He had the greatest facility with words, with the creation of metaphor (cite Aristotle), and the enlargement of a single subject, in his case the moral and aesthetic function of the human imagination."

"Coleridge, in his footsteps?"

"Same problem, but with less transcendental voodoo,— subjem, objum. Mr. Stevens was an insurance man, a vice-president. Once, fortunately, I sat in his office with him, talking about poetry. I remember him clearly. A large, rather portly man, looking both businessman and aesthete. He liked literature and he liked money, and said so. One *made* both, he said."

"Hmm," Mr. Hawthorne said. "I find him a kindred soul—to that extent."

"On other scores too. Remember, you said that America was too raw, too untraditional for the fiction writer. It was a complaint often repeated. I take it to mean, partly, that the American writer is two men, half European, half American. Our inherited sensibilities are European, our experiences are American. This was Stevens. He bought French pictures from a dealer in Paris, he read French poets, he wrote poems about Rome, Paris, Geneva and Dutch painters. But not once in his long lifetime did he visit Europe—not even for two weeks!"

"Remarkable," Mr. Hawthorne said.

"Incidentally, Mr. Hawthorne, is it true that on your journey home from Italy you said you hoped the vessel kept going right on past America?"

"I enjoyed Italy," he answered quietly.

"Stevens," I said, "also wrote about Tennessee—'I placed a jar in Tennessee'—Oklahoma, Catawba, Florida, Hartford, and Minnesota. He was lonely and writing poetry, even poems about the gasworks and the city dump, made life more palatable, more orderly. Most American writers seem lonely."

"Mr. Stevens sounds a little on the aesthetic, sugary side."

"Yes and no," I said. "He had a kick like a mule. I asked him what he thought about a book by Ivor Winters. Winters had written unfavorably about Stevens. Stevens said, 'Absolutely nuts! Winters is off his rocker!' When I asked his opinion about a certain book on the baroque sensibility, he said, 'Wouldn't be found dead in bed with it!' When a reporter asked him questions about his private life, he told him abruptly to write the article about his poetry. When Stevens wrote about the dank smell of wet potato sacks, one knew he had smelled them. He was an aesthete, yes, but he knew what the underside of a rock looked like."

"So far, so good," Mr. Hawthorne said. "I take it he was a New Englander. Hartford, you said, not far from where Herman and I . . ."

"No, sir, he was a Pennsylvania Dutchman. Ancestors were religious refugees from Holland."

"Same piece of cloth," Mr. Hawthorne said, walking on.

"If you insist," I said.

"Who is this man, with the pockmarked face?" Mr. Hawthorne asked.

Looking up, I saw it was Sinclair Lewis. The sculptor had done him almost to the waist, and had Lewis' thumb and index finger pulling on the lobe of his ear, a characteristic gesture.

"He's our first Nobel Prize winner. Given to an outstanding figure in world literature."

"Do they make posthumous awards?" Mr. Hawthorne asked, as though it were an impersonal question.

"No, sir."

"What about your Lewis? Was he a descendant of Lewis of the Lewis and Clark expedition?"

"Not that I know of. This Lewis grew up in Minnesota. One of his wives, Dorothy Thompson, said he was convinced no one loved him. If I may intrude myself, she gave the commencement address to my graduating class."

"Harvard?" he asked automatically.

"No, sir, nor Yale. She was a very attractive woman. She and Lewis had a son, an actor. I saw the young man in *Look Back in Anger*, an English play."

"And Lewis himself, I assume you are getting ready to say you talked with him."

"Almost! Joseph Warren Beach, a writer and friend of mine, had a party for Sinclair Lewis and invited a number of young writers to meet him. If I remember correctly among the group were Eric Bentley, a drama critic, Bob Hivnor, a playwright, and Saul Bellow, a novelist. The great man sat on a divan in the corner of the living room and the aspirants gathered round him. He had skin cancer and his face was scarlet. Lewis turned the palms of his hands toward us and said, 'Don't anyone tell me his name. I wouldn't remember.' Then he discoursed; about what I can't recall. If he couldn't remember my name, I can't remember what he talked about. Poor Lewis didn't like himself. That's why no one could love him. He became a funny man. His talent was for mimicking and caricaturing. He had no themes, not even those that might grow out of self-hatred."

"My dear sir, don't you wonder about the assurance and the glibness of your analysis of the man's character?"

"He who hesitates is lost," I said.

"Let us," Mr. Hawthorne said, "sit there on that marble bench and ponder ponderable questions." This time his tone was clearly ironic.

He led me toward the marble bench in a dark recess of the room, and we sat down. I could feel the chill emanating from him, and the bench itself was cold.

"Ponderable questions?" I asked.

"Have you ever met a man of genius?"

"You, sir," I replied quickly.

Mr. Hawthorne sighed and lifted his hand to interrupt any further flattery.

"Does the question of genius interest you?"

"Not very much. A related question interests me, though. What happens to the sons of great men: Coleridge's son, Shelley's, Browning's, Meredith's."

"How fortunate," Mr. Hawthorne mused, "how fortunate Shakespeare left no son?"

"Exactly."

"You seem to speak from experience."

"Very little, but I do wish someone would write a book entitled Sons and Brothers of Famous Men. My one experience with the matter was with Klaus Mann. We were together at an Army base, Camp Crowder, Missouri. Klaus was terribly in awe of his father, or his father's reputation. He wanted to emulate his father, but, alas, he lacked talent, and that was everything. I can remember his chain smoking cigarettes. There was a little ring of yellow nicotine on the skin above and below his lips, as though a painter had put a daub of yellow there. He'd talk endlessly and engagingly about the writers he had known. After a while he was sent to Italy and I went to New Guinea, and shortly we lost track of each other. After the war I did write to him. The day after I mailed it there was an article in the paper saying he had tried to kill himself. A short time later, in Europe, he died of a heart attack."

"The poor young man," Mr. Hawthorne said, "he died from knowing his pen would never be enchanted. One can understand his frustration."

"But he should not have despaired. Despair is the unforgivable sin, is it not?"

"Your tone, sir! Has irreverence become a great virtue?"

"I'm afraid it has, Mr. Hawthorne."

"A few minutes ago you said Wallace Stevens, the Connecticut poet, was the most gifted poet, but only in your opinion. Who is commonly held to be the greatest figure?"

"T. S. Eliot, poet, critic, playwright."

"New England?"

"In his bones. Actually born in St. Louis, of a race of divines, school teachers, and businessmen. You'd recognize his kind."

"The New England chill?"

"Yes, sir. The kind who can sit and drink innumerable cocktails without a flutter of an eyelid or a flush rising along the jawline."

"Cocktails?" Mr. Hawthorne asked, raising one eyebrow.

"Gin and dry vermouth, chilled, plus an olive or thin curl of lemon. Those who have tried to warm old Chocorua with cocktails have a hard time. Be lucky to raise a smile on his thin lips."

"Chocorua was lovely in the spring time. After the snows. New England after the snows melted touched the heart. Is your poet an admirer of the mountain?"

"I don't know. Stevens was. Henry James too. As poet, Eliot has a fine ear, possibly the best of his generation. As a subject, unfortunately, he had the spiritual superiority of himself and his kind. That tiresome New England preoccupation with one's own journey to perfection, knowing all along that only a very few make the journey—and one knows *who they are*. In short, he's a spiritual snob."

"Yes," Mr. Hawthorne said, rather sadly, "either we were preoccupied with depravity, seeing it in our own hearts and in the hearts of others, or seeing only that we were free from it, nobly dedicated to the work of the Lord."

"Mentioning the pride of writers reminds me that Wallace Stevens once wrote me that he *had not been* influenced by T. S. Eliot. A piece over his name in *The Harvard Advocate* says otherwise, but he said it had been written for him. I guess he wanted the denial in the record."

"We can put it in the Museum's archives, if you wish," Mr. Hawthorne said.

"Thank you," I said. "Incidentally, Stevens did not have the chill. Robert Lowell, also New England, suffers from it. His warmest hopes glow inside ice, giving them a pale-bluish cast."

"And pride? He suffers from that?"

"Self-concern maybe, but not arrogance. Breaking a luncheon date—he broke one with me—can be anguish for him. It is, I suppose, inordinate self-concern to be

anguished over that. This was when he was younger,
about thirty-one or thirty-two, a boyish man trying very
hard to break through an icy morality into the sunshine."

"Did he succeed in breaking through?"

"I think not. Although others may read his work differently."

"Is secular pride to be preferred?"

"Many writers suffer from it, if suffer is the appropriate
word. Sometimes I think it is a part of the condition of
being a writer. Pride begets ambition, the will to survive
through one's own words beyond three score and ten.
Pride takes so many forms."

Mr. Hawthorne sat up straighter, throwing his shoul-
ders back. "Emerson was a prideful man. Seeing one's self
as the world's eyeball is prideful. An eyeball can be in-
flamed, swollen, covered by a film of dust. It is not solely
the organ of moral vision. There were those nights in the
forest with the Black Man. Not all it looks upon is lovely.
It is pride to believe otherwise. The eyeball should look
inward too—and what it sees there is not always lovely."

"At random almost, I can think of exhibitions of pride
that seem rather charming. Each instance involves a poet."

"Yes?" Mr. Hawthorne asked, politely but obviously
showing that he had been interrupted.

"First, Karl Shapiro. During World War II we were in
New Guinea together."

"Was your war worse than the Civil War?"

"No, I'd guess not. It wasn't as bloody and we weren't
killing each other. There was our little business of the
atomic bomb. We can't quite get it off our conscience.
And there was the wholesale murder of the Jews. That
disturbs us—it says we are still capable of mass slaughter.
Because of absurd abstractions about other human beings
we can kill them, eagerly. In your day, or a little earlier,
Catholics and Protestants killed each other with equal
righteousness. We've changed that—but righteous murder
is still in our genes. Let me not digress," I said, apologeti-
cally.

"Mr. Shapiro," Mr. Hawthorne said helpfully, "a poet
you knew in the war?"

"Yes, sir. He grew up in Baltimore. In college in the 1930's, during the Great Depression. Was drafted early and was among the first boatload of Americans, on the *Queen Mary*, to reach Australia. In Boston, early in the war, I read his *Person, Place and Thing*. Immediately I saw he was speaking for my generation. The tone, the cadence, the point-of-view—he had caught all of it. By accident in New Guinea, I discovered we were in neighboring outfits. We used to get together and talk about writing. Once, I recall, we were walking down a mountain road, the Owen Stanley Mountains, and I told him about my discovery of his book in a Boston bookstore and my reaction to it. He was delighted and did almost a little dance, despite the wet road and his heavy Army boots. His smile was pure joy, and he told me with a wonderful boyish confidence, hands in his pockets, how he had tried unsuccessfully to get Jay Laughlin, of New Directions, to recognize how damn good his poems were, and to bring out a book. He didn't pretend he had a modest opinion of his work. His bragging was sincere, justified, and a pleasure to listen to. It was like a small boy, allowed to play with older boys, and first time up at bat he hits a home run. As he runs the bases he says to himself, 'I always knew I could clobber it over the fence!' Karl knew he could hit home runs."

"Baseball?" Hawthorne asked. "Sounds like cricket."

"They started playing it over in Cooperstown, New York, in the 1830's. Mark Harris writes novels about baseball."

"Yes, now I remember," he said. "I predicted it would not last."

"It is still with us. One, two, three strikes & you're out at the old ball game!"

"Pride of accomplishment," Mr. Hawthorne said. "Whenever a story came out right I felt that kind of joy."

"And there is pride in one's reputation. Allen Tate, another of our poets, illustrates that, I think. By the way, Mr. Tate is said to look like Edgar Poe. Same large head, and small delicate body."

"I trust he has more talent than the man from Baltimore."

"Mr. Hawthorne, you are unfair to Poe. He was a genius even though a very sick and troubled one."

"You were mentioning Mr. Tate. A New Englander?"

"No, a Southerner."

"Ah, like Poe. I suppose one's residence has little to do with one's talent, although I always mistrusted the flowered rhetoric of the gentlemen south of Washington. Black flowers in the buttonhole."

"Mr. Tate would give you an argument about equating rhetoric and falsity. Consider Mr. Emerson."

"Emerson," he said, "his rhetoric? Precisely."

"We're off the point, Mr. Hawthorne, Tate is often represented in anthologies by 'Ode to the Confederate Dead,' rather than other poems. This annoys him. What do you make of it?"

"Understandable," Mr. Hawthorne said. "We write to say no to death. A single poem or two can live on and on and on. He may feel the anthologists aren't doing right by him."

Hawthorne peered down the dark corridor beyond the room.

"You'd recognize his subject. The spider's web on the tombstone, the pull of the grave, and having the right legend, the well turned phrase, on the thin ulcerated slab.

"Like Poe?"

"Yes. And rather like you also, sir."

"Your third poet," he asked, pretending not to have heard.

"Yes," I said, "a woman, Miss Marianne Moore. A fine poet within a limited range. No intending any unkindness to Miss Moore, hers is the poetry of an exceedingly refined and sensitive old maid. My experience was this. Reviewing an arty magazine in which she had published some notes from one of her journals I complimented the editor on publishing her exquisitely phrased insights. A year later, in a business letter she handled for the defunct *Dial*, she . . ."

"You mean Ralph Waldo's *Dial* was . . ." Mr. Hawthorne said brightening.

"No, sir, same name, but quite a different magazine. Miss Moore's *Dial* published 'The Waste Land.' "

" 'The Waste Land?' That's a curious title. The land unused, barren, unpeopled, untilled—what is the intention?" he asked, gazing at me from under the heavy brows.

"Barren, the land from which spiritual joy, religious belief, and nobility have disappeared. The idea is taken from the grail legends, about the unfruitful earth, and so on."

" 'The Waste Land,' " he said, "a rather good title. A poem contemporary with you. By whom?"

"Published some years ago. By T. S. Eliot."

"The man from St. Louis."

"Yes, but to get back to Miss Moore. Years later, about twelve years I believe, I had occasion to phone Miss Moore. She was then an elderly woman and had suffered a serious stroke. Upon learning who I was she immediately recalled the review and said, 'Mr. O'Connor, it was kind and generous of you to mention my journal so favorably.' I had felt uneasy about disturbing her, and she immediately put me at my ease. As they said in your day, Mr. Hawthorne, she was a gracious lady."

"But pride, you imply it must have been there. I agree. Pride in her own work, and pride enough to remember the review twelve or thirteen years earlier. Pride, self-respect, dignity . . ." he said, gesturing with his right hand.

"And generosity. That leavens the self-concern and allows others with lesser talent or no talent at all to admire freely, open-heartedly, willingly. Graciousness is a great gift."

"Graciousness can also be a weapon. And piety too. The moral superiority of an outwardly pious person! Much evil is done in the name of piety. It is a promising subject for the writer. You might consider it," he said, looking past me.

"I had taken it for granted that it has been rather well treated by you, Mr. Hawthorne."

"Thank you," he said.

"We have a writer who has handled it well too. William Faulkner. He's somewhat indebted to you. Called his poems *The Marble Faun*, and he's fond of referring to the *iron* New England dark, a term you use occasionally in *The Scarlet Letter*."

"He's welcome to both," Mr. Hawthorne said. "I had finished with them."

"Pride, we were discussing pride. Do you believe that pride was a motivating force in Thoreau's electing to live at Walden?"

"One's own achievement is inevitably seen in an aura of satisfaction. David, as you say, did not want to bathe in a woman's love or approval. Simon Stylites sat at the top of a pole, watching ordinary mortals go about their sweaty quotidian tasks, adding pence to pence. David withdrew, and watched Nature. He preferred Nature to people. He succeeded in supporting himself, at least for a time, and that must have given him satisfaction. Otherwise he would not have memorialized it in a book. But David did not have a very firm hold on living. He relinquished it at his convenience."

"The memorial, that's what we want, isn't it? We want to justify our conduct. Man must justify—and the memorial, *Walden*, was his proof that he was a just man."

"I dare say," Mr. Hawthorne replied, "David was a just man."

"We have a gifted writer, Lionel Trilling, whose way of memorializing himself interests me."

"Trilling? An odd name."

"Keats must have once sounded odd too."

"And your Mr. Yeats, rhyming with Keats."

"No," I said, "Yeats, rhymes with Bates."

"No matter," Mr. Hawthorne said.

"Mr. Trilling, a Columbia University professor, and incidentally my advisor, wrote a fine book of criticism."

"You needed advice?" Mr. Hawthorne asked, raising his left eyebrow.

"A technical term. He was my advisor on the Ph.D."

"The P.H.D., what is that?" he asked, his interest rising.

"Nothing of importance," I said. "Lionel Trilling wrote

The Liberal Imagination, a collection of literary essays. One of the most original books in American literary criticism. Then a moderately good novel, *The Middle of the Journey,* plus several excellent short stories."

"Then he ceased writing?"

"No, he continued to write criticism, but he didn't change, didn't go on to a middle period, or a later period. He remained where he was."

"You disapprove?"

"Don't you! A change, even for the worse, would have been better."

"He has his place in the Museum?" he asked, looking out at the marble busts.

"Yes, there's a bust of him over there," I said, pointing, "next to Robert Penn Warren. In my opinion Trilling and Warren are our two best, the most original and discerning literary critics."

"I fail to see what you are quarreling with," Mr. Hawthorne said. "Mr. Trilling has made his memorial. He is your just man."

"A man should not let himself become a national monument. That's for posterity to do, if it wishes. For example, a few years ago, Mr. Trilling gave a talk on Robert Frost, a New England poet."

"New England continues to dominate the poetic scene, to be the home of the Muse?" he asked.

"If you like," I said. "The South has done pretty well too. What he said about Frost's poetry was true, but it upset some people. People like J. Donald Adams, who pore treacle over the printed page, and those priss pants types who are afraid to look at the slimy amoral grubs crawling around inside their own guts. Some of the attacks on Mr. Trilling were personal, malicious, and small-minded. Most writers, so attacked, would have been angry and struck back. Trilling chose to view it all in an Olympian way as a cultural episode, a chapter in our cultural history. If Trilling had been able to swat these people in the way they deserved to be swatted, he wouldn't look and sound like a national monument. And he might write another *Liberal Imagination* or more short stories."

"You apparently feel there is not much to be said for the successful writer. Once successful, he begins the long walk on the arm of Pride, down the garden path." He paused, then added, "There might have been a story there, my sort. But that is all past," he said, sighing.

"On the other hand, there is much to be said for success. For one thing, it makes magnanimity easier. Let me illustrate. I said Mr. Trilling was my advisor for the Ph.D., the doctor of philosophy, in English and Comparative Literature. After studying many writers, like yourself, Emerson and Thoreau, Pope and Johnson, candidates take an oral examination, then write a thesis."

"Curious," he said, "writing theses on poets and novelists. Our scholarly ancestors disputed philosophical principles."

"Nowadays one can get a Ph.D. in almost anything, even bird watching," I said. "On my final oral, on the thesis, there were a number of eminent scholars and writers. They were Miss Marjorie Nicolson, Joseph Wood Krutch, Justin O'Brien, Irwin Edman, William York Tindall, Jacques Barzun, Trilling, Dumas Malone, the Jefferson scholar and editor of *The Dictionary of American Biography*, and several others. They were all people whose books were prominently reviewed, and whose reputations had long been made. Early in the examination I sensed that they were not intent on badgering me. They were content to let me exist at my own level of competence. No examiner felt obliged, for the sake of his reputation, to belittle what I had done. Therefore the examination was free from pedantry, and the questions tended to be both simple and searching. Successful writers, the good ones, are rarely pretentious. A few are.

"Speaking of magnanimity, in my thesis I had criticized some remarks Mr. Krutch had written in an early work, *The Modern Temper*, not dreaming he would be on my committee. But he was very kind. His questions pressed on the rightness or wrongness of what each of us had said—there was no malice."

"I dare say," Mr. Hawthorne said, lifting his right hand to stifle a yawn.

"Mr. Hawthorne," I said, "if I may change the subject, do you feel the American writer can turn his back on Europe?"

"He shouldn't consider Europe one way or another—he should consider the meaning of his subject. Europe will take care of itself. In my day we had the memory of the Puritans—assuredly a European heritage, yet what was more American than clutching the Bible, living in the wilderness, and dreaming of the Black Man and his dark rites in the forest? One is, willy nilly, what one is, and assertions won't change matters."

"Nowadays, you know, we say Hawthorne and others wrote romances, not novels. Americans write romances, the English social novels. You sensed something of the sort yourself. In your preface to . . ."

"Indeed," he answered, "but the European elements were not expunged from the story, nor I daresay the English elements from my style."

"In our time we have had quite a to-do about American writing being American, not European or English. William Carlos Williams, a physician in Rutherford, New Jersey, is such an advocate. He has written a deliberately mindless poetry, some of it very striking and memorable. He wants the American writer to embrace the American Psyche and hang on for dear life."

"American Psyche? If one has to hang on for dear life, then Psyche is indeed mindless and has lost her charm, poor girl," Mr. Hawthorne said, clearly pleased with himself.

"Dr. Williams," I said, trying to defend him, "is a charming, kind, and well-disposed man. I talked with him one day in his living room. He had suffered several strokes, but was still buoyant and intensely interested in writing. I asked him why he was so concerned about isolating the American element.

" 'Well,' he said, his eyes shooting dark flames through his rimless glasses, 'my father was English, a detached, phlegmatic man. My mother was Jewish and Spanish. The Orient and Spain fought in her blood. A little firecat she was. There is also a Danish strand.' Looking up, over his sharp long nose, he said in his quick yet mild voice, 'Wouldn't you be interested in knowing *who* you were?' "

"He's the child of his parents," Mr. Hawthorne said. "He can't escape them, though he may try. Did he," Mr. Hawthorne added, "did he exhibit the writer's vice-or-virtue, pride?"

"Curious that you ask," I answered. "Of all the writers I've met, he is the most unassuming, the least aggressive about his own reputation. As an example of his generosity, take his friendship with the poet Ezra Pound."

"Pound? An English poet?" Mr. Hawthorne asked.

"American. He propagandized over an enemy radio station during the last war. Radio is a little gadget we invented after your time. Pound was indicted for treason, but never tried. After thirteen or fourteen years in a mental ward, he was let go. Williams didn't agree with Pound, but he remained friendly with him. Pound said some pretty vicious as well as some true things, both in his broadcasts and in his poetry."

"A poet traitor! Sounds very promising."

"I called Pound a poet traitor in reviewing a book of his—and he had his lawyer write to the editors that they were inviting a libel suit!"

"Judgments against me can no longer be collected," Mr. Hawthorne said sadly, and I had a sense, perhaps imagined, that his body exuded an invisible cloud of cold. "What sort of man was this poet, Pound?"

"I remarked to Williams that he was guilty of letting his ego turn monstrous.

" 'No,' Dr. Williams said, 'Pound is a child. He's never been responsible for his opinions.' That was a generous view, considering that the F.B.I.—the Federal Bureau of Investigation—was suspicious of his friendship with Pound. Pound used to refer to Dr. Williams in his broadcasts."

"Charming figure," Mr. Hawthorne said.

"Yes," I said, "You could have cast him in *The Marble Faun*. He's the kind who drinks wine out of skulls."

Mr. Hawthorne was looking past me down the long dark corridor again, and seemed not to have heard. Leaning forward, he pressed his hands against the marble bench and stood up. I got up too.

"Over there," he said, "are several busts which seem to attract few visitors. I see them standing there when I come down this corridor."

"You are here every day in the Museum!" I said, "I thought . . ."

"Of course, back there in the room with Waldo and David and Herman. At night I sometimes emanate from the marble form and wander the corridors or sit, as we have been doing. Usually the janitor has locked the outside doors and no one comes in. Tonight you slipped in before he locked up."

"Amazing," I said. "To whom do you talk?"

"Not to any of these writers," he said, including them all in a circular swing of his arm. "They stay there all night. Occasionally Peter Rugg follows me about, asking for news from Boston. And sometimes his daughter comes in, harried and upset after wandering the streets. It is difficult to understand what she says. If there are storms or lightning she comes and holds my hand. The Wandering Jew walks about, peering up at these faces, studying them to see which ones might be his kin."

"Why," I asked, "is it that you alone walk about at night?"

"Why?" he asked incredulously. "Isn't it evident?"

"You were the only one who truly believed in the Museum?"

"Of course," he answered.

"Yes," I said, politely. "Mr. Hawthorne, you wanted to look at these figures over there."

He led the way.

"This man here," I said, looking up, "is Stephen Leacock, a Canadian economist and humorist. Heard him when I was an undergraduate, but I can't remember what he said."

"Humorists are not very funny to later generations. Humor that is incidental is likely to last. We have always been strange creatures, quite funny enough without making a profession of it."

"There's a smile on Mr. Leacock's face."

"I wonder why," Mr. Hawthorne said. "And this man?"

"Christopher Morley. I also heard him. At Columbia. The occasion was the Hardy Centennial. He spent his fifty minutes kidding the scholarly procedures of another speaker. It was amusing, but again I can't remember what he said. His books were popular, especially *Kitty Foyle* and *Parnassus on Wheels*, and a column he wrote called 'Bowling Green,' in the *Saturday Review*. He wrote some light verse too. He was a nice man. One felt that. He was friendly with William Rose Benét, a colleague on the *Saturday Review*. He also was a nice man, very generous with young people trying out their typewriters."

"The grim, somber types, the sober sides, are more likely to be read."

"Why?"

"Because of human clay. You dress it up, let it dance and sing, but . . ."

"Merry Mount! You felt old Endicott had the truth of things on his side, didn't you? You liked Morton and his crew, but they were living in a mirage. My age tries not to believe you."

"Your contemporaries are no longer made of clay?" he asked.

"Plastic," I said.

"Who is this man?" he asked, ignoring my reply.

"Louis Untermeyer, an anthologist. Very influential for a time. Rather antimodernist. Not that the modernists are beyond criticism!"

"You heard him too, I suppose."

"Yes, sir, he read a long poem of his own on eating. I was an undergraduate. He walked briskly back and forth across the stage gesturing. I can remember the gestures but not the words."

"Your education seems not to have helped your memory," he said.

"The biographies say you didn't exert yourself greatly at Bowdoin, either," I replied.

"True," he said, "I was slow to mature."

"Farther down here," I said, changing the subject, "is a group of women writers. In your day you complained of female scribblers."

"An honest writer couldn't find an audience," he said bitterly. "Those charlatans filled their pages with pious fustian, and sold their books!"

"They are not in the Museum. And you are."

"A few are still in the basement," he said, grudgingly. "One of these days they'll be taken out to the ash heap!" he added with relish.

"Who lasts in the Museum, year after year after year?"

"Those who wrote about anguish as opposed to happiness; they are most likely to remain."

"Mr. Ransom, that's a bust of him there, on the edge of the Southern group. He said, 'I shake, but not as a leaf.' He's written a few very good poems, about aging, and the bitterness that fills the heart, causing us to do foolish things. Then its passing. One poem, 'Parting Without a Sequel,' is about a young girl sending a venomous letter, which she knows she ought not to send, to her lover:

> *Away went the messenger's bicycle,*
> *His serpent tracks went up the hill forever,*
> *And all the time she stood there hot as fever*
> *And cold as any icicle.*

I've heard him read his poems, in a modest, detached, ironic voice. He took part in a literary movement, contributed to it, but remained free. Some of his associates in the so-called modernist movements have made excessive claims. Not Mr. Ransom. That, I think, is why he influenced so many people, unlike each other—Donald Davidson, Allen Tate, Robert Penn Warren, Randall Jarrell, Leonard Unger, and Robert Lowell. They were all students of his. A sweet tempered man."

"Yes, but these women scribblers of yours! Who is this?" he asked, looking up at Caroline Gordon.

"Caroline Gordon, for many years the wife of Allen Tate. She wrote a few excellent short stories and at least one fine novel. Her best writing is about her father, his

little war with time and the passing generations. Once, at
her home in Princeton, in a backyard to be precise, I
watched her holding her small granddaughter on her lap,
and thought how like her fiction it was. One day, when
the granddaughter is old, she may remember being held
on Caroline's lap. It would be like a handclasp or a kiss
being passed along from generation to generation."

"Yes," Mr. Hawthorne agreed.

"Once," I added, "sitting with Joseph Warren Beach
in his dark living room I listened with a kind of awe as
he told how as a young man at Harvard he had heard
William James lecture. Moreover he had sat near Henry
James, and seen the pride in his expression as the audience
clapped their approval of his older brother."

"We are very nostalgic this evening."

"It isn't every day that I can talk with Nathaniel Hawthorne," I said. "It makes the ghosts walk."

"And this woman?" he asked, looking up. "She's very
handsome."

"Katherine Anne Porter. She is, as you say, a very handsome woman. I have no explicit reason to believe it so,
but I have wondered whether her general inability to fin-
ish manuscripts is related to her beauty. She worked on
one novel for more than twenty years and every several
years a publisher—there have been a couple in the process—announced it for the following spring. Finally it was
published. Her beauty could be her flaw. That's a Hawthorne sort of theme, don't you think?"

"A variant on that of 'The Birth Mark,' I dare say.
What sort of dilatoriness does she suffer from, the beautiful lady scribbler?"

"She's more than a scribbler. There are two fine novel-
las, and a number of first-rate short stories. She's concerned with the dream world, with the worlds we imagine the 'real' world to be, with the romantic aura in
which we see our loved ones and ourselves, with the nobility of motive we assign to those whose admiration we
want. She's concerned with the difference between the
way we dream it, and the way it was, and with our need
to redream the way it was. There is an unbelieving look

in the eyes of her heroines, and the lips are petulant. There is unbelief in Miss Porter's eyes too, and the lips are petulant. Neither the beauty nor the talent has proved wholly satisfactory."

"Her dilatoriness?" Mr. Hawthorne asked, still looking at her.

"In 1953–54," I said, sighing, "my family and I were in Liège. I was a Fullbright lecturer at the University. It was decided to get an eminent writer, if possible, for the following year. I undertook to find out if Miss Porter was available, and to gather letters of recommendation. She was available. Letters of recommendation, when they came at all, were curiously restrained, but none openly said she wouldn't do a satisfactory job. Allen Tate, a friend of hers, was in Rome but he declined to answer the inquiry. Members of the writing community, I assume, are not required to give evidence against each other. Anyway, she arrived in Liège, gave the opening public lecture, and thereafter declined the gambit. The stolid, hard-working Liègeois couldn't figure out what sort of fine plumaged bird had settled into the nest. Caroline Gordon, an old friend of Miss Porter, later said in her slow drawl, 'Oh, Katherine Anne, she can't be depended on to meet a fixed obligation. What you have to do is drop in at a quarter to three and say, *Katherine Anne, let's you and I walk over to that little old class!* Then she might put on her hat and gloves and go with you. She can't meet a schedule. Not Katherine Anne!' "

"Very beautiful," Mr. Hawthorne said, looking up at Miss Porter. "In my time, lady scribblers were never beautiful."

"'This next figure is Eudora Welty, a Mississippi writer. She participated in an American Civilization Program at Cambridge in 1954, in which I had a small part. A tall woman, nice, shy, very ladylike. She'd have no trouble fitting into a small town social life, I think."

"Our English cousins are studying American culture, blimey!" Mr. Hawthorne said.

"Examining it, let us say. They are being forced to take a close look at the Yanks. They don't have much choice in the matter really: It's either us or the Russians. But we were talking about Miss Welty. She has a fine comic sense, that works best on Mississippi subjects. Hers is a comedy of pathos and the grotesque. She is good at evoking a grotesque dream world. A night blooming cereus and a wrung chicken's neck. Sometimes the humor is too cute and chichi. At her best, she is an original and gifted writer."

"She spoke at Cambridge?"

"Yes, to young English dons and the like. She was effective, but I was struck, as I have been sometimes in listening to other writers, at the difference between the analytical-critical mind and the imaginative-aesthetic mind. The former moves from analysis to theory, the latter creates, using the elements peculiar to his or her personal vision. Miss Welty does not have a theoretical mind. She has a fine sensibility, a quick humor, deep sympathy and an instinctive feeling for certain human types, and a sense for literary effects. The former type tends to teach, or to write criticism, the latter to write fiction or poetry. Occasionally a fiction writer, a Conrad or a James, has both faculties and produces a literature of a very high order. However, I can think of at least one very fine fiction writer who seems to have little gift for theory, except where it is embodied in drama or action. So perhaps my theory is slightly suspect."

"I always believed that Herman strained too hard after theory. Emerson did not strain hard enough. So writers in the South," he added, "have become more active than their Yankee cousins?"

"Well, in a sense. For a time, there was a lot of activity in the midwest, and there still is. But our writers tend not to congregate—they work alone. Many of the 'Southern writers' live in the North. The South is their subject."

"Is Boston still the literary capital, the publishing center? Seems I recall an earlier visitor, another who came in because the janitor failed to latch the door, saying publishers have moved to New York. Of course some were there in our time."

"Yes, New York is the center for publishing. And there are many writers there. Personally I feel it is a good enough place for critics to live and work. But it overwhelms. John Jay Chapman said 'New York is not a culture—it is a railroad station.' New York is for the business that attends upon writing, publishing and reviews. Not for writing fiction or poetry, and perhaps not for drama either, except for the rewriting."

"You don't live there, I see," Mr. Hawthorne said.

"No, sir. I remember, years ago, meeting Edmund Wilson and Alfred Kazin at a small party given by Babette Deutsch, the poet, and her husband, a translator of Russian literature. Karl Shapiro took me. We were both looking at the literary white lights. Wilson had sharp, piercing eyes, and I remember being surprised that his remarks were polite chit-chat. Much of it about other writers. Somehow I had expected quotable sentences. Kazin, who later evolved a fine, spare style of writing, reminded me of young New York intellectuals I had known at Columbia. Their remarks had a one-two effect, a light jab and a hard right."

Mr. Hawthorne was looking at me curiously.

"If you don't drop, you are supposed to respond in kind, one-two, a light jab and a hard right."

"A sport metaphor?" Mr. Hawthorne asked.

"Boxing," I answered. "I wasn't afraid of the big city. But I remember that Karl kept getting in and out of cabs. He was afraid of getting lost if he walked."

"That reminds me of Peter Rugg," Mr. Hawthorne replied. "Perhaps we should see what state of mind he is in. Poor lost, lonely man."

"I trust I have not tired you," I said.

"No, no, we can talk some more, as we look for our friend Mr. Rugg."

He did not move, however, and I remained standing near him.

"Another writer who rather disappointed me was Wright Morris. In his stories he's a hard-headed type, undreamy, and satiric. When I met him he talked in a pious way about influences on his work. I suppose when a writer meets an admirer he feels under the necessity to act piously."

"Indeed," Mr. Hawthorne said, "one is not skeptical before one's admirers."

"Some critic or other has said that characters in American fiction," I said, switching the subject again, "are the loneliest in all literature. Your characters in *The Scarlet Letter* are pretty lonely. The ocean at their backs, and the forest in front of them. Living in their little tract of land, with that jail and scaffold, they were isolated from each other. The community isolated Hester, Dimmesdale isolated himself, and so did Chillingworth. And little Pearl is isolated because no one will tell her the truth. The community doesn't accept her, and her father does not acknowledge her. Isolation is a theme that runs through much of American writing. We espouse the democratic order, the great brotherhood of men, and yet we remain lonely. Herman Melville's characters are lonely. Lots of other writers treat loneliness too. Why?"

"Perhaps Peter Rugg can tell us," Mr. Hawthorne said, rather sadly.

"No, he is our symbol, the man who has lost everything, who can't find the way back."

"Where is home?" Mr. Hawthorne said, almost plaintively.

"We have a poet, Theodore Roethke, who thinks home is in the grave. His human beings have crawled through the loam and deep into the earth, like that 'old mole,' the ghost of Hamlet's father. Such a lonely ghost! This is from 'The Lost Son':

> At Woodlawn I heard the dead cry:
> I was lulled by the slamming of iron,
> A slow drip over stones,
> Toads brooding in wells.
> All the leaves stuck out their tongues;
> I shook the softening chalk of my bones,
> Saying, snail, glister me forward,
> Bird, soft-sigh me home
> Worm, be with me.
> This is my hard time.

Mr. Hawthorne's eyes were closed.

"Woodlawn's a cemetery," I said.

"It is impious," he said quietly, his eyes still closed.

"Not at all, it is true. Truer than those mad revels your pious, righteous types imagined in the forest with Goodman Brown. Or the sky lighting up with a huge A. Dishonesty about what the human being is creates the Black Man stuff in the forest. Roethke knows what anguish is. No one would succeed in pulling a Puritan Midsummer Night's Dream on him. He's heard the mire in his chalky blood murmur and hum in his ears, heard it seep into the rocky ground. He knows that the salty spirit sweats."

"Who is he, this Mr. Roethke?" Mr. Hawthorne asked, opening his eyes but looking past me.

"Looks like a retired wrestler. Huge chest, large head, balding, with hurt sad eyes. Occasionally when his mind is more tightly hemmed than he can stand, he commits himself to close medical and psychiatric care. He's a great bear, with a sensitive little kitten mewing in his chest. Sometimes the bear growls, sometimes the kitten mews. Any poet worth a damn is impious in your sense. He's worth a damn."

"The generations pass along a handclasp, a kiss. The Southern writer, Miss Gordon, meant that to you. Yes," he said, "our children write memoirs, keeping our memories green. They are treasuring the human spirit. That's why we write, to treasure the human spirit."

"Recently I met Mrs. Sherwood Anderson. The name won't mean anything to you. Sherwood Anderson was a lyric fiction writer, one who treasured human freedom, and wrote about lonely people. He's dead. His wife, a nice woman, goes to meetings of various sorts, schools and colleges, and talks about her husband's works. A kind of talking memorial."

Turning, Mr. Hawthorne walked slowly through the room, passing the marble busts.

"Here," I said, "is a row of poets. Randall Jarrell," I explained, "an epigrammatic wit. Shaking his hand is like holding cold aluminum, slightly warmed by the contact. This is John Berryman. He suffers from nerves and in-

somnia. Oh, he wrote a long poem about Anne Bradstreet
—loneliness pervades that too. You mention her husband
Bradstreet as one of the primitive statesmen in the Boston
of *The Scarlet Letter.* She'd have made a good character
for the novel. This man with the neat mustache is R. P.
Blackmur," I said as we moved on. "His work, poetry and
criticism, is half brilliance, half obfuscation. He's a professor at Princeton, although he never attended college.
Maybe that explains the half that is obfuscation. This
gentleman with the hooked nose is Lee Anderson. His
subject is the likelihood of our absolute destruction by the
bomb. He speculates about whether man's genius for language may tilt the chances in his favor . . ."

Mr. Hawthorne stopped. "Do you believe that?"

"In what else can we believe?" I asked. "Language is a
poor net in which to catch the bomb before it hits the
ground—but what other net is there?"

Mr. Hawthorne did not answer.

"Over in that corner," I said, pointing to the right, "are
a lot of academic writers, at least fifty. We don't have
men of letters nowadays, except for Malcolm Cowley and
Edmund Wilson. Most people interested in writing teach
in order to support themselves. The big question is
whether the campus helps or hinders their writing careers.
There's Leon Edel, a critic and biographer. He knew
Edith Wharton, who knew Henry James, who knew Robert Browning, who . . ."

"I see what you are implying. The museum again. You
are somewhat obsessed by the notion."

"You live here," I answered.

"By choice, yes, and by chance too."

"There's James Farrell, the novelist. He teaches at Columbia. His stories are about real people."

"That's the fundamental error for a novelist to make,"
Mr. Hawthorne said. "It's carrying the albatross around
your neck. The intention is that it fly."

"There's Mark Schorer," I said. "He's a good scholar
and critic, and fiction writer. In your day he'd probably
have devoted himself to fiction. The university may have
or may not have been good for him. I don't know."

"And who is this, with his chin lifted high?"

"Saul Bellow. He's been widely acclaimed. His subject is the free Free Hero. Not a subject for the long haul, I believe."

"Byron and Shelley did well enough with it."

"As object lessons, or how?"

"Let's not pursue the matter," he said, a little sharply I felt.

We were now in the corridor, walking back toward the Virtuoso's Collection. At the door we heard agitated voices, a young girl anxiously explaining something, then a man's answer, disappointed and sad. It was Peter Rugg and his daughter. Her face was wan, and the eyes glowed with a kind of madness. Mr. Hawthorne put his hand on my sleeve. We turned and started up the corridor again.

"She's been out," he said, "her feet looked damp. They'll both want to talk with me later."

"About what?"

"The same question."

"The same question?"

"Why I never devised a satisfactory tale returning them to Boston."

"You had trouble even introducing the possibility of getting Hester and Dimmesdale out of Boston. Robin, Major Molineux's kin, seems to be in Boston—the little Massachusetts metropolis, as you put it. Maybe Boston simply wasn't for you, Mr. Hawthorne."

"I've sometimes believed so," he said, with an air of being aggrieved. "Farther west, farther west might have been better."

"But being raised farther west might have deprived you of your subject—and you'd not be here tonight in the Museum. Although I know of writers farther west who did find a subject close to yours."

"Who, for example?"

"Robert Penn Warren. He's called himself a Methodist Atheist. That's like you, a Puritan Non-Puritan. His state was Kentucky."

"A good writer?"

"Very good. Almost too good for his own good. Once

I heard someone say, 'Red speaks all languages.' He has more talent, genius probably, than is necessary. When that's the case, talent or genius can use a writer. He's been safe thus far. He feels those forebears, and he feels the world's undertow sucking away. And he's a dedicated man. Those Methodists stomping non-Methodists at Evangelical meetings—'Stomp the son of a bitch and praise God,' one of his characters says—did that for him."

"Dedication, the writer without it usually quits before he's found himself."

"I know two intensely dedicated writers, Jim Powers, who sits down every day, working slowly away at his short stories, and Fred Manfred, who thinks, breathes, and lives writing. He blocks out the months and years ahead of him in tentative books and chapter titles. It's as though each had taken vows, like an Italian monk. 'Daily into this writing room I take with me the Will to Write, and ask not to be released until the day of my death!' "

"It is beginning to grow light," Mr. Hawthorne said. "Over there," he added, pointing to the left, "is the Modern British Room."

"Oh, could we go in there! I know I ought to leave, before the janitor comes on duty again, but . . ."

Mr. Hawthorne led me into the room.

There immediately in front of us was David Garnett.

"A friend of his," I said, "Francis Birrell, was the son of Augustine Birrell, who knew you in England."

"The world shrinks, and across the centuries the generations touch hands," he said.

"And I once sat talking with Mr. Garnett in the Reform Club in London. Henry James's club. As a boy and a young man, Garnett had known Conrad, Galsworthy, D. H. Lawrence, and many others."

"And they are . . . ?" Mr. Hawthorne asked.

"No matter. Garnett wrote a book, called *Lady Into Fox*. One evening an English farmer is out walking with his wife. His attention wanders. When he looks again his wife has changed into a vixen, and is running on all fours next to him. From then on . . ."

"Seems rather abrupt," Mr. Hawthorne said.

"Well, he would say, 'If one is going to turn a wife into a vixen, let's get on with it.' "

"Yes," Mr. Hawthorne said, slightly taken aback.

"Next to him is E. M. Forster. That summer in England I talked with him in his rooms at King's College, Cambridge. He's a fantasist. He likes, he says, to mix fantasy and the actual, after the manner of Samuel Butler, who was acquainted with Augustine Birrell. Forster likes to make it difficult to separate the actual from fantasy. That's more like your dish of tea. Not quite the alternative possibilities, superstition or all phenomena dutifully accounted for—and take your pick. But rather like it. The best we can do in our present state of disbelief."

"You believe in the Museum?" Mr. Hawthorne asked, leading me out into the corridor again.

"I'm here," I said.

He led me, without further talk, down the corridor. The sun was beginning to be pinkish on the windows, and the skylight had a faint orange glow. Mr. Hawthorne's skin was a deep brown, so that his gray eyes seemed even tawny.

At the top of the stairway, he gave me his hand. Either it was warmer than before, or I had grown used to its chill.

"May I come back again, for another visit?"

"You won't be able to find the Museum. No one ever can, at least not during his lifetime."

"Why not?" I asked, impatiently. "What's the name of the Museum? What is it?"

"As you go out, look over the door. You'll see. Goodbye," he said.

I went quickly down the stairs, knowing he had already turned and started down the corridor. Hurriedly I pushed open the door and went out. Looking up I saw the name deeply cut into the granite arch. THE HAWTHORNE MUSEUM. When I tried to open the door I found it was locked.

Turning I walked up the dark street quickly. Halfway along the block I looked back, for another glance at the Museum. It had already disappeared.

Aug 10'70

3798

PS121 O2 c. 1
  +The grotesque: a+O'Connor, Willia

0 00 02 0197419 3
MIDDLEBURY COLLEGE